AERODYNAMIC

TRADING

BY

CONSTANCE M. BROWN

PUBLISHED BY

NEW CLASSICS LIBRARY

AERODYNAMIC TRADING

First Edition: December 1995
Manufactured in the United States of America

For information, address the publishers:
New Classics Library
Post Office Box 1618
Gainesville, Georgia 30503 USA

Library of Congress Catalog Card Number: 95-74771
ISBN: 0-932750-42-7

ACKNOWLEDGMENTS

A first-time author does not suddenly dig deep and find the polished skills to write clearly and concisely. The flow of ideas, pace and timing is the behind-the-scene talents of the editor. Sherm Eagan, President of Connecticut Yankee International, 9 Mott Avenue, Suite 107, Norwalk, CT 06850, was the editor of this book. He is a skilled writer and highly regarded Executive Producer for television whose talents have been recognized by the industry with two Emmy Awards. This book would not have been presentable for publication without his help, hours of work, patience, and supporting friendship.

This book has been dedicated to Dennis Meyers. Denny was a close friend and influential mentor. He was an exceptional S&P trader and giving man. For a year, we spent hours on the phone debating and clarifying the concepts offered in this book. When repressed memories became my writing obstacles, it was Denny who pulled and prodded the deep corners of my mind until the facts became clear enough for me to continue. Denny taught me much about the markets and life itself. Much of his enthusiasm for living life to the fullest is expressed within the pages that follow. While he read early drafts, I regret he never had an opportunity to see the finished project. I am most grateful to Denny's former chief trader, Ed DiMaso, for stepping forward to critique the final draft.

Paige Eagan actually planted the early seeds in my mind as our open discussions explored the more difficult concepts for one trained in the sciences. She helped with research and was assisted by Mora Ritz at the Darien library. To both these ladies I am very grateful. The laborious production phase of type flow, page design and proofing was handled by Jane Estes and Sally Webb. Stephanie White contributed many hours producing a first draft from which Sherm Eagan could begin to apply his editing and wordsmithing skills. Pam Kimmons was the graphic artist who contributed to the intricate charts and graphic rendition of the plane.

Finally, four individuals in particular stand out in my mind as influential contributors. Every project of this magnitude eventually reaches a juncture that will ultimately mean the difference between continuation or stagnation. Both Dave Allman and Robert Folsom championed the first outlines with unconditional support. They were especially supportive of the thrust of this book when so many wanted a technical manual. In addition, Joel Berman injected a charge that reignited the project at a critical phase. Their early enthusiasm was joined by the most crucial supporter...the individual who gave the go-ahead on publishing the book...Robert R. Prechter, Jr.

CONTENTS

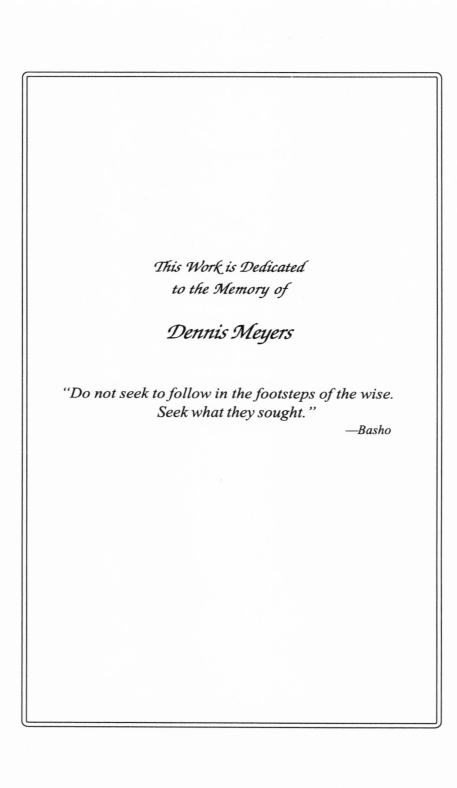

*This Work is Dedicated
to the Memory of*

Dennis Meyers

*"Do not seek to follow in the footsteps of the wise.
Seek what they sought."*

—*Basho*

FOREWORD

FOREWORD

There are five universal languages in this world: money, politics, art, sex and sport. Sport, increasingly through the past century, has absorbed the elements of the other four. In a recent Spontaneous Awareness survey conducted on behalf of sponsors of international events (Coca-Cola, Kodak, 3M, Visa International, and IBM), the Olympic Games carried a recognition factor of 71 percent, twice the impact of the second-ranked event; the World Cup in football. The global impact of the Olympic Games was three times greater than that of the Wimbledon Tennis Championships, in third place, and four times that of the Formula One Motor Racing Grand Prix, in fourth. The Olympic Games rated six times higher than the Tour de France, and ten times higher than the American Super Bowl and World Series of Baseball.

The Olympic Games are serious business. The stakes are high for all involved. It is no surprise that athletes training for the Olympic Games must develop the inner foundation to tackle the really tough obstacles such as stress, failure, self-sabotage, and performance slumps. To excel in such a high stakes competitive environment takes more than natural ability or finely tuned technique, more than confidence, and much, much more than discipline. Without discipline a competitor cannot even develop the easiest aspect of his game: the technique. The competitive pressures to excel within any arena driven by huge financial rewards establishes a common battlefield. The high stakes arena for the trader is no different than that of the athlete. Competition in a trading room is as intense as in any high stakes athletic event. I know. I have competed in both arenas.

As an internationally ranked athlete, my coaches continued to develop my technical skills as they worked to carve away, or streamline, the inner baggage of my mind. They were preparing me to compete in the 1976 Olympic Games. It is a ludicrous assumption people make when they say, "they must have wanted it more," when an athlete just edges out their competition. Believe me, once you have excelled to a level of international proficiency you want it, "it" being the win and all that is tied to the victory. So what really makes the difference? Once technique has been mastered little improvement occurs. The difference boils down to who is mentally tougher. Who is most mentally aerodynamic? Who has the least cerebral drag? It is the inner baggage we carry inside ourselves which takes away from our skills and saps our energy. The competitor with the least inner baggage wins.

The training progression used by coaches to train international and professional athletes applies equally to trading. Their techniques will make you mentally tough, and it is their methods that I will share with you in the pages that follow. You are about to learn, *do*, and then see these techniques applied to trading. In a sense, I am excited for you. If you have not been involved with top coaches and their training techniques for creating champions, then you are in for an exciting journey to new awareness. Once you become aware, there is no turning back. The inner skills and outlook you develop to win within *any competitive environment* will be changed forever.

As a final note, reality and brevity took precedence in this book over political correctness. To my few female colleagues I apologize for my repeated use of his/him pronouns. The use of "his/her" is so awkward to read that, as on the trading room floor, you have to do what works best at any given instant. Most times, "his" or "him" worked best.

PART I

The Preparation: Adopting the Beginner's Mindset

It was 6 AM when we began to collect beside one of the fastest swimming pools in the world for an international training clinic. We had arrived from Australia, Canada, Great Britain, and the United States. Nearly all of us would compete in our respective countries' Olympic Trials the following Spring. Some would meet again at the Games next summer. The bleachers were buzzing as one of the top coaches in the world stepped out on the deck. He had trained several Olympic Champions. Expectations were high that he would pass on his secrets for success to the new group of young hopefuls sitting before him today. The opening remarks were expected to be motivational, uplifting to the demands ahead, and cognizant of the talent which had just assembled. Sounds of excitement were quickly replaced with silence as the coach stepped forward to speak.

A successful swimmer went to a Zen master and announced he had come to learn all about Zen. The master invited the young man to sit down and have tea. As the master poured the tea, it overflowed. The young man shouted, "It's spilling, it's spilling!" To which the master replied, "Precisely...you came with a full cup. Your cup is already spilling over, so how can I give you anything? Unless you come with emptiness, I can give you nothing."

The coach then walked away out of sight. He left behind a stunned and confused group of swimmers on the bleachers that were not permitted to even enter the water for the first workout until we had settled down and begun to ponder what he had just said. In hindsight, two swimmers that took his opening comments more seriously than most of us are the same two swimmers that became Olympic medalists the following year.

Performance excellence in athletics and trading markets share common roots. It is not difficult to offer examples that can easily demonstrate the similarities: the drive to win, the accompanying anxiety to produce, the stress associated with past failures, the belief that you have to sustain a consistent degree of performance excellence. It should not be surprising therefore, that much of what is taught to the high performance athlete can be of benefit to the trader. Once the trader has mastered the technical skills, for the athlete the physical, the difference in improving one's performance becomes psychological. In a nutshell, it all comes down to how well we can learn to control our inner distractions and fears. As our experience grows, so do the obstacles we put in front of ourselves. Imagine a market that you believe has topped. A position is established in anticipation of a decline. However, you are proven wrong when the market continues to advance. A second attempt is made to establish a short position. Again you are stopped out. After having lost money on your prior short positions, fear immobilizes you from selling the third time. Insult to injury occurs when that third short position you just failed to establish then turns into one of the biggest winners for the current year. The anxiety to catch up forces you to enter trades that you otherwise may not have taken, causing a compounding loss and spiral decline. I know the pattern. I make the same mistakes. Fortunately, my early coaching has provided the foundation needed to break the spiral quickly and return to a more profitable course when this happens.

The journey toward performance excellence begins when you empty your mind of all the preconceived notions and ideals you have accumulated that clutter your mind. If you enter these pages with a full mind, there will be little I can offer you. Eastern philosophies, specifically the precepts of Taoism, express entering a mindset called the Beginner's Mind. Renouncing our restrictive beliefs opens our potential to unlimited boundaries. Keep an open mind, the beginner's mind, and I will share with you techniques and approaches given to me by international coaches that extend beyond sport and our trading activities. Untapped inner strength and control for performance excellence can be at your command.

PART II

The Framework for Extraordinary Performance in Athletics or Trading

Competition and Winning

Sport is a perfect metaphor for trading. It has the same ups and downs, the jubilation and the emptiness, the anger and the exhilaration, the chaos and the calm, the success and the failure. Our competitive society has a multitude of competitive systems that form the obstacles that hinder our development and diminish our potential. It is important to identify these walls and break them down before any real progress can be made.

Media slogans such as "the thrill of victory, the agony of defeat" instill performance pressures early in our childhood. A young child letting a baseball pass through his legs in a little league game is met with looks of failure from his young teammates and is then often met with harsh words from a coach who may damage his confidence, bruise his self-image, and instill in him a fear of failure.

In 1908, Baron Pierre de Coubertin declared that "the goal of the Olympic Games is not winning but taking part." This is a goal that has never been achieved, nor will it. We have strayed so far from this goal that now our nationalistic desires to win have led professionals from all nations to become reinstated as amateurs. I was once barred from swimming in a major international meet as a protest of professionalism was explored and a question of eligibility was evaluated. Back then it was just a competitive tactic. It was a single trump card that could be played once against any individual. The issue was resolved in my favor, but not in time to swim in that particular competition. The tactics and behind-the-scene maneuvers to gain a competitive edge would sometimes go beyond all reason. There is a favorite story in the Olympic swimming community about the 1972 Games when Soviet swimmers were given swim suits dipped in an adhesive that molded the suits to their bodies. The team members put on their suits with only the knowledge that tests showed fractions of a second could be removed from their sprint times by simply reducing the friction of their suits. They had not been told that there was no solvent to easily take the suits off afterwards. As the suits had been dipped in the adhesive, most had to endure the pain of skin being torn off with their swim suits from the most sensitive parts of their bodies, women and men alike.

As you squirm and become uneasy at the thought of how painful that must have been, it is natural to first think how could anyone go through such an ordeal just to win? To some extent we are all being subjected to similar competitive pressures. Stop to think for just a moment. As a professional trader, you have recently fallen into a trading slump with your end-of-month P/L statement only three days away. You are all too aware that your firm has been making cutbacks throughout the organization. On a personal level, suppressed to the back of your mind is the next mortgage payment and the knowledge that the equity in your home no longer exists because of tumbling real estate prices in your area. This job means retaining your standard of living and self-image. Now with the proper backdrop and the stage set, you might ask to what extreme measure would you be willing to go, if it promised to be the single factor to change your current monthly P/L from the red column to a healthy positive return? Suddenly the swim suit example is not as painful to imagine.

Athletic pressures spill over into all other endeavors of performance and especially those in the corporate and business environment. Professional athletes and professional traders both become the statistics from which new business flourishes. We become endorsements, performance track records, or walking billboards for a corporate sponsor, employer, or portfolio identity. Big time athletics is serious business, trading is also serious business, and both disregard the well-being and health of the individual. All that matters is the score. It is the result, "Who won?" that has become everything. Such an approach is directly responsible for creating a number of nonproductive, dysfunctional behavior patterns which high performance athletes are coached to recognize and take control of in order to allow further performance development. These behavior patterns, characterized by inner struggles and insecurities, all contribute to a background of negative noise. The noise causes a loss of concentration and loss of confidence which negatively impacts our ability. Such behavior patterns are common in athletes. I have since learned that they are equally common traits for traders as well. Consider the following examples:

> Our self-worth can be diminished because of a poor performance which failed to meet our expectations. This leads to the loss of our inner balance. We judge our self-worth solely on the outcome of our performance in sport, or in direct proportion to our current profit/loss bottom line. Performance in sport applies to the weekend golf or tennis enthusiast. Have you ever noticed how your golf game reflects your recent trading performance, and vice versa? The better your trading performance, the better your golf or tennis game. These activities of sports and trading will be effortless or disastrous at the same time. A great deal of attention will be given to help you understand why this phenomenon occurs. Not understanding why these activities are linked can lead to a very dangerous and incorrect assumption.

> Athletes and traders both frequently treat their goals as something which must be conquered, thereby expending valuable energy in a useless endeavor.

Unrealistic performance expectations lead to frustration and disappointment.

We tend to struggle for external recognition rather than internal satisfaction.

We place demands on ourselves for perfection in every task or trade. Perfection assumes there will be a point of completion, an ending, a point at which something cannot be improved or bettered in any way with time or technique. However, perfection is static and cannot apply to a personal skill in sport or trading because ability always evolves and changes. Markets will always evolve and change so trading techniques and analytic methodologies that seem perfect today will not be so in the future. Perfection doesn't apply in relation to markets because there is no finish line and no final destination for our trading ability. Our trading experiences today will help build our resources and skills for tomorrow's trading session. The progression is simply a journey, and the first steps of the journey are better viewed as a transition to excellence.

It is too easy to blame others when things go wrong. By blaming others we relinquish control and are no longer accountable for our own actions. As a result, we cannot change or improve them. It becomes a vicious cycle which is difficult to break.

Traders, like athletes, are fragile. Our worst critic is frequently ourselves, unmerciful and unforgiving of failures, setbacks, and mistakes.

None of these performance crippling similarities between athletes and traders have any relation to their potential physical or technical skills. However, psychological barriers are more restrictive than lack of technical skill for traders or physical skill for athletes. When the technical/physical barriers are down *at the same time* that the self-imposed unconscious obstacles are down, or what Don Gambril, a former Head Coach of the U.S. Olympic Swim Team, described as "taking control of the inner demons of the spirit which hinder your concentration," the impossible then becomes the reality.

In sport, the goal is to achieve a harmony and balance between the physical and spirit. Absolute balance is rare, and in my own swimming career, I recall only three times when it occurred. Balance is experienced when there is no fear of past failures or of future consequences. It is a time of complete and total concentration on the present when you can be totally oblivious to any and all distractions. On one of these rare occasions of total balance, my most treasured gold medal was won in Tokyo. It does not represent the memories of a past victory but what can be achieved now, today, when inner balance is attained. When absolute inner balance occurs, exertion becomes effortless, the mind, spirit and body are inseparable, and on that day, at that moment, no one can beat you. *No person or market.* There becomes an effortless flow, and you can be taught how to tap into this reservoir. You push beyond the envelope of self-imposed limitations and tap an unlimited universe of energy. Roger Bannister, in his book *Breaking the Four-Minute Mile*, describes this balance like few have been able to do: "The earth seemed to move with me... a fresh rhythm entered my body. No longer conscious of my movement I discovered a new unity with nature...a new source of power...a source I never knew existed." Miler Roger Bannister will always be known as the man who broke through the four-minute barrier, but you may not be aware that the sub-four-minute mile was then repeated by no fewer than *forty-five runners within the next eighteen months*. Do you think all these athletes improved their running technique within that short period of time? No way.

Once the barrier was broken, they changed their attitude from "it can't be done," to one of believing "it can be done." The psychological barrier had been removed and as a result forty-five runners broke through to a new level of personal performance excellence.

Inner and outer goals require specific training techniques and preparation to attain balance on demand. A balanced trader is a synonym for a balanced athlete. Both have limited cerebral drag and are inwardly aerodynamic. Both will experience a similar level of achievement excellence.

Balanced traders/athletes enjoy the following characteristics:

- They are individualistic.
- They have the courage to risk failure.
- They learn and grow from past setbacks and mistakes.
- They possess a multidimensional approach to competition.
- They see their competitors as partners who can facilitate improvement in their own performance level.
- They focus on how the game is played. (In trading this is the process itself, as opposed to the outcome or P/L bottom line. The score board is always a time horizon of the future, trade within the present. We'll go into this later in far more detail.)
- They use the game to gain a greater self-realization.
- They train their minds to see through the complexity of inner trappings.
- They blend with forces so as not to create a counterforce. They work through fatigue by re-

laxing, rather than focusing on it and aggravating the problem by adding more stress.

- They know their vulnerabilities and train to strengthen them.

- They understand that performance is a roller coaster and have the patience to ride the ups and downs.

- They visualize, allowing dreams to become possibilities and reality.

- They enjoy their sport or market environment for the pleasure it gives.

No one will ever be balanced and aligned at all times. My colleagues at Elliott Wave International will be the first to agree that I am far from being a calm, "in-control-at-all-times" kind of person. Judging from acquaintances and friends who trade as a profession, we all tend to be passionate, strong willed and display emotional swings outside the trading room — even in the trading room (which really should never happen). I remember flinging a telephone across a room as the phone system went down for the "umpteenth" time. (Fortunately it was thrown in my private office, and others were not at risk. It was also only one of four phones tied to independent phone services so I was not jeopardizing my trading link.) When you do lose balance, and we all do sometimes, know that you must gain the ability to return to center and regrasp the characteristics listed above.

Competition among traders on a trading floor is as intense as any high stakes athletic event. More money rides on many trades than the difference between winning and losing at Wimbledon, The Masters, or the Super Bowl. Other traders can seem threatening and may create a sense of fear that you will be judged inferior to them, be it through your P/L performance, trading activity, or intellectual methodology. This environment of competition breeds a killer instinct among many traders. Frequently the more insecure the trader, the stronger will be their killer instinct. This is not the path to success. True strength, like water, blends with other forces. Practitioners of the martial art aikido actually defeat their challenger by blending with the force of their opponent. The opponent in this case is your own fear. To transcend fear requires preparation. Every trader knows fear; the difference is how you live with it and how you prepare and train for it. Fear will always be with you. This book will offer specific techniques that will help you learn how to work with your individual fears and use them to your advantage. Philosopher Alan Watts states, "The other side of every fear is freedom." In Part III, titled "Inner Aerodynamics: Enhanced Trading Skills Through Professional and Olympic Coaching Techniques," we will discuss which specific techniques to use to help us calm our inner anxieties and relinquish our fears.

The secret about competitive environments is learning to blend with your competitors and to become aware that they will help you rise to the occasion. Appreciate that they contribute to attaining your highest level of ability, rather than focusing on who was right or wrong, or who won or lost. For instance, the contrarian nature of trading with the Elliott Wave Principle presents some unique challenges and opportunities. When the market completes a rising diagonal triangle pattern disguised as a bullish breakout formation above a major resistance level, you will experience other traders squirming in their chairs and hear them feverishly accessing their computers to see why you are selling the market when they are buying it.

Many will decide that you are marching to your own funeral with outward glee. For them it is clearly a bullish breakout formation. Don't try to ignore their activity; this will only contribute to your own level of stress. Accept it, let their hubbub

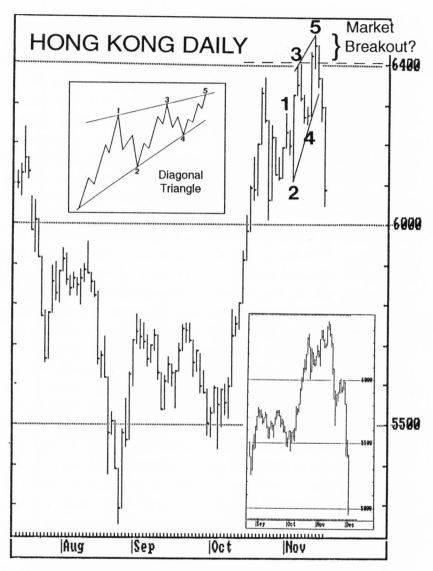

This daily chart of Hong Kong's Hang Sang Index illustrates the fatal error in judgment a buyer could make by assuming the market was breaking out above 6400 to continue the prior rally. The market rarely offers a gracious exit for a buyer caught long near the top of a diagonal triangle pattern. If the buyer decided to be patient, losses would have continued (lower insert).

of activity flow through you, then smile to yourself and perhaps sell some more! You are selling into the high of a fifth wave diagonal triangle which suggests a market top to a larger rally. If you are wrong, there will most likely be a gracious level to cover the position with a marginal profit. As for the traders who were long the market, they would be trapped. The weakness is theirs, not yours. They view other traders as their competitors, as opponents, which must be crushed or annihilated in order to give themselves the illusion that they are better. This activity is only wasted energy and contributes to the clatter of internal noise, which can break your concentration.

Much can be learned from a former Olympic Champion who is regarded as a Champions' Champion, Jesse Owens. In the 1936 Olympic Games in Berlin, which had been staged by Adolf Hitler to demonstrate to the world the superiority of the German race, a story of incredible partnership is told. Jesse Owens, a black athlete from the United States, was the world record holder in the long jump. Owens was on the edge of elimination after having fouled his first two jump attempts. Germany's top jumper, Lutz Long, rushed to his side and suggested making a technical change to Owens' approach. Owens followed Long's advice and qualified on the next jump for the finals. In the finals they continued to push one another. It was on Owens' last jump that he set the Olympic record of 1936. Film footage of the event then shows Lutz Long holding Owens' hand high in front of thousands of cheering spectators. Both walked arm-in-arm around the giant Berlin stadium, astonishing the huge audience. "It took a lot of courage for Long to befriend me in front of Hitler," Owens was later quoted.[1]

Elite athletes work as partners and blend to attain optimal performance. The Head Trader who motivates his brokers to

---

[1] *Olympic Controversies*, by Harvey Frommer, published by Franklin Watts.

Lutz Long and Jesse Owens
1936 Olympic Games, Berlin

focus on the annihilation of an "opposing" desk, is in turn setting up the very environment which will yield a lower return. A general theme which many top coaches express about fellow competitors is to use the level of their excellence as a key to self-improvement. Don't be hindered through intimidation; extend your own boundaries. If the trader next to you is a whiz on stop placement, ask for his advice.

Sometimes when you ask for help, your questions will be met with an air of, "Well, don't you know that?" The other trader has used your request for help to fuel his own ego trip by putting you down. Recognize this response for what it is. Don't withdraw with feelings of inferiority. You have in some way been intimidating this trader, and your request for help has actually exposed his vulnerability. You can't lose by asking. By trying to blend with your opponent, you will either gain a part of the skill that you perceived earlier to be threatening, or you reveal that he is vulnerable. Either way, you win. You improved your own skill level, or you diminished a source of intimidation that distracted from your own trading. The other trader may have a strong technical skill, but lack the mindset to fully use it. That trader may ultimately defeat himself from within.

As confidence in your ability grows and your skills improve, you will then experience a new challenge: mastering the complexities of winning itself.

The outcome of any trade, any point in a game, is important but not an end in itself. The scoreboard is one measure of our performance throughout the "event." The trap is developing an *obsessive need* to win every trade or point. Let's get real: you aren't going to be right with every trade; that's why strong money management skills are a vital aspect of trading. You can't allow a loss to influence or impact your performance on the next trade; that unnecessarily compounds the element of risk. Once that need becomes overpowering, you lose the joy of the process and the satisfaction that comes with a high level of performance. As an example, it is entirely possible to win the Formula One World Championship by consistent high performance, but never finishing first in any single Grand Prix race. Let go of the obsessive desire to produce; be in the moment; focus on the flow and joy that comes with performance excellence.

For the trader, there is a feeling of exhilaration when we are in close synchronization with the flow and rhythm of a market. During these periods we are totally focused on the current moment of activity on our computer screens. There are no thoughts of our commute to work that morning, or errands we need run after the markets close, and no concern about how the outcome of a current trade will impact our bottom line. Attention to the *now* with total immersion in the details of the present will lead to performance excellence and a consistently rising equity curve. Focusing on the present moment without distractions is the real key. Disregard conflicting thoughts creeping into your consciousness and tune out that familiar song playing on the radio of your mind. You know the song, the words go something like this: "I-could-a, would-a, should-a, what-if-I-had-a."

We'll discuss how to work with these distracting thoughts at a later time. There will be specific activities defined to help you develop skills for dealing with such energy draining mind gremlins. For now, just begin to recognize such thoughts for what they are: distractions.

The Three Selves

You cannot transcend
what you do not know.
To go beyond yourself,
you must know yourself.

—*Sri Nisargadatta Majaraj*[1]

From Luke Skywalker to the ancient Lamas of India, people have tried to understand and tap a source of strength and energy greater than mere physical power. They have been seeking "The Force." Roger Bannister's description of tapping into "a new source of power...a source I never knew existed" when he broke the four-minute barrier has been expressed by other athletes who surpassed old boundaries. The source of inner strength needed to excel to new levels of extraordinary performance has to originate from more than an extra bowl of Wheaties.

Our needs, wants, and goals are complex because each of us is made up of three distinct individual beings. Varying cultures, religions, and even medicines all have different terms, yet similar definitions, for our three inner selves: our unconscious self, our conscious self, and soul. (Stick with me on this one, I promise not to jump off the "deep-end" on you.)

Some of the originating sources where we find references to our three selves date much earlier than religions of the modern

---

[1] From the book *Sacred Journey of the Peaceful Warrior*, © 1991 by Dan Millman. Reprinted by permission of H. J. Kramer, P.O. Box 1082, Tiburon, CA. All rights reserved.

world that are relatively new. Mohammedanism is about 1500 years old, Christianity is 2000 years old, Judaism is much older than that, and the roots of Buddhism began around 500 BC. It might be said that our western civilization is more advanced in materialistic comforts than the Asian civilization. The Asian cultures are far more advanced than we are spiritually. (OK, what does this have to do with trading? It becomes the very foundation of our ability to achieve excellence. So hang in there.)

These ancient spiritual cultures, that are still powerful forces in our modern world, have a common belief that there is a common thread connecting all peoples. It is a kind of universal energy that individuals can tap — "The Force." Two widely distant peoples share common beliefs about a universal Life Force; the Native American Tribes of North America and the Tibetan Buddhists. They share a common philosophy and remarkably similar prophecies. They both believe the individual is able to accomplish seemingly impossible feats by tapping into this universal energy. A Cherokee woman, Dhyani Ywahoo, is a modern-day Buddhist and member of the Etowah Cherokee nation. Her story tells of how her family has spiritual ties to the holy man, Padmasambhava, who founded Tibetan Buddhism thousands of years ago. Recent meetings between Native American leaders and the 14th Dalai Lama of Tibet revealed their prophecies that originated many, many thousands of years ago are nearly identical. What is even more amazing is that many of the details of those prophecies were closely guarded secrets, never before revealed outside the monasteries or tribal councils. When you really think about it, such similarities shared between such diverse peoples are astonishing and lend an element of truth to these people's individual common beliefs. As when two distant research institutions arrive at the same scientific conclusion independently, both works receive greater credence.

In the November 1986 issue of the magazine *Discover*, I came across the story of the Superstrings Theory, a theory that offers a scientific and physical basis for understanding how we are all connected and suggests that there is indeed a universal energy that can be tapped. The Superstrings Theory was developed in 1984, primarily by physicists John Schwartz and Michael Green, after more than a decade of work. This theory so captivated the scientific community it was quickly dubbed TOE, or Theory of Everything. In brief, the Superstrings Theory supports the work of Albert Einstein by showing that matter and energy are interchangeable, and ultimately, blended into a single unified field. In other words, all matter and all energy are linked. The theorists describe matter as consisting of tiny primordial lengths and loops of something like strings, and they claim energy arises from the actions and interactions among these strings. These so-called superstrings connect everything to everything and apparently exist in ten dimensions: our familiar four of length, width, height, and time, plus others that cannot be observed by normal human senses. These additional dimensions operate only on the Planck scale, which in size is to the atom as the atom is to the Solar System. As *Discover* put it, "The theory has turned physicists into mathematicians, and mathematicians into physicists, and the universe into an entity in which all matter and energy, all forces, all people, planets, stars, cats, dogs, quasars, atoms, automobiles, and everything else...are the result of the actions and interactions of these infinitesimal strings."

The scientific community had finally stumbled upon what the Tibetan Buddhists and Native Americans have believed for thousands of years, that there is a universal connection or consciousness. Steven Spielberg used entertainment to explore the concept in *The Star Wars Trilogy*, as Yoda and Obi-Wan Ben Kenobi train Luke Skywalker to feel and use "The Force." The movies became widely popular. It clearly struck an inner nerve that transcended mere entertainment in a spiritually-starved Western Society.

Performance excellence is achieved through an inner balance and understanding of what makes us who we are as individuals. With minor variations, numerous ancient cultures believe in *the three selves*. It is found in so many diverse and ancient cultures that there must be an element of truth within it to perpetuate its continuance over thousands of years. Although science has not specifically confirmed the concept, several authors in the scientific community have introduced explanations of the human brain using several terms and concepts that can be synonyms for the *three selves:* Id, Ego, Super-Ego. Authors also discuss our Left-Brained and Right-Brained attributes. The work of Dr. Paul Maclean in the '40s and '50s introduced the concept of the Triune Brain. In his work the human brain comprises three components: the Limbic System, associated with emotions; the Reptilian Complex, the source of our "fight or flight" instincts (Panic! "Get me out of this trade!"); and the Neocortex, the seat of our technical and rational mind.

An excellent description of *the three selves* is offered in the writings of former World Trampoline Champion, Dan Millman. In his book, *Sacred Journey of the Peaceful Warrior* [2], Dan defines the *three selves* as the Basic Self, the Conscious Self, and the Higher Self. They each have their own distinct characteristics, wants, needs, and desires. Inner balance is experienced when the *three selves* have been satisfied equally, and their needs attended to, or at least acknowledged. Let's take a more detailed look at each of the three selves as Dan Millman defines them.

The Basic Self can be viewed as the child within us — bold with curiosity until the slightest hint of danger or unfamiliarity becomes present. The boldness is then replaced with a withdrawn and shy being until the perceived danger has past.

---

[2] From the book *Sacred Journey of the Peaceful Warrior*, © 1991 by Dan Millman. Reprinted by permission of H. J. Kramer, P.O. Box 1082, Tiburon, CA. All rights reserved.

Through the eyes of our Basic Self we experience all emotions. The Basic Self has a storehouse of endless energy that fuels unharnessed emotions. It is motivated by a primitive impulse to survive, seek shelter from discomfort, to seek pleasure, avoid pain, and to have fun. The Basic Self is unrefined by culture, rules, or logic. There is no perceived higher purpose or refined beauty, only good feelings and bad feelings. The Basic Self demands attention to its own agenda of wants and desires. It can be characterized by an extroverted desire to explore and have fun, yet rapidly withdraws and becomes insecure when it gets in trouble by facing anything that is unfamiliar, and then seeks guidance from some other source. It becomes the source of our need for reassurance, and it is capable of childlike temper-tantrums to bring attention to its demands. When we are in front of a trading screen, it is the Basic Self that expresses feelings of excitement and exhilaration that this is fun. It is equally capable of panic and fear. When things start to go wrong, it is the voice of the Basic Self that screams "cover the position, run, take cover" and find safety on the sidelines.

Our health and ability to heal is linked to the Basic Self. As we become physically run down by stress, anxiety, and over work, it is the Basic Self which needs release and craves a little fun. Even when ignored, the Basic Self eventually gets attention and rest after we have broken down, with a flu bug, an ulcer, or worse. Our nutritional requirements are dictated by the Basic Self.

The Conscious Self is like an android or robot. The early character of Spock in *Star Trek* is a most fitting example. Through the eyes of the Conscious Self the world is seen objectively and in icy calm. It is expressionless as it sorts information and weighs the best course of action. When the Basic Self has a compelling need for guidance, the need for someone to interpret, to reassure and direct it, the Conscious Self will formulate a solution to appease and suppress it. The Conscious

Self is untroubled by emotions or sentiment; its world is orderly, structured, and terribly limited. It seeks only what is useful and constructive. Beauty becomes a definition, a category. The body is seen as a necessary burden, a machine that enables movement and reproduction. The Conscious Self is immune to emotion, yet, without the playful spirit, the emotional energy, and the vitality of the child, or Basic Self, it does not live. Only the sterile world of problems and solutions exist, confined within boundaries of pure logic. It is the Conscious Self that thrives on analytic testing and provides the discipline to work endlessly to research new techniques and acquire scientific understanding. Learning, reasoning, and logical deduction are the abilities of the Conscious Self. When the markets turn into chaos on our screens and we react with robot-like analysis and icy calm, it is the Conscious Self which is in control. It is addicted to the endless cycle of problem definition and solution identification. If the Conscious Self is always in complete control we rapidly progress towards burnout, lose balance and sight of our self-worth, and become overly self-critical with our lack of perfection.

The Conscious Self knows nothing of the Higher Self. The Higher Self is a far and distant voice. Without it, life feels insipid, shallow, and incomplete. The sense that there is a higher purpose is the search for our Higher Self. The traps which block and prevent us from finding our Higher Self are selfishness, ego, and greed. The internal radiation of warmth we feel when we give of ourselves freely is a glimpse of the Higher Self. It is our conscience, intuition, and spiritual guide in the larger scheme of things. Without it, our trading activities become the world of the Conscious Self, the gray world of problems and solutions. Eventually we become overwhelmed with the sense that trading is no longer fun, but hollow, and leaves us barren and empty. No matter how hard we concentrate or try to re-ignite the inner spark and drive, our trading performance declines.

Performance excellence requires balancing the *three selves*. All three need to be nourished and developed to attain extraordinary performance on demand. An example of how the *three selves* interact together in our daily trading activities may help demonstrate how we all experience them in some form. Part of what follows will be blatantly obvious, while other aspects will need to be given attention in later chapters. Let me share a trading experience with you that I had in 1991.

The alarm clock went off at the usual time of 5:15 AM, blissfully ending a restless night of tossing and turning. The foggy haze of the hour was abruptly cut with the sharp knife of reality as I recalled that the Gulf War had begun last night. The usual groggy stumble into the shower was replaced with a frantic dash to the television to view CNN and hear the overnight developments in Baghdad.

Just one day before hostilities broke out I had established positions of short Yen, long Crude, and short 400 S&P contracts. I first learned that war had broken out during a phone call to the office from Grand Central Station in New York. My commute home from the Wall Street district to Darien, Connecticut caused two communication blackout periods when I could not be contacted. (Back then I did not carry a cellular phone.) Nagging instincts throughout the Lexington Uptown subway ride had prompted me to phone the office from Grand Central Station. Instinct proved to be correct. We were at war and I was torn between the disbelief and horror that Washington was actually bombing Baghdad, and the jubilation of my positions rapidly moving in my favor. I adjusted my stop levels and prepared for the second leg and longest communication blackout period of my commute home. The bar car was the place to be that night. The train ride on Metro-North from New

York to Darien took the usual hour; another fifteen minutes by car and I was home. As I walked in my door and turned on the television, the trading desk phoned to inform me that the markets had already proclaimed a winner. The Coalition Forces had attained complete air domination, a scenario I could not have considered in my wildest imagination. I was educated in the Sciences, not military strategy. While my Yen and Crude positions had been unwound at nearly break-even because of the earlier stop adjustments made from Grand Central, there was nothing that could be done that night for my 400 S&P contracts. A gap up opening for the S&P market was already being called for in the morning.

It was not going to be an easy day. The news confirmed what the markets had already deduced the previous evening; the War, in essence, was over. The commute back to Wall Street the next morning seemed particularly short. The time was quickly consumed with an inner conflict between *two selves,* each with different approaches to my S&P problem. The Basic Self part of me was filled with the fears and survival instincts of a child. It was an inner voice trying to convince me to throw in the towel right on open and take my losses quickly. It was chanting, "Don't forget big mistakes will get bigger with time." The android, or robot part of me was a computer in action. It took charge of the chaos of emotions and brought a sense of order and control. The evaluation of options available to me and ways to unwind 400 S&P contracts eventually dominated and suppressed my childlike fear and flight-to-safety instincts. My Conscious Self took control by asking a string of questions.

"Visualize the worst case situation on the screen now while you're on this train. What would that be? How will you react to it?"

The answer is simple. The worst situation is that *there is no market*; a limit move occurs right on open.

"So what are you going to do?" the internal android asks.

"Faint," my Basic Self interjected, beginning to panic.

"No you don't," corrected the Conscious Self.

"OK, I know, work the back month."

"How? Give me specifics. Never mind, too slow, I'll figure out the details."

The internal conversation continued and finally a limit move was considered unlikely. Several other scenarios are then considered, evaluated, and potential game plans are constructed for the different outcomes that may occur.

I began to notice that the speed and pitch of the train was changing. We were crossing the East River Bridge leading to the 125th Street Station. Winter in New York always seemed to be harsher and colder in this area. The season has no color, just shades of gray. The train moved past buildings which are hollow shells, blackened by fire. They are ruins, barren and empty, but still the building facades show exquisite artistry and architectural details of craftsmen long forgotten. Had these artists emigrated from Germany, Ireland, or perhaps Italy? I often wondered what country had donated such skill. The train moved on to numerous buildings facing the tracks with broken windows. They are still inhabited and residents tape plastic over the windows in an effort to block the biting cold. A group of black men were huddled around a small fire shooting up from a metal barrel positioned in the center of an empty lot filled with bricks, tires, and unwanted articles. As this scene passed outside the moving train's window, a third voice from within me began to speak to the inner child and android.

"Listen Child, you too, Android. You two guys had better keep this image in mind today. Whatever happens in the market on any given day is unimportant.

So you're going to lose some money today. What's that in the larger scheme of things? Nothing! What about those guys shivering by the barrel? Do you really think you have problems?" Poof, my Higher Self stepped out of view and its voice disappeared as quickly as it entered the conversation. For a brief moment a sense of perspective was attained.

As the train plunged into the blackness of the Park Avenue tunnel, the android regained control.

"OK, what's another likely scenario for your S&P's? How about an open just above the third major resistance zone from the close? Maybe. The fourth zone did contain numerous Fibonacci relationships."
"Yeah, equivalent to The Great Wall of China..." piped in the Basic Self.
"Enough about walls," the android abruptly cut in. "Where is the third resistance zone located?"
"Let's see, 750 above the close."
"Gasp, I just want to dig a hole and hide in it today. This has to be a bad dream. I think I'm going to be sick," whines the Basic Self.
"No you're not. Snap out of it. So where will the market retrace and what will you do? Will there be any orders within those levels to fill your size? Should you reverse this short mess and go long?"

Rapidly the multiple scenarios with varying degrees of initial shock are replaced with a game plan formulated to fit the differing market opening possibilities. All possibilities were rehearsed and ready to go as the train pulled into the last station. The doors of the train flew open, and like the starter's gate holding back several finely tuned explosive Thoroughbreds, the race began with a bolt forward. It was not going to be an easy day, but whatever the computer screen handed me on open, I would be ready to react to it. There would not be time to think, just do.

As I walked down the narrow isle of multiple computer screens in the trading room, many traders were already at their desks. Just ahead was Marcus, displaying that familiar grin of satisfaction when he knew someone else was up to their neck in trouble. Not this morning. I really did not want to deal with his abuse today. For some reason the walk down that aisle brought back a very old memory.

Eight of us walked single file on the green carpet covering the marble pool deck for the final heat of our event at the Yoyogi National Stadium in Tokyo. The anxiety and pressure created an internal chatter and noise that became deafening. I was drowning in a pool of emotions. Then the training and preparation began to wedge between the inner folds of chaos. "Remember to focus. Imagine the tunnel around you." A calm begins to quiet the inner turmoil, a voice has stepped in to take control. "Focus on only the end of the tunnel, a tube extends from you to the end of the tunnel. Everything within the tunnel is in sharpest of detail." Everything outside the tube fades into a soft focus. "Don't fight the distraction, be aware of it, but let the distraction pass through the tunnel and out again. Accept it, then let it go. The distraction is only a tactic to pull you off center. Stay focused; there is only the *now*. Live the current moment to the fullest, feel and relish all the details within the tunnel as you walk. Now visualize the start, feel the stroke mechanics to

the smallest detail. Stay focused; you have a job to
do." Eight swimmers stepped up on their respective
blocks.

As I arrived at my own desk, one of the game plans rehearsed
on the train began to unfold. The only question remaining was
if this short position should be reversed. In my current frame of
mind I couldn't objectively consider going long, so I analyzed
the charts upside down and made the conclusion that I should
look for an opportunity to go net long.

The time was 9:29 AM, the starter's gun in my brain was
about to go off. "Release the tension, take three deep breaths.
In through the nose, out through your mouth. Now focus."
The first tick hit the screen above the second major resistance
zone. I was in trouble, but there were several other scenarios
that could have been much worse. As the charts updated, only
the process was in focus. What's the count? Where's the retracement? "Pay 40 for 100," done. "Pay 20 for 80," done,
done, done. All 400 contracts had been unwound; it was now
9:41 AM. Earlier thoughts began to distract me, and my mind
wandered away from the trading room.

The swimming event in Tokyo was the 200 meter backstroke, four laps of the pool. I still remember my
thoughts as I entered the second turn. "You're only
finishing the second lap. Stay focused on the details,
dig in, don't ease up now." The second turn then led
to a shearing sharp pain that radiated up my left pointer
finger, hand, and into my lower arm. A split second
error into the wall and I knew I had broken a finger
again. "OK pain, I know I can't block you out. I
accept that you're there. Your timing to visit is horrible. I'll tend to you later. For now stay focused, just
pay attention to the details of the stroke, feel the rhythm

return, yield to the pain, then push past it." Like a flawless computer, the stroke mechanics returned with renewed, effortless power. Water flowed around and over me without resistance. The sensation began to energize, replenish, and sustain me, there was no one else present, it was no longer a race, there was just the sensation of water rushing by effortlessly without sound, unrestricted by boundaries of time.

It was 9:43 AM and the Conscious Self was calling. "Hello. Where are you? You're in the hole on that last trade, eh? So what, the damage is done. It's behind you. Remember when you hit the wall in Tokyo? Today is like Tokyo, this race is not over. Now dig in and re-focus!"

"Take a deep breath."
"What's happening with the thirty minute charts?"
"The wave count is...and the technical indicators are forming a bottom...the market is trading at a premium still...the resistance and support tables need to be re-calculated."
"Do I want to go long? At what level will I be wrong? Where will the stops go? Where do I get in?"

The trading day fell back into a nearly normal rhythm.

I hardly recall the day ending or how I moved from the office to Grand Central Station. I stepped on board the train for Darien and found an empty seat by the window. Wedging my knees up behind the seat in front of me, it didn't take long before I was asleep. I don't even remember leaving the station.

The crisis was history, but tomorrow would be a new chapter.

Goal Setting

SO YOU SAY YOU WANT A TELEPHONE?

To: VITALY KOROTICH, Editor in Chief of *Ogonyok* Magazine, Moscow

New apartments are being built in Alushta, and telephones are being installed for people who are coming to live in the city. Our district was built in the 1950s, but underground telephone cables were not planned for, so we were left with no telephone. I have lived in the city for thirty-two years, worked hard all my life, and grew old here. You can imagine how angry I became when I asked a telephone worker when our street was finally going to get telephones, and he said, "Buy a telephone pole, put it up, buy a telephone cable, string it up, buy a telephone set — and then we'll hook you up."

Excuse me, where can I get a telephone pole?

—T. ZAKHAROVA, Alushta[1]

As professional traders, we sit before our circus of computer screens, network news displays, and assembly line of telephones. It seems inconceivable that someone in this age is without the simplest of technological necessities: a telephone. The letter

---

[1] Reprinted with the permission of Simon & Schuster, Inc. from *SMALL FIRES* by Christopher Cerf and Marina Albee. Copyright 1990 by Christopher Cerf and the Editors of *Ogonyok* Magazine.

from Mr. Zakharova serves as a reality check for all that we take for granted. His letter also illustrates perfectly how to attain a goal. If the first obstacle you need to overcome, no matter how strange it may seem, is to acquire a telephone pole, then start asking where to get one! As two-sided is the sword of Mr. Zakharova's final question, it serves to illustrate how to transcend the first obstacle most people fail to accomplish in reaching their goals: *he takes action*.

Goals motivate us into action to write letters, picket for a cause, face the difficulties in changing our careers to trading for a living from one that may have been totally unrelated, or provide us with the strength to sustain years of effort so that we may inch gradually closer to any goal we have defined for ourselves. Emotion accompanies goals.

Yes, emotion. That is our motivational force. It is our passion that minimizes the size of the obstacles blocking us from reaching our goals and fuels us through the periods of exhaustion. So why is it then that this chapter, the very one that should be filled with passion and emotion has become the most difficult for me to put into words for you?

Click.

The fifth attempt for this chapter has just been obliterated forever with a click of the computer's mouse button.

Mr. Zakharova, how many times did you write your letter before the words came together to clearly represent your thoughts? I have really struggled to understand why this area of the book had become so difficult for me. I eventually began to realize it was based on a ten minute incident that changed the direction of my future. The incident itself will be shared with you later, but what is more important is to understand how that brief incident in 1976 nearly kept me from writing this chapter. Why?

It is one thing to find and understand what ignites a passion within us; it is quite another thing to sustain the effort and energy required to keep us on our path towards fulfilling our goal. While passion sparks the formation of our goals, how do we turn the passion off so we can let go of a goal? Do we have to let go of old goals in order to fully adopt and become committed to new goals? The answer is yes.

Most discussions I've read about goal setting failed to address the important element of letting go. Goals are so much harder to let go of than to set. A long term goal is sometimes never attained, *and never will be.* Goals are easy to establish. It's not that easy to walk away from something you may have passionately pursued for several years. The more time you spend trying to reach the individual milestones that lead toward a goal, the harder it becomes to avoid being fully consumed by that goal. I'll give you some specific examples shortly. The way you resolve unmet goals will have a major impact on your future decisions. They can define the direction you decide to take at life's future crossroads. Let's begin with taking a look at some important aspects of setting a goal.

If goals are derived from motivations and desires, then you may think acquiring money is a goal. It is not. Acquiring wealth is a goal. Money is just a milestone along the way. I'll address money itself in the next chapter on motivation.

A long term goal has to be accompanied by short term milestones. It is these milestones that help build our confidence and allow us to measure our progress towards the longer term goal. Milestones also help us believe that a seemingly impossible long term goal will be reached some day. We just need to keep taking small steps in the right direction to get there. The goal itself, with its accompanying milestones, should be defined *on paper*. There's no room for generic, conceptual fuzziness. To quote Mr. T. Zakharova, of Alushta ... "Excuse me, where can I get a telephone pole?"

John Naber, four-time Olympic gold medalist, spoke at the International Swimming Hall of Fame. His message eased the pressure for many young swimmers. Simply put, he said keep in mind that you may some day want to hold a World Record, but for next week's swim meet all I want to see is 2/10ths of a second off your best time. (He got everyone to agree that was realistic.) He then said multiply that time reduction by the number of meets you know are scheduled over the next five years, and you'll find that the current World Records will be shattered. There's even room for a slump. It made sense then. It makes sense now. It even applies now as I sit at the keyboard writing this book... certainly the hardest thing I have ever attempted. So I began to treat those thousands of random torn scraps of paper containing ideas for this book as those 2/10ths of a second improvements. Elaborating upon each idea, a small milestone, leading to the goal itself, a book. If you are reading this now in print form, the goal to have these ideas published for others to use was met.

We need both short and long term goals. The components of a goal cannot be fuzzy. Specific elements are required to allow measurement. An example might be, you want to enter your first golf tournament within two years. (Not win it, get real, just qualify for it.) This goal has a time element allowing a precise measurement. If you've never swung a golf club before, this is a formidable challenge. The first milestone is to drive over to the course and schedule a series of golf lessons. When you start to play, actually chart your score by the individual hole. Don't monitor your progress over the whole course with just your final score. You may find you're a whiz at the par 5... but a disaster at the short water hole.

Tennis players get down on themselves when their game falls apart, but the whole game rarely falls apart. It may be the serve, maybe the footwork, follow-through on the backhand...maybe just your bond trades...I suspect you've caught on. Break the task down into smaller elements. Keep track of your P/L by market traded, rather than by simply focusing on a cumulative bottom line. I have learned not to trade anything with roots or hooves, or the last two days before my end-of-month statement, or when I'm sick.

The *three selves*, introduced in the previous chapter, need to be given individual attention. Goals and milestones need to be established for all *three selves* or we will be unable to sustain a high degree of performance or stretch ourselves to attain the extraordinary. Trust me on this one. You may think you don't have enough time to give attention to the three different Selves within you; just ignore them and they will make the time. You will eventually discover this when you are emotionally and physically burnt out from trading. Ignore the Basic Self and the stress *will*, *not may*, put an abrupt end to your trading.

A major player in the S&P market warned me to take time out to have fun. I didn't heed his warnings... I was too busy trading. Not long after, when I was unable to keep food down or sleep, my friend called me at the office and said, "You're through. It's all over. That's the simple part, and it's already been decided for you. It eventually happens to all of us. You're done. But you'll come back much stronger for it. Now re-sign!" He was right.

I was a short horizon trader that focused on the markets around the clock. As soon as the S&P closed, there was time for a quick break before Tokyo opened...and then on to London's FTSE 100. Carrying the duties of both analyst and trader was disastrous. Physical exhaustion drove my health straight down the drain and my P/L along with it. I can only hope you will heed the warning better than I did. Some burnt out traders (and I'm sure you know a few) never return to trading.

Now that I've tried the scare tactic, let me give you a few ideas of how to set goals for the *three selves* to keep you in the game. Your Conscious Self may want to manage a large fund and is satisfied by the day-to-day progress of learning technical analysis and any element which increases your skill for attaining that goal. Great, but what about the Basic Self? How about a goal to run the Colorado rapids, hike to Mt. Fuji, or build your stamina for a two week bicycle ride next summer through Europe? Maybe learn to sail, play golf, or throw a pot on a potter's wheel? The best traders know when to tell the Conscious Self to take a hike and then do something for fun like read a comic book or watch cartoons. (*The Rocky & Bullwinkle Show* is my favorite...with the gang of Boris, Natasha, Sherman and Professor Peabody...and I love that moose! Maybe my Canadian roots?) You've really arrived when you can do it without guilt. To attain balance we need to recognize that all three selves need to be nourished, exercised, and motivated.

So what about the Higher Self? It is reassuring that the goal doesn't have to be grand. You don't have to personally save the rain forests. Stay within the boundaries of your comfort level. Saving the rain forests may not be your bag, especially when you live in a high-rise in Manhattan and the only forest you identify with is Central Park. So find something else that makes you more comfortable. Make time in your schedule to help a friend. Donate a day to AmeriCares or Habitat For Humanity to build or repair a home for a needy family. Coaching a baseball team or teaching someone to read through a literacy program may be more appealing. Pass on something you know to someone else. Give a few sandwiches and apples to the homeless at the Times Square subway station or in Battery Park. Anything. The point is contribute your time in a way that is beneficial to someone else *without expecting some kind of payment*. It feels really good, and besides, an improved self-image can contribute to some awesome trading returns.

Beware that goals can become overpowering and have the ability to own us. When your trading activities allow you to buy that Hatteras yacht, enjoy it for the fun it brings you. If you truly don't enjoy being alone on the yacht, find that you never use it unless you have people with you, but fear others may think less of you if you didn't have it as a trophy, you may have fallen into the trap of being owned by the possession, rather than vice-versa. Being owned by possessions will increase your base level of stress *and will thereby negatively affect your trading*. A "Catch-22" isn't it? Trading bought those goodies in the first place, and now it could be the goodies that are negatively affecting your trading. That yacht may not be a release for tension, but a source of it, an Albatross that increases your tension and stress.

When you *want* to sell the trophies, a great feeling of freedom comes along with it. It took me quite a while to identify my own trophies. We all have them. One summer day I was sitting on the deck of my Connecticut home, sipping a rum & Coke, looking out at the picture postcard view of sail boats gliding by on the Sound, when I realized this just wasn't me. Boring. I wanted to be out riding a horse somewhere. The possessions I had accumulated had left me feeling empty and asking myself, "So now what?" A very empty feeling after years of work. I was guilty of creating a stage setting that our culture and geographic area had defined as the image of "success," but it wasn't *my* definition of success. As a result when the stage was set, it was empty, and I had done nothing to enrich or bring warmth into my life. The house, along with all the trappings surrounding it, owned me. I sold everything.

I moved to a small isolated log home in the country: stone fire place, quilts, old pine furnishings you could put your feet on, surrounded by four-legged friends with wagging tails. The house was hard to get to, difficult to find, and was just what I always wanted. My friends thought I had finally lost it. What they didn't realize is that I had finally found it, and "it" had been a very expensive lesson for me to learn. I had incorrectly believed that my goal was the image defined for me by others in the Wall Street community. However, what my soul needed was something entirely different.

Trophies are not necessarily materialistic. We hoard psychological trophies as well. We cling to successes associated with a prior year's gains, a degree acquired from an Ivy League school, a prestigious or fashionable address. They are all forms of trophies, baggage we carry that is not constructive. These trophies are all inner obstacles that drain our ability to reach our maximum potential. At a later time we'll focus on just how damaging these inner obstacles can be. More importantly, we'll also address how to work with them.

If the smallest step leading toward a milestone presents itself, take it, even if it seems to be through a back door. It takes courage to ignore all the reasons that our Conscious Self will throw at us to explain why this is not the right time or convenient moment to change directions. The Conscious Self likes total control of all situations, but the perfect conditions will never be present, so take the first opportunity when it comes. The Basic Self needs security; change is an immediate threat. So that means two components of the *three selves* are at odds with one another. It causes tremendous turmoil and inner conflict. In such situations, Asian and Native American writings explain that it is the Higher Self which is pushing us into unfamiliar situations that we otherwise would not have taken. Goals on the surface seem to be tangible, but are in fact road maps to a better understanding of ourselves and lead to a sense of higher purpose. *What we learn along the way while trying to attain a goal is far more valuable than the goal itself.* A goal to win a gold medal for the purpose of simply owning the medal to impress others is a great deal of work and a great waste of time for something you might simply buy from a pawn shop.

The Higher Self can make us so uncomfortable that somehow we find the ability to pull up stakes, possibly sell everything, and head off into the unknown. The motivation and drive may not be clear to us at the time; all we know is that it is the right thing to do.

An important step towards reaching any goal you may have is being able to imagine the process. In athletics we are trained to visualize. Visualizing is like daydreaming, replaying and imagining yourself successfully pursuing the goal you've set out for yourself. See yourself successful at whatever that goal is, and then visualize all elements leading up to that goal. There are many applications for visualization. Visualization is an activity that you choose to view images in your mind's eye that will influence your emotions and energy. Our central nervous system cannot distinguish between real and imagined events. For example, close your eyes right now and imagine a juicy, sour yellow lemon. In your mind, slice a big wedge from the lemon and place it in your mouth. Bite down into the wedge, feel the sour juices fill your mouth. Did you find yourself salivating or your mouth trying to pucker? In sport, results are frequently dictated by the images and visions we have of ourselves. If you see yourself missing that golf shot, you will create tension and anxiety that will have a negative impact on your performance. If you carry images of success, you create an inner calm, confidence, and relaxation that contributes positively to your success. Jack Nicklaus, in his book *Golf My Way*, talks about having very sharp, distinct images in his mind before making a single shot.

> First I 'see' the ball where I want it to finish, nice and white and sitting up high on bright green grass. Then the scene quickly changes and I 'see' the ball going there: its trajectory, and shape, even its behavior on landing. Then there is a sort of fade-out, and the next scene shows me making the kind of swing that will turn the previous images into reality.

In the last chapter about the Three Selves, I described my visualization process for unwinding the S&P position I held as the Gulf War started. I "saw" the computer screen and rehearsed how to respond to each scenario even though I was on the train. Visualization is not psychological hocus-pocus, it is a learned skill which needs practice. This will be discussed in greater detail at a later time.

The last area for discussion is adjusting goals, or when to raise the bar. You raise the bar, or establish a new goal before reaching a major goal. Never touch the "golden ring" of your desire. The glitter, passion, and emotions that motivated you to reach a distant goal may turn to dust. Goals need to be revised and continually kept just out of reach. When a very long term goal is attained, it should become a celebration of having reached a major milestone towards a new goal already defined. *Don't ever let the goal itself become the final destination.* If you reach your goal without something else to strive for next, you will find that the passion and drive dies, and in its place is left an empty void. It took me some time to learn that the real enjoyment is the moment-to-moment process of the journey, rather than the arrival at the goal itself. The reason the glitter and excitement fades at the moment you reach your objective is that the goal instantly melts into our pool of knowledge and past experiences.

The guys in the NACA tracking van interrupted to report that they heard what sounded like distant thunder: my sonic boom! The first one by an airplane ever heard on earth.

And that was it. I sat up there feeling kind of numb, but elated. After all the anticipation to achieve this moment, it really was a let-down. It took a damned instrument meter to tell me what I'd done. There should have been a bump on the road, something to let you know you had just punched a nice clean hole through the sonic barrier. The Ughknown was a poke through Jello. Later on, I realized that this mission had to end in a let-down, because the real barrier wasn't the sky, but in our knowledge and experience of supersonic flight.

—General Chuck Yeager,
First Man to Break Mach 1: the sound barrier
Yeager: An Autobiography
Reprinted by permission of Bantam Books

When I reached a long term goal for the second time, this time it was to manage a commodity portfolio. It was only then that I began to understand what had happened many years ago after working eleven years for the Eastman Kodak Company. From the time I was in University, I had wanted only one thing... to have some kind of responsibility for Kodak's Color Films. My major in University was based on early contacts I had made with the placement office for Kodak Canada Ltd. I joined Kodak right out of school and proceeded to learn every discipline of the business. I loved it and every aspect of working directly with professional photographers. When I learned that Kodak Canada primarily implemented the marketing plans created in Rochester, New York, I left Canada, my home and my family, and joined Eastman Kodak — a move viewed by Kodak Canada at that time to be equivalent to a defection. The pain and conflicts were enormous. Eventually after several brief assignments in the United States, I entered Kodak's management training program, which led to the responsibility that had been my long term career goal since school: Product, or what some corporations call Brand Manager of all Kodak Professional Color Films, representing a substantial portion of our division's earnings at that time. In hindsight, had I never been given that particular job, I might still be working for Kodak today. In essence, I had reached my dream...and there was nothing beyond it. I settled into the cyclical transition of marketing plans, implementation, and launch activities. Our launch activities included changing the name of KODAK VRG Film (a manufacturing name that stuck with the product, meaning Variable Resolution Grains) to KODAK GOLD. The name wasn't original; we stole it from Kodak Limited in England. That single strategic change in name, coupled with a launch prior to the 1988 Olympics, doubled film sales. In addition we launched the highly successful KODAK COLOR WATCH marketing strategy. Sales generated by this strategy outstripped manufacturing capacity and required building a new production line. You likely know the program: in North America, Bill Cosby displayed the KODAK COLOR WATCH seal in commercials for years. The marketing strategy is still being used today.

While our team grew the business for our division a staggering percentage, the process became automated. The passion was gone. Unknowingly at that time, my golden ring — the goal to head Kodak's marketing activities for their professional color films — had turned to dust. There was nothing else to strive for within the firm. The next rungs of the corporate ladder seemed to lead to more bureaucracy, fierce political battles, longer hours to be pushed into a punishing schedule that already consumed seven days a week, and worse...I didn't want to spend the rest of my working days in Rochester, New York, under sunless skies three-quarters of the year. We all believed George Eastman had built Kodak in Rochester because of the constant 18% gray skies — a shade of gray which represents perfect balance between the three emulsion layers which make up color films. The gray skies matched my spirits. I became the good corporate soldier. Management incorrectly thought I had finally developed management skills and had matured. In actual fact, I was willing to just let things take their own course rather than rattle management's cage and fight to move things ahead faster than a corporate bureaucracy could generally accommodate. I settled down, accepted the limitations, avoided the political traps, and resigned to growing old...just after my thirty-fourth birthday. *Don't ever let the goal itself become the final destination.* When you reach a goal, it should be a milestone towards something new that you keep out of reach.

When I worked for Kodak and stopped trying to buck the system, everything became routine. The Hunt Brothers silver crisis was unfolding in the market at that time, and my products became strongly affected by the spiraling costs. It was also around that time that I became far more aware of foreign currency exchange rate exposure, and gradually I moved farther and farther away from marketing and closer and closer to the financial markets. A new spark was ignited, and I steamed through each day in anticipation of that night's chapter in a new home study course preparing for a useless series 6 and 7 exam. (I was such a novice, I didn't know that series 6 and 7 had little to no resemblance to trading reality.) I didn't care that brokers needed a sponsor to take the exams.

I saw my first chart on FNN, a new station for Rochester Cablevision, and I understood it! Charts for photographic films are called D Log E curves, or density vs. log exposure curves. On these charts, the smallest shift on the x-axis or change of slope between any one of the three color emulsions plotted will predict an image change recorded by that film. As little as a two degree shift of a curve was considered a major displacement. These guys on FNN were looking for plotted curves that actually *crossed* or diverged! There seemed to be some promise with...what did they call it... technical analysis.

The new goal to leave Kodak became more defined when I attached a time element to it. I wanted to work on Wall Street within three years. I wanted to trade, that's all I knew. I was unaware there was a sellside or a buyside. Wall Street all seemed more interesting, energetic and exciting than Kodak in Rochester. All I knew was that I wanted in.

The career change came in some respects after me rather than vice-versa. I was merely receptive to a change and any opportunity that might bridge the immense canyon between photography and Wall Street. Opportunities generally pop up when you're not looking.

Coming home from a business trip to Minneapolis in late February, my flight arrived into Chicago late, and I missed my connection to Rochester, New York. Finally settling in on the next USAir flight I noticed a tall man struggling to reach the seat beside mine. We both complained about the tight quarters as there was insufficient room for our knees and briefcases. So far it was a typical business flight. Shortly after the flight took off the man sitting beside me began to squirm and fight with his briefcase, a case that looked like it had been on safari through the Serengeti in Africa. As the man opened his case, I became aware that I was totally fixated on its contents. He had a pile of bond indentures, 10K, and 10Q reports. I had only read about such things in my home study course and had never actually seen one. (A game I still play on airplanes is to try and guess what someone does for a living and where they are from. Too many Sherlock Holmes books as a kid, I guess.) This man was definitely in some way involved with the financial world I had only begun to learn about. As the flight continued, we began to talk. After he learned what I did for Kodak, he asked me many questions about the strengths and weaknesses of two marketing plans described within sections of his reports. He also asked if the marketing plans complemented one another. I remember they did. I reciprocated with a string of stupid questions about bonds... and learned that a bond issue was the 17s *of* 2001, rather than *in* 2001. (It still seems strange; bonds mature *in* a particular year, not *of* a year.) He asked me for my business card and he in turn gave me his...all four of them. Chairman of this, President of that... I had never heard of him from my universe of photography. His name was Stanford N. Phelps from Greenwich, Connecticut. At a later time he told me his story of how he had once hired some young guy by the name of Michael Milken into Drexel Lambert. I had been sitting on the plane next to one of Wall Street's junk bond kings. I had no idea at the time just where that flight from Chicago would eventually take me.

Two days later the courtship began when a bouquet of flowers was delivered to my office at Kodak's head office. Within three months I was saying my good-byes to friends, meeting real estate agents to sell my house, and giving many belongings away as I prepared to move from my Victorian home into a small apartment. The company was in shock because no one had ever returned the key to the firm's family jewels before. My family to this day can't believe I walked away from what appeared back then to be corporate security for life. To change jobs because of an acquaintance made on an airplane was considered unbelievable. For several years my parents wailed if only my flight from Minneapolis to Chicago had not been late. There were days when I have to admit that I had wished for the same thing. I learned to hate the sellside of the market, junk and corporate bonds alike. I didn't last long, but it was worth it. I had bridged the Grand Canyon between photography and Wall Street.

If you are new to the financial industry, you will quickly discover that few people enter this field right out of school. The stories are as diverse as the people and markets themselves. What is of greatest interest is not the diverse industries that were crossed but the catalysts which led the individual to make such a major move. I jumped into the junk bond frying pan because I was afraid another opportunity might never come along again. Who was going to hire a total greenhorn with a photography background to trade? Don't call us, we'll call you. So when the first train to Wall Street seemed to cross my path I jumped on board. Anyway, I had only just learned what a bond was... Junk bonds weren't covered in my home study course. Apparently I was hired based on two credentials. The first was that I could and did match up several takeover candidates with my marketing training. The second was that I had once been a competitive swimmer. I was later told it was primarily the latter that led to the job offer. Did he think I was a natural for swimming with the sharks? Kidding aside, if you have been an athlete, you developed the same skills as those needed for trading. Take the exercises and lessons in the next section very seriously if you're on the outside of the "looking-glass" now and want to get into this business.

This leads me back to where this chapter began, with a discussion of how to let go of goals that cannot be reached. We have to let go of old goals sometimes so we can move on to new ones. The absolute worst advice someone can offer another is, *"just move forward and leave the past behind you."* The early struggles I experienced with writing this chapter eventually homed in on this single fact: that unresolved goals from the past can't be shed by just walking away from them. It is not that easy. Goals that are improperly put to rest can and do impact your judgment in future situations.

One of my former unresolved goals became the catalyst for leaving Kodak. The fear of missing an opportunity that would leave me asking "what-if" was the only motivation I needed to take action when S.N. Phelps came after me. There were numerous factors involved, but the primary catalyst was that ten minute incident I referred to in the beginning of this chapter that finally got me to sell everything, leave Kodak, and jump into the unknown. Fear is one of the strongest catalysts for moving us toward a goal.

What was the fear that motivated me to leave the familiar Kodak womb and go to Wall Street? I did not make the 1976 Olympic swim team. The Olympic trials are held so close to the Olympic Games themselves that final events can be sold out before the team is even selected. Swimmers who place third in the finals of the Trials become Olympic team alternates. Alternates were not allowed on the pool deck because there was insufficient room. I had decided that if I couldn't swim, I'd go to the Games in some other capacity. I submitted a portfolio of photographs to the accreditation office in hopes of attaining an official pass as a photographer. This is just about as competitive as finding a spot on the team as an athlete. Needless to say I didn't make it. So I drove from Toronto to Montreal with a new portfolio prepared and arrived at the accreditation office to try one more time to get in. This time I was met with a "Get out to Bromont...you're covering the three-day event...and you're late!" I wasn't selected to swim, but I was a photographer at the Games and did cartwheels as I rushed to where the equestrian events were being held. This site was about as far as anyone could possibly be from the Olympic swimming pool in Montreal. I was grateful for this small blessing.

One night, another photographer and I drove back to Montreal to pick up our transparencies from the lab. We walked down a different path from prior evenings and came upon a large structure emitting an odor that my nose immediately identified: chlorine. The pool was right in front of us. During the Montreal Olympics the outer construction of the pool was incomplete, and we had stopped by a construction entrance, closed off by a large metal fence. To this day I can still remember looking over the plywood construction wall just beyond the top of the fence to see people in the distance sitting all the way up to the top bleachers, bright banners hanging down from the pool ceiling, and the top of the high diving platform with the flags of several nations flying. The pool itself was out of view, but the sounds and echoes of cheers were not. As the photographer beside me used the single overhanging construction light bulb to sort the day's films, I saw a security guard walk towards us. He started to send us on our way but for some reason stopped. I surely had a strange expression on my face because he turned to me and asked if we wanted to slip in to watch the next event from the top bleachers? I paused for a moment and began to walk forward as he opened the gate. I'd never said anything to the photographer I was with as to why I was so interested in the swimming pool. Just as I stepped forward, I remember the photographer beside me grabbed my arm and said he really had to get back to make a phone call to his magazine, he had already kept them waiting a half hour. Foolishly, I stepped back, thanked the security guard for his kindness, and began to walk away. I didn't hear a word the other photographer was saying. There was only a chant between my ears repeating, "Time to move forward, don't look behind, it's all over, move on to something new." I thought it was some kind of test and the consoling words from my coach were being replayed. I could hear the security guard slam the metal chain fence, wrap the heavy chain, and lock the gate behind us. The metallic sound seemed to reverberate up and down my spine. In closing the gate the guard had accidentally hit the construction light causing the only bright light source to begin swinging. Our long shadows in front of us began to swing from left to right as we walked away. All the while I was repeating, "Don't look behind, it's all over, move on to something else." We walked into a parking lot that was completely black. There were no lights. We were swallowed by total blackness. I thought I had silently closed that chapter in my life as the metal fence slammed shut that night. Or so I thought then.

That incident and the sounds of the fence are still with me. Not continually, but every time I may be missing an opportunity, the image and sounds of that metal gate slamming at the Montreal Olympics comes to mind. The incident took on added significance when I later learned I had passed up seeing the actual event I had been training eleven years to swim. The pain associated with that new piece of information was indescribable. Time should have put a new perspective on the incident, but it never did. The nightmares about looking through the fence at the pool, my view blocked, but still hearing the sounds and smelling the chlorine, followed by the metal fence closing, our swinging shadows swallowed by the blackness of that parking lot, all return every four years. I'll finally put this one behind me soon. In 1996 the Olympics are coming to Atlanta. I now live near Atlanta. Coincidence? Fate? Who's to tell? It has taken exactly twenty years to have another opportunity to walk through that metal gate... some goals we just have to resolve completely before we can put them behind us and move on.

Don't confuse failing to reach the goal as the underlying source of the pain that needs resolution. You can reach your goal and still experience similar inner turmoil. The source of this deep anguish is being denied an opportunity.

Consider the story of American runner Billy Mills who stunned the 75,000 people witnessing the 1964 Olympic Games unfold in Tokyo's National Stadium. His story is one of the most unforgettable comebacks in Olympic history. In the home stretch of the 10,000 meter race, Mills unleashed a frantic sprint from far back in the pack, bringing the crowd to its feet, and pulled past the field to post a three meter victory.

In the bedlam that followed, Mills was denied the opportunity for the traditional victory lap. Although he had won, he anguished and felt unfulfilled for twenty years until 1984, when he and his wife, Pat, revisited Tokyo's National Stadium.

> "I knew what I wanted. I needed my moment," he recalls. "So I went down to the track, and as I started around, I lived the race. I could sense the people in the stadium. Toward the end of the lap, I heard one person clapping. It was Pat, and I started to cry. It was raining, so I turned my face to the sky and regained my composure. It was the most satisfying lap I've ever run."
>
> *—From an interview with Billy Mills by Joe Drape, for the Atlanta Committee for the Olympic Games*

Motivation and Self-Improvement

" You Can Only Win One for the Gipper Once"
—Red Auerbach, Former President of the Boston Celtics

Remember that Ronald Reagan movie when the dying football player, George Gipp, asks Knute Rockne, Notre Dame's legendary coach, to tell the team to win that big game "for the Gipper"? The story goes that Rockne used the Gipper speech to inspire the Irish to a famous come-from-behind victory over Army several years later.

In Red Auerbach's book, *MBA: Management By Auerbach*, he expresses his thoughts about this approach. "It probably did work — once. My question is: What did Rockne do for an encore? He could only ask his team once to win one for the Gipper." Auerbach goes on to explain that there are too many "big games" in the course of an NBA season and that the magic formula is not an eloquently delivered message in the locker room. He states, "If your players aren't sufficiently motivated at that point, nothing you say or do is going to make the difference...*First of all, you can't motivate a team or a group. You have to motivate an individual.* We're all too different. What gets one person going can turn off another. There's also no quick fix when it comes to motivation. It's a gradual process that starts in the initial recruitment of a player and builds throughout a career."

An individual's motivation comes from loving what they do. True, the money is important for both professional athletes and traders, but it can't keep you motivated in the financial or sports arena. If your own career is at a crossroads, imagine getting paid for doing something you'd love to do anyway. Then if you are fortunate enough to be paid for doing what you love, the key is learning the strategies which can keep that inner spark alive. It is not necessarily a question of "how can I get motivated?" as much as it is "how do I stay motivated?"

While profit is assumed to be the primary motivation for anyone in finance, this assumption makes it difficult to explain the trader or investor who finds a profitable trading system and then abandons that system for another when something new appears to have greater promise. We are all driven by several different motivating factors.

One motivation is discovering the perfect system. For these individuals, profit is not their primary motivation. System hopscotch is a symptom of someone who is in the business for investigative research. They have a greater driving force to satisfy their scientific curiosity than to accumulate profits. When they have a winning streak, they tend to go out and purchase higher powered computers with new improved trading software with exponentially more features. They are driven to test all the new bells and whistles that their new software offers. The logic is that if they made a profit with one system, just think what wealth they could accumulate if they learn to master all the indicators! Andrew Cardwell is a technical analyst renowned for his work and development of the Relative Strength Index (RSI). Andrew developed a valuable price forecasting methodology from specific RSI patterns he calls Positive and Negative Reversals. He commented that the original RSI indicator itself was passed on to him by a client of his when he was a commodities broker. The client made money from this technical indicator, but abandoned using it. Why? He found something else that looked more attractive and appeared to have greater financial reward. Cardwell has since put a lifetime into the research and successful development of this analytic method using RSI. What became of the client that first gave him this information? He apparently eroded his account to zero as he pursued his need to find the perfect indicator. Such individuals are motivated by trying to find the "perfect" system; they fool themselves into thinking they are strictly motivated by money. Profit alone will not sustain their drive; they will continue to tweak and test indicators for their entire trading careers to fulfill their need to satisfy their scientific curiosity.

What about motivation for the intellectual challenge? The intellectual challenge is coupled with the motivation or drive to "beat the game," a game that we are all too aware few are capable of winning. When I was beginning to trade, one of my mentors stated that the S&P was the most difficult market to trade. As this comment was reinforced by watching traders shy away from S&P futures (generally trend followers), it only served to fuel my motivation to win at the game of trading S&Ps. That's probably why my trading career has evolved towards the S&P futures market. I've always been motivated to go after what was labeled "the toughest," so why should trading be any different? If I had been told soybeans was the toughest market out there, and reinforcement from others had backed that claim, I would have likely burnt the midnight oil studying the factors and influences of the soybean market, instead of the S&P and financial markets.

We all have motivations in varying degrees. Remember, we are made up of three distinct individuals; it is no surprise they have different needs to be satisfied. The Basic Self will establish a motivation for the excitement alone. The Basic Self, our inner child, likes to have fun. When there is an imbalance, it can manifest itself in an addiction to the adrenaline rush associated with the "trading game," similar to excessive gambling. The symptom to watch out for is a need to play the trading game all the time. Is it difficult to step to the side and watch a fast market develop? Do you have to be part of every significant intraday move? Are you able to take a week off and not watch the markets? No papers, no news, no phone calls back to the office to find out what's happening in the markets? I used to go through withdrawal symptoms the first three days of a one week vacation. How about you? Do you have a sense of relief, an actual sense that you have reduced your stress level because you have just established a position or are no longer flat? Look out if you answer some of these questions "Yes." Obsessive traders will be unable physically to sustain the pressures of the trading game for long. Their longevity will be extremely limited. I have this obsessive trait and know it for what it is, one of my weak links that has to be consciously kept in check. Obsessive motivations must be kept in check so they do not cause an imbalance among the *three selves*.

Don't forget to consider ego as a motivational force. To some degree we all have an ego and need one to believe we can succeed where so many others have failed. However, if ego is not in check and is an imbalance to your other motivational traits, the markets will destroy you until humility and respect enter into your line of perspective. One trading room I worked in, early in my career, had a trader who would periodically announce: "I can do no wrong." When that phrase was uttered, it was my signal to fade this trader. I didn't trade this particular market often, but this was an exception. His ego usually led him to a huge loss when he knew he "could do no wrong." Fading him until his major hit occurred usually led to a very profitable gain in a very short period. When that one trade finally cost him dearly, I knew not to fade him any longer, and directed no further attention to his trading activities. (We'll address why this was incredibly foolish for me to have done at a later time.)

Everyone is different and, as Auerbach notes, no one thing motivates all. Actually, motivation stems from *multiple* reasons. Multiple motivations explain why we establish multiple goals to satisfy each of our *three selves*. It is more than important, it is essential to know what motivates us. This has a direct impact on how we trade. As another example, I will never be a long term horizon investor because part of my own drive is the excitement of the markets. My personality needs to see results fairly quickly. I do not fit the profile of someone willing to sit and wait through a corporate restructuring for a junk bond to be revalued. That is as exciting to me as watching paint dry, even though the financial rewards are tremendous. I just don't have the patience for it.

The temperament you have becomes an extremely important factor to the trading horizon you should focus on. It will have a significant impact on the potential you will have to make a profit. If you are trading a weekly horizon, but your trading personality is a closer fit to a six hour horizon, it won't matter how much you know about money management. Proven money management principles will most likely be thrown out the window as the trader who is forced to trade longer horizons begins to over bet in the need to satisfy his motivational drive for excitement. A great money management myth is that there is less risk associated with a short term horizon trade compared to longer term horizons. The standard deviation of prices will be greater with longer time horizon positions, *but the market drawdown will be about the same*. The reason for this is that the short horizon player generally holds much larger positions than the longer term investor.

It is extremely important to understand what fuels your own motivational fires. I recall an employer, whose capital I was trading, walked into my office to view the screens. (A situation to be avoided if at all possible.) I was looking at a five minute S&P chart, it was a thin market during lunch time, and some novice trader entered a market order to buy 50 cars. The pit locals had a field day on this order and ran the market a dollar ($500 per contract). My employer knew we had a sizable short position at that time and began to panic. I called the floor; I knew it was a market order that was being worked, and at the same time that the locals finished pressing the market for this order, the pit became deathly silent in the background — a sign that there was no other paper entering the pit. I entered a limit order to sell another 20 cars immediately, and I thought my employer was going to have a stroke. The short lived rally was indeed over. We had actually found an ideal level to sell and add to our current position. The market did retrace the entire move up, and my employer survived the crisis he had perceived on a five minute chart. His logic, however, was surprising: he said that is why he much preferred us to focus on just the weekly charts and longer horizon trades...*they were less risky.* He was very serious too!

So what differences are there between someone who eventually drops out, having lost sight of their goal, and another who continues on through all the slumps, back-testing, and emotional ups and downs that we traders experience? As with athletes, the individual who sticks with it likely knows where he's going and values his goal. The professional basketball player that already has his multi-million dollar NBA contract signed is no longer motivated by the money. What keeps him going? In professional trading the same analogy can apply. Regardless of what drives us, there will be times when our motivation hits skid row. It's during these lulls, or down times, that there are specific strategies my coaches used to reignite the motivation. These strategies do apply to trading.

The first strategy is actually harder for an athlete to accept than a trader. The trader's advantage is that he is already familiar with cycles and accepts that they exist. It is immaterial if you believe they are reliable enough to trade from or not. So if you accept that there are cycles in the markets, it is not difficult to make the association that there are cycles within ourselves. Our motivations will have their seasons. There are going to be some down times. Accept it. There will be cyclical development periods of our Three Selves as well. We may be at times loud, boisterous, extroverted, and outwardly highly productive.

At other times, a cycle will influence a time when we experience an inner reflective and quiet nature that will offset the early stress and tension from the crest of the prior cycle. *Development of our inner self is cyclical.* Sometimes we just want to goof off and play, and at other times we may be very attentive, driven and methodical about our intellectual research and trading activities. It is important not to become too rigid within a trading schedule. For example, there are many disciplines associated with trading that we need to spend time on: money management skills, analysis back-testing, trading technique, market research, etc. Utilize the variations to your advantage. Learn to recognize and accept your own cycles of development and accompanying ups and downs. Coaches teach athletes that it is natural to lose it, "it" being your balance, your drive, your edge, or perhaps even your skill for a while. Have patience; it will return. This is natural. It is important to yield to these personal cycles rather than fight them. You may be able to offset the timing of an expected cycle low or crest, but you won't be able to avoid it. The lows in sports are called slumps, and there's never a good time for them. The crests are called peaks, but there is definitely a right time to peak. Peak too early or too late and the "big game" is lost. No one can sustain peak performance all of the time. If that's what you're after, forget it! *No one can sustain peak performance all of the time.* It is extremely important to accept this, otherwise you set yourself up for an emotional setback. If you judge yourself harshly or unjustly during these setbacks, then nagging thoughts arise that will question why you should continue?

In Fred Rohe's book, *The Zen of Running*, he describes:

> "If the dance of the run isn't fun
> then discover another dance,
> because without fun the good of the run is undone,
> and a suffering runner always quits, sooner or later."

Our motivation is directly proportional to the pleasure and personal rewards we allow ourselves. Go back and re-read that last sentence...it is loaded. We have to allow ourselves a personal reward. I'll address this in more detail as it is the source of one of our trading obstacles that we need to overcome: self-sabotage. Do you reach a certain level of profit in your trading account, and then begin to change your trading style so it leads to a major loss? This is a form of self-sabotage when you don't believe you deserve a favorable outcome or reward. We'll come back to this discussion of self-sabotage. The other factor is that our motivation is directly proportional to the pleasure we experience in striving for the milestones that lead to a goal. I intensely disliked the field of junk bonds and had to change. I not only had to change the market I was involved with, but I also recognized I wanted to switch from the sellside to the buyside.

> For those new to the financial industry, the sellside of the market requires a broker ideally to find both a seller and buyer to execute a cross trade simultaneously. In a cross transaction, settlement passes from the seller straight over to the buyer. Therefore no, or very limited, capital exposure exists for the firm in the middle of these cross transactions. As a result of the lower risk, the firm can justify higher commissions for a cross transaction and thereby establishes the motivation for the broker to find both sides of the trade. On the buyside, you risk your own, or your firm's capital. You don't go out into the market to find someone that can take the other side of your trade.

A change does not necessarily have to be from the sellside to the buyside, or to a different discipline or market within the business. It is equally important to change your routine, give yourself a reward, or introduce new elements into your schedule to keep you vigilant towards a goal. The hardest reward to give ourselves is time off. It's important. Actually, it's essential! When our trading seems to be on a hot streak we can't leave for fear the momentum will be broken. When we are in a trading slump, especially if we're on a trading desk, we can't afford to take the time off when we are down. We promise ourselves we will take time when the slump is over. Quality time is never found in such situations because there is no in between, we are either on a hot streak or in a slump. It's not often we trade on a flat line. No one can trade all of the time. The fastest way to make many principal investors crazy is to show inactivity in their account. I've learned that for many investors *losses are more acceptable than account inactivity*. This is nuts.

Another important reward is to buy ourselves an occasional gift. Go buy that speed boat that invigorates your soul. Then when you hit a slump, and we all do, you won't get caught at home wishing you had bought it when you could have, rather than having given all the money back to the market.

If after a string of trading losses you experience a drastic decline in your motivation, you are likely being affected by a specific problem — investing too much ego into the activity. We then measure our own self-worth by the results of our trading, or sport, thereby allowing the result to become a dangerous mechanism for ego-deflation. Good coaches have many different ways of picking athletes out of the dust when this happens, but their objective is always the same: to understand that excellence is achieved by improving upon an error. Without loss we would be unable to reach greater heights. We need to learn how to lose before we can learn how to win. Learning to cope with a loss and learning to constructively use our down cycles, lays the foundation for our successes. Knowing how to lose and knowing how to cope with the loss will remove the fear of potentially experiencing a failure when you try. It's going to happen, it's cyclical. Coaches teach athletes to blend with these cycles of ups and downs, not to fight them. View a loss as an opportunity to improve, and it will be far less damaging to your ego.

Frequently we are called upon to motivate ourselves to do something that we really don't want to do. This is very different from when we want to create a motivation, or identify what our motives and goals are for doing something in the first place. But when the task is viewed as unpleasant, the trick is to break the task into small, manageable segments. When a job seems easier to do, when we believe it is possible, motivation is more available. Analyzing government bond spreads is one area I have a hard time getting excited about. By breaking certain steps down, or integrating other aspects which are more enjoyable, it becomes a lot more manageable. For longer tasks set up a system of rewards. Give yourself a payoff when you pass a milestone. For example, a dinner out, a live show, or my favorite...a chocolate fudge brownie. (Government bond spreads can be very fattening.)

Be cautious about being motivated to accomplish goals simply for the sake of achievement alone. This creates extreme tension and pressure. Continually being fixated on reaching a goal will actually build a serious obstacle which will prevent you from attaining that goal. The limitation is that you will put more attention towards the future and never be able to fully live, concentrate, or immerse yourself completely in the current moment. This in turn may become the flaw that holds you back from performing to your best ability and thereby hinders your improvement.

The first chapter introduced the Tao mindset of the Beginner's Mind. If you believe you have all the answers, you impose a false limit on yourself. Self-improvement happens in an infinite number of ways — be open to them. Try to consciously see yourself as a beginner, and protect yourself from thinking you know it all. For a period of time I designed trading models for numerous Foreign Exchange traders working for major firms in New York, Chicago, and Los Angeles. There were at least one hundred different models I designed for individual traders. (Can you think of any better way of exposing yourself to a wide variety of traders from which to learn?) Some approaches the traders used were very unique applications to common problems. Other traders used methods which were variations of common indicators. The top traders I encountered all seemed to have a similar trait: they were all trying to learn something new each day. The traders often posed questions to find out if I really knew my stuff. Once I was accepted, these traders became relentless learners. They had endless energy for trying new ideas and finding other ways to profit test their approaches. On the other hand, I frequently found that those traders who already knew everything and were highly skeptical about being given anything new, had serious flaws within their indicator setup. They frequently used the pre-defined variables that are established as default limits by their quote vendor and discarded new approaches which could have resolved timing or reduced false market signals for them.

As a totally inexperienced greenhorn when I left Kodak, the trading room and brokers were extremely intimidating. Eventually I caught on that by learning just one small thing a day, your abilities will soon surpass many around you. The reason is that many reach a plateau of achievement, and then they stand still, or maintain a holding pattern, thinking they have learned all there is to know. Those who have stagnated will be passed.

I gave a presentation at a conference in Las Vegas that involved a trading demonstration. I was setting up the overhead materials, waiting for the audience to settle in. As is normally the case, I tend to scan the audience. My eyes and heart stopped when I recognized one individual sitting near the front. George Lane was in attendance. My presentation included a rather graphic example of when his Stochastics indicator would reliably fail. I had planned to include this failure as a signal for when traders of size could fade the smaller trader. It would be the smaller traders that would supply the volume for a larger order coming into the market on the other side. George Lane had created the Stochastics indicator. He is recognized as one of the best lecturers among all analysts, and is also well known for not being shy about expressing his opinion when he audits a lecture. He cheers robustly for someone presenting well crafted new research. Flaws in logic are brought to the audience's attention with equal fervor. He also makes sure the speaker does not move on until a topic is distinctly covered for the audience. George Lane's presence is formidable. In this setting, my first reaction was mild panic. I considered skipping my examples of when to fade Stochastics, but then thought better of this flight-to-safety instinct and charged ahead with the original game plan. I was confident that I had done my homework, confident that I had done enough testing to rebut any challenges that George may have raised during my lecture. So I charged ahead. To my relief, and somewhat surprise, George Lane became my supporter, sharing his boisterous and warm enthusiasm openly. He was one of the most outspoken individuals in attendance. His inquisitive comments and questions contributed to everyone present. George is in his seventies, but he still has the curiosity to learn, share, and listen to new ideas. He doesn't stop learning or asking questions. He comes to the table with his teacup ready to be filled and exemplifies the Beginner's Mindset that was mentioned in the first few pages.

We need to take the time to reflect and learn from our current progress and mistakes. A client of mine, referred to in Jack Schwager's book, *Market Wizards*, once had an unprofitable trade during a contract rollover in the S&P market. This individual has been in the business for a great deal of time and is highly respected throughout the Industry. The trade did not lose much money, but regardless, he struggled to understand why that trade went wrong. He soon recalled an identical circumstance from when the cost of carry was out of line in a similar manner. Not in the last year mind you, several years back. Longevity in this business is rare. I attribute his market success and survival to his assertive attitude to reflect upon past errors and successes and to learn from them. One day when I was moaning to him about an error I had made with a trading strategy, he asked how old I was? When I answered he told me, "You better be making errors. How else are you going to learn?" His commitment to learn from every winning and losing trade has made quite an impact on my trading approach.

Reflection takes time and practice. Reflect on your feelings towards trading, its patterns and rhythms as they present themselves to you. Also work on understanding the interaction of your personal life with your trading performance. This interaction contributes directly to our trading performance fluctuations. Reflection can also help you get a grip on reality. If you are physically exhausted and drained, your trading performance is going to decline. One year I took a terrible nose dive with my trading track record. Until that time it had maintained a steady growth that ranged between a 27% to 43% annual return. It was too late when I finally took the time to reflect on what contributed to this trading disaster. It boiled down to two weaknesses actually.

I learned not to trade the last day preceding an end-of-month statement, and also never to trade when I was sick. After evaluating every single trade, I discovered that by removing those particular days from my bottom line would have produced a net profit of +34% for the year, rather than a negative return. Before this evaluation, I was unaware I took greater risks in front of a P/L statement and unaware of how illness caused me to lose my intuitive timing and instincts.

While I was struggling to understand the factors that contributed to my worst trading year, I had uncovered a beat up, old coaches' manual for track. In it was a section to help a coach try to understand why an athlete's performance had suddenly taken a turn for the worse. It offered this list to test if the athlete had been presented with any new distractions to account for the decline in his recent performance. My jaw dropped when I read it... *I could answer yes to every question...* Think back on when you have had a trading slump. How well would you fare on this list? Be honest with yourself.

- Have you experienced changes in sleep patterns?
- Has there been a death or loss of a close relationship,
- or major illness of a close family member?
- Have you had an increase in financial responsibility?
- Have you recently relocated?
- Has your social life taken on a new dimension?
- Has your interest in [trading] changed in any way?
- Have you recently been injured or excessively ill?

Answering yes to one or more of these questions was suggested in the manual to have sufficient negative effect to interfere with the athlete's capabilities, attitudes, and performance ability in track. As performance in sports and trading are impacted by similar psychological factors, this list clearly applies to trading. If one or two are proven to have an effect, just think what happens when you can answer yes to all of them! All of these questions actually help to identify performance obstacles. So does experiencing an equity curve change just before an end-of-month or end-of-week statement. Each needs to be handled in a specific and different manner, which will be fully discussed in Part III, "Inner Aerodynamics: Enhanced Trading Skills Through Professional and Olympic Coaching Techniques."

Psychological Tactics

The yielding can triumph over the inflexible;
The weak can triumph over the strong.
Fish should not be taken from deep waters;
Nor should organizations make obvious their advantages.
—*Tao Te Ching, no.36 (Original Chinese source)*

Trading for a firm in Boston whose roots were based in Hong Kong and whose principals are Chinese made me very curious about Asian learning approaches. This led to my introduction of the very ancient Tao Te Ching. In traditional Chinese learning, the cyclic transformation of all aspects of life is understood as constant movement. This process is the Tao. To be really good at something requires the presence and participation of your mind, body, and spirit in total synchronization, with spontaneity and centered awareness. I can think of numerous coaches who unknowingly adopted the Tao Te Ching, or were silent students themselves. Most of what they taught me in sport, which applies to trading and business, is defined in the Tao Te Ching.

Coaches spend time not only training the athlete's body but training the mind as well. We are taught strategies to prevent being psyched-out by an opponent and tactics to enhance your own position in a competitive environment. These are given a great deal of attention. Most of these tactics, or game plans, are derived from two simple strategies also suggested by The Tao. The first is to conceal any advantages. Concealment does not promote any resistance or counter force. The second is to overcome those who are inflexible by yielding. Let me explain.

In trading rooms where traders are closely packed together, a competitive environment is created that is no different psychologically from any holding area created for competitors prior to a high-stakes sporting event. The similarity finally dawned on me when a trader began to express similar lines and tactics I had experienced in locker rooms prior to swim meets.

Fading cold traders or shadowing hot ones will continue as long as there are traders. I managed to get away with fading the trader that exclaimed, "I can do no wrong", but I was wrong to have paid any attention to him. As confidence in my own abilities grew, I stopped taking any notice of others around me. My mentors all share a common belief — that the best traders are *completely independent* and don't care what another trader's opinion might be. For the majority however, let the head games begin. By being aware of the games being played, it becomes easier to blend with them and ignore them or apply them in other ways. One New York trader I heard say, "I'm tired, I've had no rest, I just lost a bundle on that last trade," when in fact he hadn't closed a position at all, but was opening one. At the end of the month we learned this guy just had the best month on the desk and had "dropped" nearly everyone behind in the process. His low profile caught those who fade or shadow a trader off guard. He gave the appearance of being nonconfrontational, not at his peak, and vulnerable to making errors. This subterfuge gave that trader a competitive advantage. However, the real advantage is retained by the trader who is completely independent and pays no attention to others.

Shadowing and fading occurs in the pits as well. There are tactical strategies used between traders of large positions against the exchange floor locals. The same tactics apply. Big players cannot show a physical stop. There are times of course that you have to place physical stops, but as a general rule it is best not to show all your cards. If you think an order is quietly held in the hands of a broker waiting to be revealed and executed at an appropriate time... Ha! Time to shed the scales from your eyes. Standing beside the S&P pit you can see orders passed from a desk to the runner. Larger orders then start a vocal outcry from the top tier of the pit. An announcement is heard about whose order has just been received, what size, and at what level. Put a few juicy carrots in front of the locals during a thin market that offers them the opportunity to position themselves favorably... and you get a run on stops. A wash and rinse cycle, so to speak, where all the stops are washed out and the traders have to reposition themselves at a higher/lower level than they might otherwise have had prior to the run.

There are tactics where this knowledge becomes an advantage. Bidding a market up to have a more favorable sale for larger orders is fairly common practice. In essence this is no different from what the pit locals are doing by running stops. A small, well-placed market order in the S&P pit during the lunch time lull will sometimes become the "sacrifice fly ball" to fill a larger order coming into the market on the opposite side. This would not be the situation for much larger market spikes. You need to intimately know the character and mechanics of the market you are trading. It is easy to make incorrect assumptions about what is contributing to a market's move. As an example, a big deal is made throughout the S&P trading community when the pit reveals an order is being worked for Paul Tudor Jones that leads to a sharp market spike. The pit and many traders will assume Jones' firm is bailing out of a large position in trouble. Their assumption is most likely wrong. More often while the pit is forming that sharp spike, the real play is a cash order being worked for Jones' firm. The S&P pit is only seeing the dollar neutral hedge being worked as a much larger cash order is being executed simultaneously through the Daisy computer that handles block orders for the NYSE. As a result, the pit incorrectly assumes that the trader has been caught on the wrong side of the market, when in actual fact, he has established a hedged position or a net position on the other side of the market. The pit and smaller traders' erroneous assumptions are reinforced because the market may then develop a sharp move in the opposite direction. However, the real point is: you shouldn't care. Trade your own game and disregard who is trading what for whom. If that spike occurred just after you established your own position, resulting in your position being stopped out, reestablish it. FAST! Don't waste time trying to figure out if Tudor is in trouble or not. It doesn't come off your bottom-line, or for that matter, contribute to it either if he is right.

Once you have been marked or identified as a significant trader based on the action and size of your orders (or if you frequently identify the market's pivot levels), then it becomes a different ball game for that trader or firm. It is not enough to evaluate the direction of the market; you must then learn to contend with the added complexities of disguising your orders so the pit doesn't identify you. The pit would then shadow your orders, making it difficult to be filled. There is a great deal of truth to the saying, "if the locals fill you easily...you're probably wrong."

Most psyche-out tactics are counterproductive. That is, until you are taught how to use them as controlling tactics. The difference is that most psyche-out tactics have a negative effect caused by belligerent techniques. Successful tactics strive for minimum conflict. In long distance running and swimming races, there is a great deal of strategy and tactical activity. Taking the lead is often followed by losing the lead. An athlete fully prepared and trained looks beyond the moment of holding the lead or falling behind. Understanding this can help you gain the advantage and enhance your position over an opponent. In trading, who is the opponent? The market, everyone else, but primarily ourselves when we have lost our center of balance. Here are a few other points common to both athletics and trading:

- When you let go of an obsessive need to win, you decrease your tension, stress, and anxiety level and increase your probability of winning.

- When you want to run faster or be stronger, don't force it — relax instead.

- Insecure athletes and traders promote themselves; they attempt to appear strong, when in reality they're not.

- Trying to quicken your rise to the top sets you back. Evolve slowly as an athlete.

- When you meet with rigidity, become flexible.

- When you want to achieve in sport or trading, you must give — time, effort, and yourself.

- Give the appearance of vulnerability, and you'll be stronger.

- Conceal your advantages to catch others off guard.

Experience and continued exposure to psychological tactics will certainly prepare us to deal more effectively with new tactical maneuvers; however, the key is not to create a counter force. On the other hand, psyche-out tactics will be successful if we never stand our ground. So how can you avoid becoming a wimp? By learning to deflect incoming tactical maneuvers. Over time this book will establish the foundation and knowledge required to deflect such maneuvers. Then you can counter with an unexpected surprise, having concealed your advantages.

PART III

Inner Aerodynamics: Enhanced Trading Skills through Professional and Olympic Coaching Techniques

Try not. Do. Or do not. There is no try.
— *Yoda*

OK, up to now you have been involved in a passive way, able to sit in your easy chair, read at your own leisure, and have no demands placed upon you. Your passive role has just come to an end. Now the training begins. Oh sure, you may still remain passive, but then you will not improve your skills or establish the essential foundation needed to tackle the really tough obstacles such as stress, failure, decision paralysis, and performance slumps. In a sense, I am excited for you. If you have not been involved with top coaches and their techniques for creating champions, then you are in for an exciting journey to new awareness. Once you become aware, there is no turning back. The outlook you currently have towards winning within *any competitive environment* will be changed forever.

You are about to enter a private training clinic. It is essential that you allow yourself to become involved. In this clinic, a variety of exercises will be presented for you to practice. The exercises will collectively provide for you a shift in your focus that will make the difference between stagnating at the skill level you currently have versus rapidly building upon and enhancing your abilities. You will learn how to filter and minimize external distractions, and then how to filter distracting thoughts. We will work on your ability to focus, concentrate, and center yourself *on demand* within highly demanding and stressful situations.

Of course that assumes you actually DO the exercises. Preceding an exercise there will always be an explanation with examples to provide you with the necessary foundation and understanding. Then you will be asked to take an active role. To satisfy the Conscious Self, the purpose for each exercise will be given. Some of the exercises will make you feel uneasy, others will be fun, and some will require thought, pen, and paper. All are important. You can't skip any of the steps or you will likely choose to skip the very aspect that you need most to help yourself. Give them all a chance and know you are working directly on the basic foundation of your trading skills. These attributes for success are proven, they work, and they will have greater ramifications than you may first realize.

I hope you have learned that mastering a specific indicator, or a trading technique, will never be enough. By gaining this awareness you have prepared yourself to move on. *Now you are ready to train your mind.* You are ready to acquire the inner skills you need to establish your edge.

As with any top coaching clinic, we begin by first watching and listening to a Master. This is usually accomplished by viewing a film or video. Then the components of the skill are broken down and fully analyzed. This is the approach we will take together now. The words of this particular coach, or Master, are words you have heard before. However, at your first introduction it is very possible that you did not fully comprehend the meaning and depth of his words and actions. You will.

This training clinic begins with an excerpt from a film script written by Lawrence Kasdan and Leigh Brackett from a story by George Lucas. Get comfortable, enjoy the multidimensional symbolism, have fun with it once again...

...We have begun...

THE EMPIRE STRIKES BACK

EXTERIOR: DAGOBAH - CREATURE'S HOUSE - NIGHT

A heavy downpour of rain pounds through the gnarled trees. A strange baroque mud house sits on a moss-covered knoll on the edge of a small lagoon. The small, gnomish structure radiates a warm glow from its thick glass windows. As the rain tap dances a merry tune on Artoo's head, the stubby little android rises up on his tip-toes to peek into one of the glowing portals.

INTERIOR: CREATURE'S HOUSE

Artoo, peeking in the windows, sees the inside of the house - a very plain, but cozy dwelling. Everything is in the same scale as the creature. The only thing out of place in the miniature room is Luke, whose height makes the four foot ceiling seem even lower. He sits cross-legged on the floor of the living room.

The creature is in an adjoining area - his little kitchen - cooking up an incredible meal. The stove is a steaming hodgepodge of pots and pans. The wizened little host scurries about chopping this, shredding that, and showering everything with exotic herbs and spices. He rushes back and forth putting platters on the table in front of Luke, who watches the creature impatiently.

LUKE: Look, I'm sure it's delicious. I just don't understand why we can't see Yoda now.

CREATURE: Patience! For the Jedi it is time to eat as well. Eat, eat. Hot. Good food, hm? Good, hmm?

Moving with some difficulty in the cramped quarters, Luke sits down near the fire and serves himself from the pot. Tasting the unfamiliar concoction, he is pleasantly surprised.

LUKE: How far away is Yoda? Will it take us long to get there?

CREATURE: Not far. Yoda not far. Patience soon you will be with him.

(*tasting food from the pot*) Rootleaf, I cook. Why wish you become Jedi? Hm?

LUKE: Mostly because of my father, I guess.

CREATURE: Ah, your father. Powerful Jedi was he, powerful Jedi, mmm.

LUKE: (*a little angry*) Oh, come on. How could you know my father? You don't even know who I am. (*fed up.*) Oh, I don't know what I'm doing here. We're wasting our time.

The creature turns away from Luke and speaks to a third party.

CREATURE: (*irritated*) I cannot teach him. The boy has no patience.

Luke's head spins in the direction the creature faces. But there is no one there. The boy is bewildered, but it gradually dawns on him that the little creature is Yoda, the Jedi Master, and that he is speaking with Ben.

BEN'S VOICE: He will learn patience.

YODA: Hmmm. Much anger in him, like his father.

BEN'S VOICE: Was I any different when you taught me?

YODA: Hah. He is not ready.

LUKE: Yoda! I am ready. I...Ben! I can be a Jedi. Ben, tell him I'm ready.

Trying to see Ben, Luke starts to get up but hits his head on the low ceiling.

YODA: Ready, are you? What know you of ready? For eight hundred years have I trained Jedi. My own counsel will I keep on who is to be trained! A Jedi must have the deepest commitment, the most serious mind.

(*to the invisible Ben, indicating Luke*) This one a long time have I watched. All his life has he looked away... to the future, to the horizon. Never his mind on where he was. Hmm? What he was doing. Humph. Adventure. Heh! Excitement. Heh! A Jedi craves not these things.

(*turning to Luke*) You are reckless!

Luke looks down. He knows it is true.

BEN'S VOICE: So was I, if you'll remember.

YODA: He is too old. Yes, too old to begin the training.

Luke thinks he detects a subtle softening in Yoda's voice.

LUKE: But I've learned so much.

Yoda turns his piercing gaze on Luke, as though the Jedi Master's huge eyes could somehow determine how much the boy has learned. After a long moment, the little Jedi turns toward where he alone sees Ben.

YODA: (*sighs*) Will he finish what he begins?

LUKE: I won't fail you - I'm not afraid.

YODA: (*turns slowly toward him*) Oh, you will be. You will be.

(The film cuts away to various scenes and then returns to Luke and Yoda.)

EXTERIOR: DAGOBAH - BOG - DAY

Luke's face is upside-down and showing enormous strain. He stands on his hands, with Yoda perched on his feet. Opposite Luke and Yoda are two rocks the size of bowling balls. Luke stares at the rocks and concentrates. One of the rocks lifts from the ground and floats up to rest on the other.

YODA: Use the Force. Yes...

Yoda taps Luke's leg. Quickly, Luke lifts one hand from the ground. His body wavers, but he maintains his balance. Artoo, standing nearby, is whistling and beeping frantically.

YODA: Now... the stone. Feel it.

Luke concentrates on trying to lift the top rock. It rises a few feet, shaking under the strain. But, distracted by Artoo's frantic beeping, Luke loses his balance and finally collapses. Yoda jumps clear.

YODA: Concentrate!

Annoyed at the disturbance, Luke looks over at Artoo, who is rocking urgently back and forth in front of him.

Artoo waddles closer to Luke, chirping wildly, then scoots over to the edge of the swamp. Catching on, Luke rushes to the water's edge. The X-wing fighter has sunk, and only the tip of its nose shows above the lake's surface.

LUKE: Oh, no. We'll never get it out now.

Yoda stamps his foot in irritation.

YODA: So certain are you. Always with you it cannot be done. Hear you nothing that I say?

Luke looks uncertainly out at the ship.

LUKE: Master, moving stones around is one thing. This is totally different.

YODA: No! No different! Only different in your mind. You must unlearn what you have learned.

LUKE: (*focusing, quietly*) All right, I'll give it a try.

YODA: NO! Try not. *Do*. Or do not. There is no try.

Luke closes his eyes and concentrates on thinking the ship out. Slowly, the X-wing's nose begins to rise above the water. It hovers for a moment and then slides back, disappearing once again.

LUKE: (*panting heavily*) I can't. It's too big.

YODA: Size matters not. Look at me. Judge me by my size, do you? Hm? Hmmm.

Luke shakes his head.

YODA: And well you should not. For my ally is the Force. And a powerful ally it is. Life creates it, makes it grow. Its energy surrounds us and binds us. Luminous beings are we ... (*Yoda pinches Luke's shoulder*) ... not this crude matter. (*a sweeping gesture*) You must feel the Force around you. (*gesturing*) Here, between you ...me ...the tree ...the rock ...everywhere! Yes, even between this land and that ship!

LUKE: (*discouraged*) You want the impossible.

Quietly, Yoda turns toward the sunken X-wing fighter. With his eyes closed and his head bowed, he raises his arm and points at the ship.
   Soon, the fighter rises above the water and moves forward as Artoo beeps in terror and scoots away.
   The entire X-wing moves majestically, surely, toward the shore. Yoda stands on a tree root and guides the fighter carefully down toward the beach.
   Luke stares in astonishment as the fighter settles gently onto the shore. He walks toward Yoda.

LUKE: I don't... I don't believe it.

YODA: That is why you fail.

Yoda's training put emphasis on skills of concentration, full attention to the present moment, and belief in one's own ability. They are without question the skills and attitudes that differentiate the average performer from an individual with extraordinary ability. We are not born with these skills; they are taught. Since they are acquired skills, the good news is that anyone can learn them. But the catch is, do you have the desire *and ability to take the necessary action* to develop these attributes? Yoda questioned Luke if he could finish what he started. Can you? Make a commitment to yourself to *do*, not just try, the exercises that follow.

People want success, money, or their definition of the good life on easy street. They want it handed to them without any effort, energy, or commitment on their part. It has frequently been stated by high achievers that success is 10% skill and 90% hard work. I experienced this first hand when I once offered a friend the means to earn thousands of dollars. John had the skill, but would have to apply himself for many hours to thoroughly learn what was being offered to him. After a brief attempt to try and learn, he never practiced again and gave up... even though he knew I had just bought a new Nissan 300ZX through this technique.

Let me explain more fully. As you think about this experience, ask yourself if you would have invested 80-120 hours of your time to simply learn the mechanics of a profitable game? If you do not think you could apply yourself that long to learn a winning system that was being handed to you on a silver platter, your trading career will end before you've even begun.

I had discovered my aptitude for counting cards at Blackjack when Kodak sent me to my first convention in Las Vegas. Fred, my friend and good Kodak customer, played Blackjack until dawn one night as I played along with him on a single twenty dollar bill. I had never played Blackjack before. My twenty dollar bill survived until dawn. I watched in fascination as Fred's green and black chips grew and diminished. The house allowed my two dollar bets to float in and out of the game (Good thing too... two dollars is a very high element of ruin for a twenty dollar bank roll!). Meanwhile my customer gradually returned all his earlier winnings back to the house. As the night progressed into the early hours of the morning, it became clear to me that by simply betting when our six deck shoe seemed to be rich in face cards, my meager two dollar bets had a high return that helped me through the losing streaks. That observation is what really kept my original twenty dollar bill alive that night. I had little knowledge then of how to play Blackjack, but a lot of intuitive money management skill and luck. At the end of 8-9 hours of play I recall leaving the table ahead 10%... or with 22 dollars. Fred walked away with a $5000+ loss. This first experience at the tables was all it took to whet my appetite to spend endless hours learning how Blackjack should be played.

I read and studied all the Blackjack Masters I could find when I returned home from the convention. Ken Uston, Stanford Wong, Bryce Carlson, Lawrence Revere, Julian Braun, and Dr. Edward Thorp, who originated the *optimal f unit*, or optimum number of units to bet given the probability of varying outcomes in a favorable game. I studied. I practiced. I learned. I practiced some more. I had a computer program written to evaluate minor strategy variations as they applied to varying casino rules throughout Las Vegas and Reno. I counted down decks of cards until they were paper thin and dog-eared. The books all said you had to have speed. Uston defined the time limits and I practiced until I could beat them. I could count down and remember a six deck shoe in less than 140 seconds. Eventually my old IBM-AT computer was churning money management comparisons and playing with the various strategies against itself for weeks at a time. Soon I thought I knew which were the most favorable games offered in Vegas and how to play them. (Sound like defining the probability of various market moves? Indeed it is. However, you can see that applying yourself so intensely can also appear to be obsessive behavior.) After much preparation, I was ready to count down six decks of cards if need be, alter the playing strategy as the game swings shifted between the player and the house, and then apply the correct money management betting strategy for a particular count to minimize the risk with my fixed bank roll. I was ready to take on Las Vegas. I arrived. I played. I lost!

I was able to play Blackjack with lethal accuracy at home. It was confirmed by my computer testing. But in the casino, the outcome was entirely different. The noise, the distractions, the fear I felt when I was down, and the under betting as a result of that fear when the cards were again in my favor, all led to the complete loss of my bank roll. Sounds like a trading room scenario, doesn't it? It certainly was.

What I had failed to learn was how to concentrate and maintain my level of skill within the casino's environment, the only place it counted. I was not mentally prepared and lost the professional card counters' marginal advantage. Even though I only made a few errors per hour, that was enough. My old swimming coaches would probably not have been surprised to know that it was their techniques that solved my concentration problems and fears in the casino environment. The same methods used to excel at Blackjack apply equally to trading.

So I went back to work after my first loss at the Blackjack tables. This time to train my mind. I practiced with blaring music and noise in the background. I learned to carry on an uninterrupted conversation with a friend as they dealt through the six decks of cards as fast as they could. People told me I was crazy to even try again.

The next trip to Vegas was very different. Soon I learned winning was more than fun, it was exhausting work. Blackjack is very mechanical, hard work, and actually boring as you play each hand mechanically to a predetermined set of rules established by statistical outcome. For all my practice hours and hard work, Las Vegas showed its appreciation by barring me from several of its finest Casinos. It became nearly impossible to sit down at any table. Eventually I even went to the extreme of enrolling in a class for dealers so that I might learn what dealers are taught to look for when screening for professional card counters. I learned not to show large betting swings and to increase the number of hands played at a time, rather than bet big on a single hand when the game was in my favor. Sound like an introduction to portfolio diversification and money management? It certainly became the foundation of a new career in trading.

Eventually the welcome mat in Las Vegas was pulled, and around that time a friend introduced me to a futures contract. I turned my attention from counting cards to trading cars. I tried to teach several friends how to play Blackjack, but each time when it came down to taking the time to count down decks of cards, they all quit.

Do you have the energy and persistence to pursue your goal step-by-step? Let's see... go for it!

Long after I had stopped playing Blackjack and was deeply engrossed in my career as a trader, I met an individual after work that I had met before. We were discussing trading and money management over a beer when he surprised me by asking: "Have you ever played Blackjack?" I took the easy way out and just said, "Yes." This individual was always thinking, always pushing to learn. His drive for information soon had me sharing my views about the similarities between Blackjack, money management techniques, and trading. One weekend at a seminar in Atlantic City, we ran into one another again.

We decided to venture into a few casinos together. Sure enough, within minutes, the "friendly" pit bosses would step over and ask me their familiar "routine" questions. After the first shoe of cards was dealt, we adjourned to a seminar room to go over more extensive details about Blackjack strategy. We both came to the conclusion that it was a game in which you could control the outcome with skill and preparation, but the work required for defining strategy through back-testing, table diversification, and money management was just too similar to our jobs. It was not a stress release, as it was just more of the same. We wanted a break when we removed ourselves from the financial environment. That's the reason I have no interest in playing Blackjack today. My Blackjack partner on that occasion was the Senior Technical Analyst of the Fidelity Management Company in Boston, the largest asset management corporation in the United States.

There is an important lesson to be taken from those Blackjack tables. Regardless of the skill level we acquire for playing Blackjack, or trading, without an ability to concentrate fully, we limit ourselves. This is very similar to defining the outcome associated with a trade before establishing the position. If 'x' expectation has a 60% probability of happening, then the probability for that outcome to occur has already been reduced by 40%. But now consider this. If an individual's skill level is at a high 80%, and then he only gives that ability 60% of his concentration, the outcome will be the same. That skill level just dropped from 80 to 48, a 40% reduction in capability. *A trader with lesser skill and ability, but with greater concentration and focus, can and will outperform the more skilled trader.*

So how do you go about training your mind? The first step in training your mind is to adopt a tangible concept of what the mind is. Don Talbot described the mind as a radio. This is because our minds are somewhat like radios, channel surfing constantly through different stations. Some stations will be much stronger than others, while others will be weak and then gradually fade in and overpower the stronger station we had been listening to first. These multiple stations are always transmitting just under our consciousness, as it is our unconscious, the Basic Self, that has the ability to program all the frequencies and transmit to open channels.

The radio analogy is an exceptionally good one because of the association with waves. As radios receive sound waves, science identifies our Basic Self as propagating the Beta waves of our brain. The Conscious Self would be our Alpha waves. (Science still hasn't figured out at what frequency to find the Higher Self. That one is being left for priests to define.) As our attention wanders to these subliminal thoughts, the interference or distractions they pose can significantly diminish our ability to perform, to stay focused on a single station and perform to our fullest potential. If you have ever lived in the Caribbean or Florida, it is similar to when the sun goes down at night; Cuban stations become much stronger and overpower local stations or cause extreme interference. It is this same background noise within our minds that creates the physical stress knots and emotional anxieties when we try to ignore or suppress the distraction. Attempting to ignore a distraction that pops up in our mind, or an external distraction such as a noise, will consume more energy than if it is simply acknowledged as being present. We need all our energy to focus on the abilities and skills we are trying to use. Distractions are a serious energy drain.

Through training we learn that the flow of distracting thoughts will never leave us. However, we can learn how to identify the distraction and then utilize the most effective technique to allow ourselves to let go of it. The key is to identify and then let go. The first step is identification of mind distractions. Through conscious identification we can then eliminate the repetitive interference of the same thought. The second step requires different techniques based on the type of distraction. We will discuss these techniques shortly, but the bottom line is that through the appropriate technique we can learn to live with the distraction without it having a negative impact on our performance.

The key will be to identify it, *accept it*, and then let go of it. This is the same principle as scanning past a radio station you don't want to stop and listen to further.

The effort we expend to suppress and ignore inner distractions is a major source of stress that accumulates and remains as an uncomfortable nagging anxiety within us. The anxiety itself becomes a distraction until the originating cause is more fully acknowledged. Left unattended, the stress creates *physical* knots in the muscles of our necks, chest, and lower back. Eventually these knots become extremely painful, and we attempt to put a bandage over the problem by seeking the help of a chiropractor, physical therapist, or some other pressure release. Pressure valves are energy releases for the body which temporarily reduce the pain.

Our suppressed and sequestered thoughts, concerns, and fears form energy blockages. Don Gambril, a former United States Olympic Swimming Coach, explained this concept of energy blockage within ourselves in the following way. Imagine a garden hose with the water pouring freely through it. Energy flowed through us this easily when we were small toddlers. We did not judge; we just accepted things as they were in our physical world. We would focus and then just let go as we moved on to something new. Now imagine a garden hose with a stone in it. Tremendous water pressure builds behind the obstruction and the little water that does pass around it comes out ineffectively and without much control.

The stone in the hose is similar to an obstacle in our mind. It robs us of energy, and there are only a few solutions. We remove the stone. We find an alternate way to release the pressure caused by that obstacle, such as turning off the faucet, but that minimizes the energy that should have been directed at the primary task at hand. The pressure release reduces the associated discomfort, and we therefore associate feeling better with that activity. The relief is only temporary. It is easy to associate the adrenaline rush associated with racing cars, other high risk sports, the emotional swings of a horror movie, or any physical activity as successful solutions to minimize our inner discomforts. The displaced, or temporary, energy release is incorrectly assumed to be a release from the original discomfort. It does help, but it does nothing to break down the original obstacle. This is similar to finding an alternate route for the river that is trapped behind a hydroelectric dam. The energy is lost, as is the water if the pressure is released through a creek upstream. The obstacles within our mind rob us of energy and diminish our ability to concentrate.

When Luke Skywalker was doing a handstand while Yoda was perched on his feet, the scene offered a visual representation of striving for inner balance. Distractions, in this case the beeps from R2D2 directed at Luke about the sinking X-Wing, serve to represent any external or inner distraction capable of breaking our concentration. The phrase "Try not. DO. Or do not, there is no try," means you must give 100% to the present moment. If you are trading and thinking about other unrelated market scenarios, or thinking about the argument you may have had with a spouse as you left home that morning, you will most likely have a trading loss that day because your mind is not on what you are trading.

The mind is also a sneaky trickster. It can make us believe that misconceptions are our reality. As an example, if the Basic Self has decided you will lose today, *or do not deserve to win today,* guess what the outcome will be? That's right, a loss. That's not the only trick it plays on us. It can also mislead us into thinking we are dealing with inner obstructions and stress effectively, when in actual fact we are building immense inner dams of obstacles that interweave and reinforce one another.

We are misled again into thinking we are reducing stress by minimizing the amount of work we do for a period of time. This is similar to an alternate way of reducing the pressure in the hose with a stone in it: reduce the amount of water forced through the hose. We actually do the same thing by reducing the number of markets we might trade that day, maybe go on a vacation for a week, or find a way to temporarily change the pace of our normal routine. Just like the hose however, as soon as the water is turned back on full force, the pressure behind the obstruction returns. Left alone, the hose finally splits...just behind the obstruction. We break down.

Coaches that get outstanding results have an ability to train an individual to filter out mind noise and erase inner obstacles or anxieties that cause these energy blocks and stress points. The approaches are far more subtle than the highly structured workout schedules they prepare for physical development, but they are no less demanding. Just like it is easier to work on the technique of your backhand in tennis, it is easier to work on the optimum period for an indicator than it is to change the very inner foundation of who we are so we can execute the technique better. The coaching that is offered to change an inner attribute is usually offered privately at the time it is most needed for that individual. Never in a group setting. It was not until later that I discovered that all these techniques had been a part of everyone's training schedule, just asked of us at different times.

You are about to prove to yourself through the following series of exercises that our ability for performance excellence comes from our Basic Self, our unconscious mind. One of the most important elements to recognize about our unconscious mind is that it is unable to differentiate its reality from the reality of the Conscious Self. *All the reason and logic offered by our Conscious Self to argue convincingly that we have the ability to trade or accomplish a task and win will be sabotaged if our Basic Self, our inner ego and self-image, does not also agree we are capable of achieving or doing that same task.* It means if you think you can allow your Conscious Self alone to motivate you through elaborate back-testing of indicators to be a successful trader, you have another thought coming... you've just set yourself up for failure. It is the Basic Self which always wins, not our Conscious Self with its long string of logical reasons for success. If our inner child refuses to go along, it will prevent us from succeeding.

Have you ever entered a trade only to say to yourself after a loss: "I can't believe I did that same thing again!" We rarely learn things the first time around and need time to change. This is especially true when developing our inner skills. These are much more challenging than learning about the mechanics of a technical indicator as dictated by the Conscious Self. Our unconscious mind learns and accepts change slowly, and as experience brings fear into our trading, the "game" becomes more complex for our Basic Self.

Once we have a certain level of technical ability to trade, our problems associated with trading losses are usually related to an inner weakness rather than a lack of technical skill. Sadly, most traders never do get beyond their suspicions about their technical indicators or the fundamentals when they fall short. *But you are already miles ahead of most traders by simply recognizing that you need to evaluate your inner skills first.*

An introspective evaluation is much harder to do and requires a lot of patience. It takes some understanding about the process itself in order to be successful. The following excerpt from "An Autobiography in Five Short Chapters" by Portia Nelson is an ideal analogy for the way we learn and adapt to changes.

Chapter One:
I walk down the street and come to a deep hole in the sidewalk. I fall in; I feel lost, helpless, but it's not my fault. It takes forever to find my way out.

Chapter Two:

I walk down the same street and come to a deep hole in the sidewalk.

I pretend I don't see it, and fall in again. I can't believe I'm in the same place - but it isn't my responsibility. It still takes a long time to get out.

Chapter Three:

I walk down the same street and come to a deep hole in the sidewalk. I see it - but I still fall in. By now it's a habit. But now my eyes are open; I know where I am. I take full responsibility; I get out immediately.

Chapter Four:

I walk down the same street and come to a deep hole in the sidewalk.

I walk around it.

Chapter Five:

I walk down another street.

Our Basic Self, the unconscious self, likes familiar patterns and routines. Familiar routines become habits, and we cling to them because the familiar is a comfort to us. We cling to the familiar even when we don't like the situation we find ourselves in. We may know a job is not right for us or a relationship makes us feel uncomfortable, but we stick to it because we know what to expect. Change means we have to abandon the comfort associated with knowing what to expect and jump into the frying pan and pain of the unknown. Change doesn't get easier; the process becomes easier as we learn to accept the progression and learn to recognize its stepping stones.

So be patient with yourself... but relentless in your pursuit to master the skills that follow.

Distortions of Reality and Ability

The Golden Eagle

*A man found an eagle's egg and put it in the
nest of a backyard hen. The eagle had hatched with a
brood of chicks and grew up with them.*

*Believing himself to be a backyard chicken, he clucked
and cackled. He thrashed his wings and flew a few
feet into the air, just like a good chicken. He scratched
the earth for worms and insects.*

*Years passed and the eagle grew old. One day he
noticed a magnificent bird soaring in the heavens in
graceful majesty. The old eagle gazed up in awe.*

*"Who is that?" he said to his neighbor.
"That's the eagle, the king of birds," said the neighbor.*

*"Wouldn't it be wonderful if we could soar like
that up in the heavens?"
"Don't give it another thought," the chicken replied
— "you and I are chickens."*

*So the eagle never gave it another thought.
He lived and he died thinking he was a backyard chicken.*

—Anthony Demello, *The Song of the Bird*

In this phase of our training clinic, you will be asked to stop and think about what your perceptions are about yourself. Are you also an eagle that has become comfortable within the confined boundaries of a chicken coop? The eagle's spirit lives within each of us. Sadly, much of our environment and early conditioning teaches us to suppress that spirit. This is an example: if as a child, we are told that we aren't good at math, then it is not long before we begin to believe it and assume the role of a math incompetent. We assume the role that our Basic Self feels most comfortable with, even if that image promotes an image of incompetence.

Darien, Connecticut is a small, very well-to-do, preppie, Ivy League community on the shore of Long Island Sound. Before you think I'm throwing darts at this town, know it was once my home. Darien offers a beautiful country setting of elegant homes built throughout twisting country hills covered with thick New England forests. It is a dramatic contrast to New York City, which is only an hour away. The entry level for purchasing a home within this community begins near $300,000. The average sale price is $641,770 (June, 1995 YTD). It is similar to nearby Greenwich and shares the humble honor of apparently having the highest income per capita in the United States. It is within this setting that the story of the eagle was fully exemplified at one of the many parties in Greenwich.

It is fascinating to listen to the teenagers of this community, normal American teenagers with all the usual insecurities of who they are and what they will do when they grow up. The difference between these adolescents, and others of a different geographic area in the U.S., is the image they have of themselves in later years. They were born eagles and know it. Able to succeed at any venture they decide to choose. Success surrounds them. At one party I became fascinated listening to these teenagers. One teenager talked about which industry she were considering to *manage*, or which Wall Street firm he wanted to join because of *the firm's* financial potential. Another was waiting to hear if a professional hockey club was going to make him an offer, so he could then turn down the first contract offered by a second string team. One teenager didn't discuss how to buy a car, he wanted to know how to setup a network to *deal in antique cars*. There was no discussion of smaller objectives or of potential obstacles in their way. If you brought a more realistic progression of steps into the conversation, the milestones were rapidly dismissed as details to be ironed out later when the implementation plans were formulated. Those teenagers presumed success for themselves, and they were beginning to act out those roles of success.

Greenwich and Darien are affluent communities, but many families in those communities are now house poor after the staggering game of real estate hopscotch that occurred throughout the affluent 1980s. Many Wall Streeters, with those huge bonuses from the Reagan years, propelled Fairfield County real estate values skyward at a rate of 2% per month until the bonuses dried up in 1987. Property prices then dropped as much as 40%. That recession created a negative equity for many families with million dollar homes. They (make that 'we') kept rolling over their entire equity and savings into successively higher priced homes as a means to protect capital. The real estate implosion literally wiped out families' entire savings. (Similar to the bubble bursts in Tokyo, California, or the oil patch of Texas to the Mountain States.) So for many teenagers, only the image remains. The families no longer have abundant cash and riches to go out and buy these dreams for their kids as they once could have. Those teenagers knew economic changes had affected their families, but not their young dreams. In the face of adversity, they remained confident of success because of the roles played out around them. Sure, like all kids, some of these teenagers will elect to shun the opportunities they have and retreat into a period of denial or rejection, but their inner image of themselves will not change. They will always be eagles with the ability to step out of the chicken suit and slip back into the role of a successful person, whenever they choose to reassume that role and image.

Most of us are eagles. (If you are trading, you are an eagle. You didn't get there by being a chicken.) Still many of us were raised within the chicken coop of our own design. We limit ourselves because we only see ourselves playing one role in life, the role defined for us during our early years. Our image and the role we choose to experience in life is to a large degree dependent on *what we allow ourselves to experience*. This is dependent upon how deserving of success we feel we are.

Early in my swimming career, a coach of mine worked on changing the poor self-image I had about my ability to do any sport. I had always been overlooked by big name coaches until high school when a National coach commented that I could use my arms to swim. What a concept! His attention greatly improved my speed and technique in practice, but I fell short in competition because I did not have a winning self-image at that time.

The same problem occurs for traders. Some traders are successful up to a certain profit level, and then they start to experience a progression of losses or one big hit that wipes out a string of small winners. The Basic Self will unconsciously sabotage our success if our growing profits are in conflict with what we unconsciously believe we deserve. That sense of self-worth will dictate the level of ability we will attain. Once a realization dawns within us that our self-image is nothing more than a concept, the path ahead becomes unlimited and unrestricted. The reality is that work and practice will lead to success in trading, golf, business, whatever. The boundaries for attaining the goal we set for ourselves are genuinely confined by our concept of self-worth. For this reason trading skills are inseparable from self-image.

The gap between knowing and doing remains the weak link in most of our lives. Knowing what to do is usually not the problem; it is translating intentions into action, and resolutions into results. A frequent lament by those who conduct trading seminars is that traders can't pull the trigger. At the very moment these traders should enter or exit a trade they freeze. As traders, we may wish for the results, we may be confident in the outcome, we will even have a pretty good idea of the best method needed for executing the trade. But we wait for "permission" from some inner voice to take the necessary action. As a result many individuals wait until fear, self-doubt, and their insecurities dissolve. They never do. The motivation and conviction needed to take the necessary action doesn't step forward until our inner adversaries go away. They don't go until we've faced them.

We know that our brain has two hemispheres that perform different functions: a linear, rational left brain, and a more holistic, imaginative, and creative right brain. The specialized cells of the brain allow us to store data, to compare and discriminate, and to perform the miraculous number of processes we call thinking. We can consciously will ourselves to calculate the Fibonacci retracements, remember an incident from the past, or recall a hypothesis of a potential intermarket relationship.

We have to contend with unintentional thoughts that are just below our field of awareness. It is these thoughts, or background noises, that we need to learn to control. Often these thoughts carry with them a negative emotional charge. They are the anxieties and old images we'd rather not think about. These thoughts have the power to lift us up, bring us down, promote a feeling that we are trading with effortless ease, or freeze us from taking action as we become captive to a moment of indecision. These random thoughts and images reflect a natural discharge of stressful impressions and memories. Our

Basic Self cannot tell which images are real or artificial, so we end up reacting to these artificial images by creating physical tension and imbalance.

Our Conscious Self then interprets our world through a biased filter. This is what causes us to misread or misinterpret the meanings of real events and makes trading far more problematic and complex than it already is. We confuse, misunderstand, misinterpret, and find it increasingly difficult to identify what is reality and what is Disneyland. The trap is that the mind will manipulate abstract concepts into a web of illusions that have little or no bearing on reality. What is needed is a skill that allows us to filter, or down play, the mind's incessant chatter so that we no longer pay attention to it. We still have the thoughts. We still have the beliefs and associations. We still interpret and make value judgments, *but we don't mistake these thoughts for reality.*

Pre-conditioning can thoroughly mislead us. My Wall Street commute had numbed me to the common day occurrences of swearing taxi cab drivers, gestures from seemingly otherwise passive people, or audible abuses when driving anywhere in or near the city. When I moved to a more rural community in Georgia, there was a period of adjustment to be made within this new culture. One day, driving toward the North Georgia mountains, I approached a narrow bridge on a winding road. As I approached the last bend in the road prior to the bridge, another car came around that turn. As we passed, the driver made gestures with his arm out the window and yelled, "HOG!" He quickly drove by, and I became upset that he seemed so angry with my driving. I was clearly on my side of the road and had not taken, or hogged, more than my fair share. Maybe it was my New York plates that so irritated him. Without more time to think, I made the last sharp turn towards the narrow bridge. I narrowly missed hitting the largest hog I had ever seen in my life! The immense porker was standing right in the middle of the single lane bridge. That driver's one single word warning had produced a string of emotions, artificial images, and false assumptions. The reality? There was a pig in the road — a "Hog!" I had attached all the other words, connotations and incorrect meanings around that word because of my prior conditioning in New York.

Events are just that — events. Depending on what is inside us, we can feel differently about that same event. Some sunny days when I was walking in New York, the city was beautiful. The architecture, the people, the hustle of the city, it was all exciting. On a different sunny day, all I could see on the exact same streets were the homeless, the garbage, the needed repairs, and foul smells. On my negative days, the city was broken down and filled with impersonal cold faces rushing by me. These very different perceptions would both occur on sunny days. Weather was not a factor. The difference depended on what was happening inside of me. We see things not as *they* are, but as *we* are. However, a hog is just a hog, as a buy order is simply that, a buy order. We have to discard and dump all the peripheral baggage that comes along with one word... buy it, or sell it, hog, or HOG!

Objective: Separating Virtual Image from Reality.

Purpose: To identify what is important to you in the present moment and deserves your attention, versus what should be viewed as a distraction.

Exercise: Ask yourself these few simple questions when unconscious mind chatter begins to come into focus as a distraction. By asking these few simple questions for each distracting thought while you are trading, you will be able to improve your concentration.

1. Does knowing this help my position ?
Answer no, promise yourself to come back to it at another time.

2. Does knowing this right now make a difference to my position?
Answer no, promise yourself to come back to it at another time.

3. Can this help improve my relationships, help me support my family, reach my goal, or add to my happiness?
If the answer is no, put it aside for now. If the answer is yes, re-ask the second question. This shortens the time horizon to the here and now.

By acknowledging the distraction and then telling yourself it can be given attention at another time, you reduce the stress associated with that distraction. If you try to suppress it, the inner child will throw the concern back at you, and you won't be able to temporarily shelve the distraction. You'll end up having to deal with an emotional storm from your unconscious self that will demand attention when you can least afford the distraction. These inner temper-tantrums can yield disastrous trading results.

In Chapter 2, "The Three Selves," I recalled breaking my finger in a swim meet. Pain, real physical pain, becomes a by-product of stress when we are trading. It is a very powerful distraction that demands attention. You can use the same questions in either situation.

When I broke my finger it was not life threatening, it served no purpose to focus on it in the middle of a race, and there was nothing I could do about it short of stopping. Breaking a finger requires attention, but by accepting the discomfort, I could then let go of it by changing the direction of my focus. I promised myself the problem would be given my full attention in the very near future.

Your mind cannot differentiate between emotion and reality. After the series of questions listed in the previous exercise, I focused on what was important at that moment. I literally did not feel the pain in my hand again. When I stopped however, I saw I had a compound fracture, a small bone was poking through the side of my finger, and it certainly became the center of my focus then. There was little doubt of the reality after actually seeing the problem. Had I seen the reality moments before, I would not have been able to filter out the pain. Unseen, my mind could trick the body long enough to play the game and carry on.

Those three questions are very powerful. You can block out of your mind just about anything. Just tell your Basic Self you will give the matter your full attention later. Continual repetition of a thought or image in your mind cannot be permanently pushed back into your unconscious and shelved. You eventually have to resolve it. Then when you do, give it your full attention. Be prepared to try and understand what your Basic Self is trying to bring to the surface of your awareness. Once fully addressed, you have just permanently removed one of the obstacles in the hose of your psyche. The sensation you will feel is like someone has just released the pressure on a pinched nerve in your spine. The relief is immediate, but soon the pressure builds again behind the next inner obstacle that is encountered.

Expectations and Other Mind Traps

There is nothing either good or bad
but thinking makes it so.

—*Shakespeare*

The last chapter demonstrated how we could be significantly misled by our preconditioning, thereby making it difficult for us to identify what is real. We addressed distractions that break our concentration and have little or no bearing on what we are trying to accomplish. To help identify what is most important and relative to the current moment we asked a series of questions that act as a filter. The method we will explore next takes a different approach — it will *transform* the distraction, not just temporarily filter it.

Filtering out irrelevant thoughts that come to our attention at inappropriate times is a method that is effective for isolated or random thoughts. Filtering is not effective when we unknowingly fabricate self-destruct mechanisms, or mind traps, that sabotage and limit our abilities.

Let's take a look at one exceptionally damaging mind trap: expectations. Expectations create a mental anxiety that immediately defines a limiting and inflexible boundary — a performance standard. The trader who hits a home run one week is frequently *expected* to repeat that performance the following week. The expectation defines the platform for failure because anything less becomes a disappointment. An expectation is an extremely inflexible standard which allows no room for alternatives.

Another example of this particular kind of trap is defining a specific expectation for a year end return. Anything less than that expected return can only be interpreted as a performance failure, regardless of the fact that a profit is just that: a PROFIT! If you didn't reach the precise target you set for yourself, then you feel a sense of disappointment. Does that make any sense if your primary market spends the entire year in a consolidation, or contracting triangle pattern, as the S&P did in 1992? You will have no control over this situation. In such a market environment, a 10% return could be viewed as exceptional, yet an unrealistic bogie of 20%, set at the first of the year, would have meant you failed to reach the target. You are left having to justify the lower return, by blaming it on the market's low volatility, rather than patting yourself on the back for profiting in an environment in which most trend-followers would have been losers. In this situation, you encountered an unpredictable factor that reduced the potential for meeting your expected return. That's hardly failure. We have to leave ourselves some flexibility for events and circumstances we have no control over.

The self-constructed mind trap of a standard setting expectation is most effectively dealt with by broadening the way we express it. Here's how to go about doing this. We enter a trading day with an expectation that the market will advance to a specific target. This expectation provides us with limited odds for success as there can only be one successful outcome. The market has to advance, and there is no other acceptable outcome as we defined it, within this expectation. By expecting the market to rally right from the open, the disappointment may well throw us off balance when that expectation fails to occur. Should the market first drop, then progress towards our target, we may trade the move poorly because our inflexible expectation did not allow for an alternate route towards our target. Our stop may have been executed based on our expectations for an immediate rally, and then we make matters worse by getting upset when we fail to reestablish the same position as a bottom forms.

We waste energy and create a distraction for ourselves further as we stew over an unexpected market open that caused a loss, that would have been a gain if we had only done nothing. (Back to the *could-a, would-a, should-a* theme song.) As we fret over a poorly placed stop (instead of viewing it as an opportunity to learn after the market closes), we then fail to observe what the market is presently doing and miss another opportunity. (You can't trade the present because you are hung-up on the past.)

This offers an example of when to apply the first exercise in the prior chapter to trading. Does an unexpected market open that has now reversed have anything to do with your opinion that a long position should be established? The answer is likely no. Drop the excess baggage, move on, and don't stew over the open. However, you would not even have to attempt to shed the baggage and the distraction caused by a disappointing, or unexpected open, if the expectation had been defined as a *preference*.

Two easy changes will remove the boundaries and accompanying poor odds associated with an expectation.

> *First,* Expect nothing, but be prepared for every potential outcome that may develop.
>
> *Second,* Rewrite the expectation as a preference. Transform it into something less restrictive and confining.

When we expect something to turnout in a precise and particular way, we so severely limit the possibilities that the odds become overwhelmingly against us. An expectation becomes our Achilles heel by preventing us from remaining flexible. Expectations are particularly damaging because they make it very easy for us to attach our ego to that expected outcome, thereby leaving us vulnerable to disappointment when it turns out differently.

OK, so here's how to neutralize this mind trap. Change *"I expect the market to rally towards an objective of 556.00"*, to *"I would prefer the S&P market to open strong from 550.00, but a decline down to 548.75 first will not jeopardize my objective of 556.00."*

The target has not changed. Our mind however has adopted an attitude that allows the price objective to be attained in various routes for getting to that level. By defining a range to work within, we neutralized the stress and anxiety that accompanies the need for a single outcome. It is similar to being told you have to match all six numbers on the lottery ticket to win, *and the six numbers have to come up in your exact sequential order.*

The next exercise helps transform expectations into something less restrictive. Work through the following list of mind trap examples and neutralize them by changing them into preferences.

Objective: Replacing Expectation Statements with Preferences.

Purpose: Preferences are less restrictive than expectations and therefore have better odds for successful outcomes.

Exercise: Rephrase crippling expectation statements into empowering preference statements.

Expectation: *Out of ten trades I only had eight winners.* Mind trap...Sorting for the negative. This is easy to do. This expectation is subliminal but shows you expected ten perfect trades, and nobody bats a thousand.

Less Restrictive Preference: *I had eight trading wins because I did "x" correctly. The other two trades could have been improved by doing "y." I'll try that next time.* You just positively reinforced what you did right and used the less desirable trades as a learning opportunity.

Expectation: *The market did not fully reach my target. I'll keep the position until the level is attained.* The expectation has setup an either/or mind trap. Either you will be right, or you will be wrong. There is no allowance for shades of gray.

Less Restrictive Preference: *The market has approached my target at "y," I'll begin to scale out of this position and take some of the profits if the market struggles at "x" level.*

Expectation: *I expect to achieve and produce x% by my next closing quarter.* Big trap... our value depends upon how much we achieve and produce, and therefore, we must achieve "x" or we will be worth less in our own self-image.

Less Restrictive Preference: *I would prefer to be up an additional 15%, but 7% would be good in a low volatile market scenario.*

Expectation: *I have been told I'm not a good trader in the Lumber market, but our analyst has identified a big trade coming.* The trap is that an expectation defined for you has become a self-defeating thought.

Less Restrictive Preference: *I know I've been labeled a poor producer in the Lumber market. I can continue to fit into this role defined for me and have limited success, or consciously recognize I have no* *interest to trade a secondary commodity, or I can improve my knowledge about the key factors that move the Lumber market.* This one is the most complex. Either you prefer to master the Lumber market or you stop trading it. You can't operate under someone else's expectation. Role playing into someone else's expectation is replaying the story of the eagle and the chicken coop.

Focusing/Concentration

You must be present to win.

So far in our training clinic we have become familiar with two techniques that help to minimize distractions so that we can improve our ability to focus and concentrate. Now we need to home in on the specifics of what focusing is really about so that we can develop it further.

Concentration refers to the degree to which we are able to focus our awareness. Like telescoping a camera lens to isolate a face from the crowd, we can focus our minds on a single task. Our ability to focus our attention over a time interval is our attention span. Both our ability to concentrate and our attention span can be improved with practice.

We can sustain a high level of skill over longer periods of time by breaking the task down into much smaller components. It becomes easier to concentrate when we have less to focus on. As an example, a sixty-four year old runner was asked by a reporter when he crossed the finish line of a 100-mile race, "How did you run such a long race?" He replied, "I didn't run a hundred miles; I ran one mile... a hundred times." What a wonderful example of how to change our perception when it is overwhelming to focus on an entire task.

An ability to focus means we can concentrate all our thoughts and actions toward one small aspect of the present moment. We won't let our minds wander and split our consciousness into fragments like refracted light through a glass prism. If we focus on a +15% to +20% gain for the year, that distant goal could appear overwhelming in relationship to the gain/loss of today's trade. (Note that the original expectation for 20% has been altered to the preferential range.) If we are currently in a net hole of -6% for the year, that distant year-end bogie could be especially unnerving.

However, if our goal comprises a much smaller step, it is easier for us to focus, and we are able to direct our attention with fewer distractions. We increase our odds for success by making smaller steps in the right direction. We become right more often. These small winners develop a trend of consistency and show up in a growing equity curve.

Centering is very different from concentrating, or focusing. Centering is the thought process of understanding how every aspect of our trading contributes to our overall development and growth as a trader and person. It is a kind of concentration that is all encompassing and will be discussed further in the next chapter.

Focus, on the other hand, is the process of narrowing our concentration in order to eliminate specific unproductive or distracting occurrences. It is the method we use to fine tune our span of attention so that we can stay in the moment.

Most of us focus and trap ourselves within a time frame that has no bearing on the present. We put too much of our attention on past and upcoming problems. We get hung up on a trade we missed, or a painful loss when our indicators showed us a similar pattern. We stew and worry about what would happen if this individual or that government did "x." There is a big difference between preparing for different scenarios that could influence and increase the risk exposure to our position, versus letting those potential scenarios haunt us and distract our attention when we are ready to execute our order to buy or sell. The only way to net a successful outcome, or positive return, is to focus on the present moment.

When the time comes to execute the order, you should know that you have prepared for the various outcomes to your very best ability. Then act. Put your entire focus and attention on the mechanics required to establish the position. Think less and act more. If you have excessive concerns about an indicator giving the wrong signal, you may have to go back to reinforce your confidence that it is still a statistically valid winner. The negative return that occurred was only an isolated outcome. Take the time to put that failed indicator signal behind you by back-testing similar results until you are once again comfortable. Otherwise you'll get stuck every time you encounter a situation that seems similar to your nagging doubts. When the time comes to establish or close a position, that is not the moment to stew over an alternate outcome because of a poor performance on a prior trade.

Concentrate on what you have control over. You can't control government intervention, comments from other traders, the weather, late train schedules, or the traffic you had to fight on your way to work that morning. So focus on what you do have control over — your own performance. Athletes who perform optimally are totally engaged in the moment. I cannot emphasize this too strongly. It is this single-mindedness which accompanies excellence. *You must be present to win.*

When we are trading well there is a flow, an ease which allows us to become oblivious to what's around us, and we become fully absorbed in our actions and thoughts for the moment. The flow and ease we feel has no room or thought for guilt about past performances, or fear of future shortcomings. This oneness with trading or a sport yields a "high," a sense of being in a time warp. It is a flowing state without any conscious need to control, or think; we react and live in the present. In actuality we do not think within the present time frame, *only act.* Here's why.

We all have varying degrees of concentration. The constant flow of mind noise cannot be entirely filtered. Some of the background radio stations of our mind do get heard slightly, but they *can only broadcast a program about the past or future*. We cannot possibly think about anything in the present moment, only act. A wandering mind draws our attention to the past or future; it always moves our attention away from and out of the present. This in turn diminishes our performance by diverting our attention from the action at present and also dissipates the energy we have for applying our skills.

Filtering and transforming distractions are two methods to improve our focus. While these methods specifically increase our ability to concentrate, visualization offers the means to train or program your Basic Self. In the story of the eagle in the chicken coop, the eagle had an image that he role-played throughout his life. Through visualization he could have corrected his inner image and experienced how to soar, even before spreading his wings to fly. Visualization is important, but we need to temporarily delay describing this technique until we've prepared a proper background.

The amount of time we are able to completely immerse ourselves in the present moment can be extended with practice. Practice itself takes commitment and time. By practicing (and we will go into details how to practice in a few pages) we are actually learning to allow our Basic Self and Conscious Self to operate in balance. These two very different selves have to come to some kind of an agreement. The flow and effortless resource of energy is the sensation we experience when the Basic Self, our unconscious, is in full agreement with and supports our Conscious Self. As a result we make our best decisions and tap our fullest potential.

Those who have been fortunate to have an exposure to Eastern philosophies and culture will already be familiar with the very ancient wisdom of the Chinese *I CHING*, which means 'Book of Changes.' The Chinese revere the I Ching and approach it as if it were a very wise person. If it is treated like a person, its replies are like personal replies. As an example:

It is of great importance to achieve an inner peace
which will allow you to act in harmony with the times...
Hold your thoughts to the present... Actions that spring
from this attitude will be appropriate.

— I CHING *no.52*

No matter how much we practice and learn to focus, or how strong-willed we may be, our minds will always wander. It is impossible to remain permanently focused, *but it is not necessary!*

Look for opportunities to give your mind a break from the rigors and stress associated with concentrating. When I was playing Blackjack, I had to practice to increase the length of time I could play error-free. There was always some point in time when I would begin to make errors. The principle of diminishing returns applies to any activity. It certainly applies to Blackjack and trading the markets. I knew I had to walk away from the tables after three hours of card counting to take a break. That was my limit. After that time I would only get sloppy, lose my concentration, and give up any advantage I had.

When the dealer shuffled the decks, I learned how to take short effective breaks to help unwind from the intense concentration. As traders, we need the same opportunity to break from the rigor. When we can only steal a few seconds to take a break, we have to be creative as to what that outlet will be. One method that worked for me was to simply put a 4" x 6" photograph near the computer screens of a particularly favorite hiking path. I would "walk" that twisted and curved path near Henry David Thoreau's famous Walden Pond. This photograph would serve as my mind's window of escape. Another method for taking a very short break without leaving the trading desk is to shift activities from thinking to doing. Make something. I learned to fold and design various paper airplanes. Our office was filled with aerodynamic planes that became very popular throughout the trading room. The paper plane itself became a starting point to allow my mind to navigate its own flight plan of day dreams. A favorite paper plane design is illustrated in the photograph I took for the cover of this book. The instructions on how to make this same plane follow. If paper airplanes aren't your thing, use a different sense. Put a CD on your player and kick back for a few minutes.

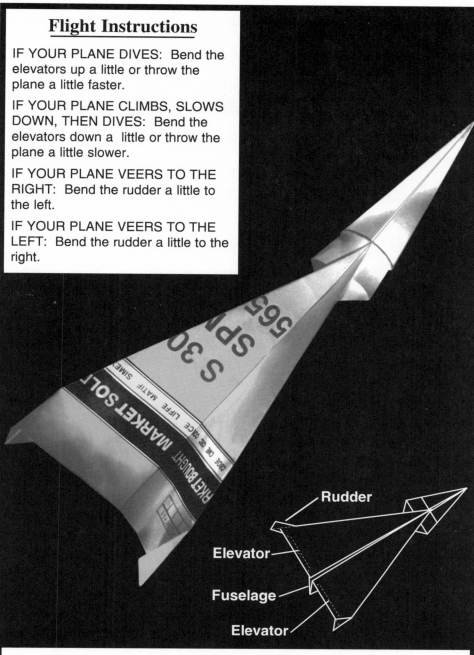

Rudder

Elevator

Fuselage

Elevator

Paper Airplane On The Cover

This plane is formed from a single 8½" by 11" sheet of paper, two pieces of tape and two staples. The delta wing design is similar to the XB-70 Valkyrie — a 2,000-miles-per-hour experimental United States Air Force bomber tested in the 1960s. A little up elevator is needed to attain maximum distance and accuracy.

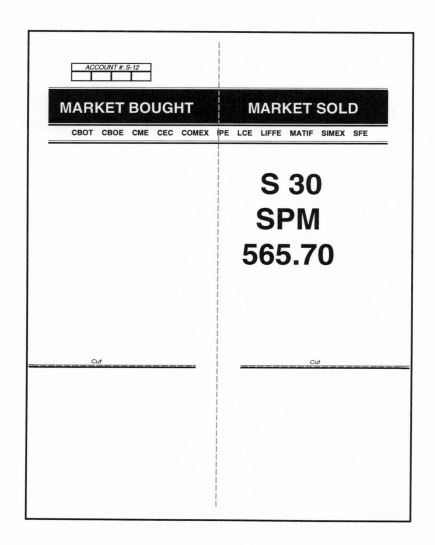

You may photocopy this page to create a template for your airplane. Align top edge of drawing to top edge of copier and enlarge 200%.

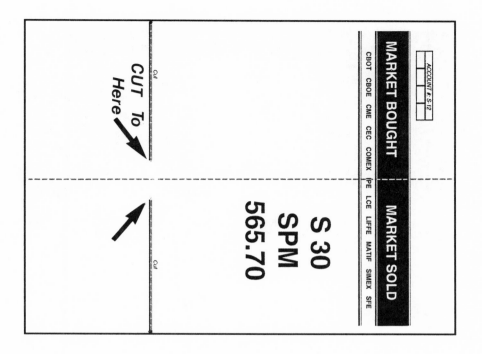

1. Cut solid lines.

2. Fold paper in half along dotted line so printing is on the inside.

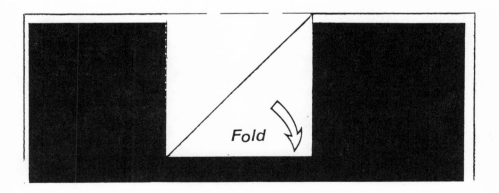

3. Fold paper down as shown to form a diagonal edge.

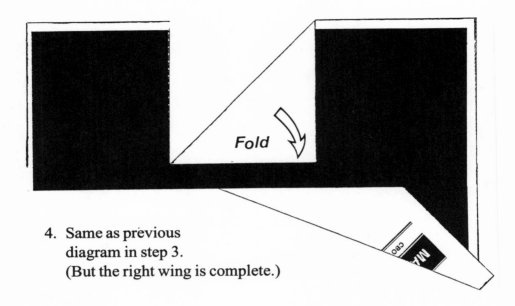

4. Same as previous
   diagram in step 3.
   (But the right wing is complete.)

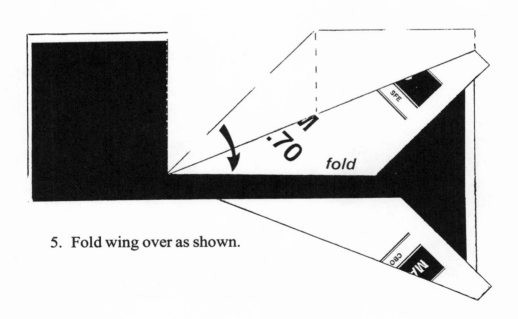

5. Fold wing over as shown.

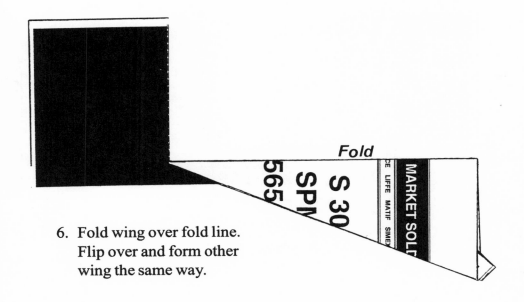

6. Fold wing over fold line.
   Flip over and form other
   wing the same way.

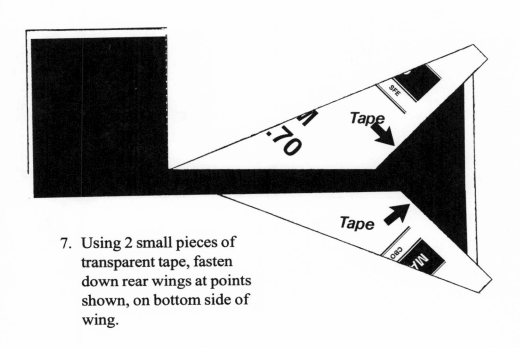

7. Using 2 small pieces of
   transparent tape, fasten
   down rear wings at points
   shown, on bottom side of
   wing.

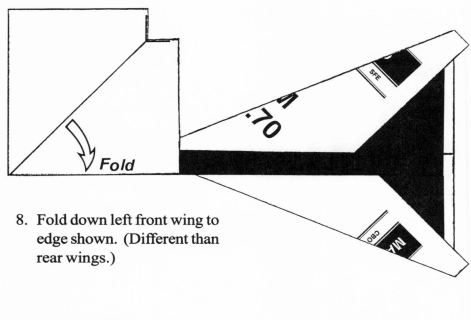

8. Fold down left front wing to
   edge shown. (Different than
   rear wings.)

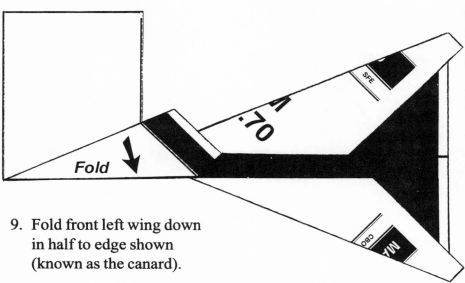

9. Fold front left wing down
   in half to edge shown
   (known as the canard).

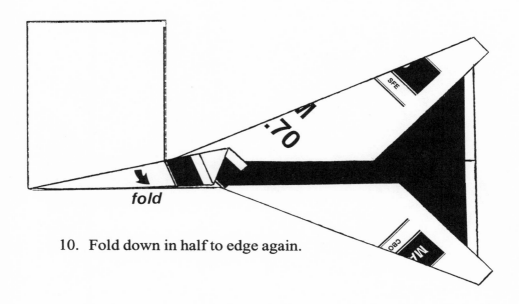

10. Fold down in half to edge again.

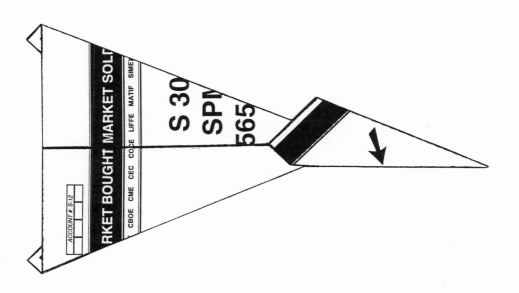

11. Flip plane over to form front right wing.

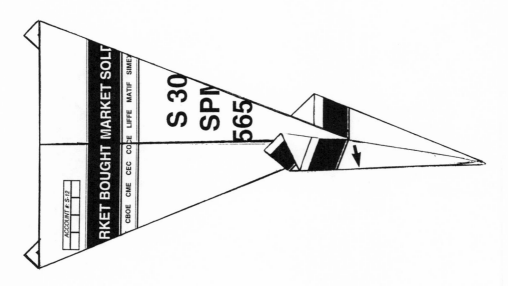

12. The final fold over is easier if front left wing is open as shown.

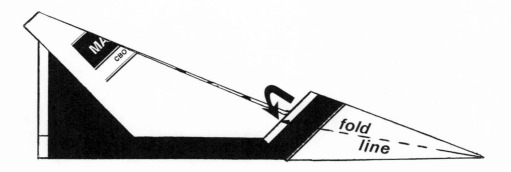

13. Align the trailing edge of the canard wing so that it is underneath the main wing.

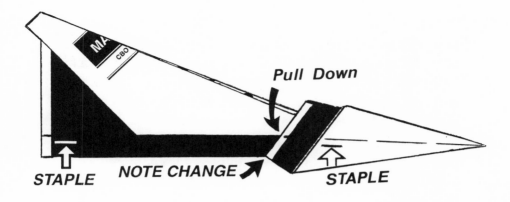

STAPLE   NOTE CHANGE   STAPLE

14. Nestle the top edge of the canard into the fold line of the main wing and staple as shown. Add a staple at the rear fuselage for weight.

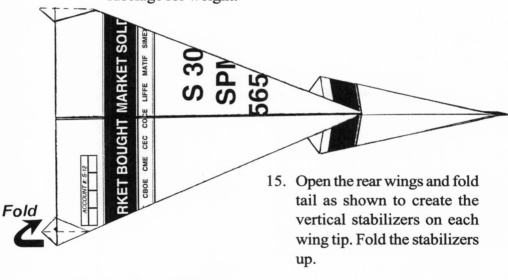

15. Open the rear wings and fold tail as shown to create the vertical stabilizers on each wing tip. Fold the stabilizers up.

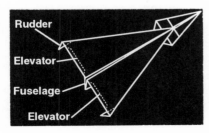

16. Fold rear elevators up. (See page 127 for flight instructions.)

While your Basic Self will get all excited about anything that seems fun, it also demands nutrition. You might want to bring fruit into the trading room so you can recover from a low blood sugar attack. There are lots of small ways to take a break and still be near the computer. Some traders use computer games. While fun, they never let your eyes take a break from the computer screen, so try to diversify and allow your mind to take a break in a way that does not need the computer. The point is: after controlling all the distractions for a prolonged period, give your mind a break by embracing the distractions.

Here's the next exercise. You'll be surprised by its difficulty when you first begin, but with practice you'll be able to measure and monitor your improving attention span.

> **Objective:** Increasing your ability to stay focused on the present.

> **Purpose:** To improve and lengthen the amount of time you can sustain your abilities to concentrate.

> Have you ever experienced a time early in the morning when you suddenly found yourself walking into the building where you work, or walking into the trading room, and couldn't remember traveling from your home to that present location? It is as if we are not consciously aware of the steps in-between the activity of traveling from home to work. Like sleep walkers we unconsciously go through the motions. Maybe the routine in our lives is repeated so often that it just blurs all together.

> From Darien to Wall Street it requires two different trains to cover the distance. Occasionally, I could hardly recall the transfer from one train at Grand Central to the next one in the Lexington subway to finish

the commute to Wall Street. If you can identify with this experience, then have I got the perfect exercise for you. But if you have not experienced something similar, you're not off the hook, do it anyway.

Exercise: Pick a period of time, like a commute from home to work, which is extremely repetitive in your day-to-day routine. This exercise needs an element of distance, a fixed interval of time, and repetition; therefore, a frequent commute is ideal.

Now set up small milestones for yourself to break the distance into smaller segments. The time from getting in my car to when the train picks me up on the platform in Darien; then the distance from Darien to when the train crosses the bridge at Old Greenwich; from that bridge to the 125th Street Station; etc. You get the idea, even if you are not familiar with the train route between Darien and Manhattan. From the starting point to the first milestone, you only focus on what is happening to you.

Pay attention to the people around you. Treat that time like you are passively viewing a movie screen. Pay attention to every detail. What other people are wearing, which landmarks you passed, the change in pitch of the train wheels as you approach, then cross the bridge. Filter out any distracting thought that tries to pull you away from the present and your conscious observation post. You will eventually slip into the past or future by wondering what people do, or remembering an incident in the past, or formulating hypotheses about what will happen to you in the future. When this happens, think of how far you traveled before your concentration was broken. Mentally give yourself an immediate pat on the back for trying such an exercise.

Be aware that simply doing the exercise has put you on the road to pass most of those sitting around you. You gave your full attention consciously to the present, even if only for a short distance before your mind lost focus and you lapsed into the past or future. You also made the transition from *wanting* to *doing* something about improving your concentration. Focus again and try to stay within the present a little longer.

> The next day repeat the exercise and keep your attention on the present for a longer time, over a farther distance. The long term goal is to be able to concentrate the entire distance between your home and work without being pulled into the past or future.

In the present you react to what you are experiencing; you aren't focused on what you are about to do in the office, or what you did the prior night. This last exercise is very hard to do, but I think you can understand the value of it.

Centering

Without Oars (of the same length)
You Cannot Cross in a Boat
—*Japanese Proverb*

Centering is a thought process which develops understanding of how every aspect in our life contributes to our overall development, growth, and ability to trade. When we are centered, there is an inner core of strength and calm. Distractions and events which don't fall in our favor are unable to pull us from a solid inner foundation. When centered, we remain in control; off center we lose control. As an example, a questionable line call for a centered tennis player will have no effect. *There will also be no break in their ability to concentrate on the next point to be played.* With the law of averages, maybe a lucky net cord bounce will eventually occur to even out the bad line call at a later time. However, if the questionable call pulls the player off balance, that resulting break of concentration will likely have a negative effect on future points in the game.

The same situation develops for traders. One bad trade or a horrible fill can pull you off center if you let it. One morning before the market opened, the floor called me to change my fill on 100 cars in the S&P market by 3 full handles (points). There was a fast market the previous day, but it wasn't *that fast!* If you are unfamiliar with the S&P market, this was notice that I had lost $150,000 in my account before the new trading session had even begun. (The firm did not tape record our orders so there was no recourse on our part when the tape from the floor was found to be inaudible. Tape recorders had been viewed as an unnecessary expense by the firm I was working for...that was, until that incident occurred.) I was thrown off center by the incident and knew not to trade that day. I was angry to the core and stormed out of the building. Had I traded at all with a hostile attitude, the results would have been disastrous. I also recognized that I had to go back and practice an exercise that effectively prepares you for just such a situation. This exercise is effective, but we'll put off defining what it is for just a few more pages.

Keeping our center of balance also means retaining our perspective. Our trading ability is never as good as our best winner, nor as bad as our worst loss. Even the most centered occasionally will be pulled off balance and overreact. When this happens, rather than become self-critical, congratulate yourself that you became aware of the imbalance. Recognizing the weakness is the first real step in strengthening it.

The movie *Ghost* has a rather memorable and sensual scene around a potter's wheel as the two principal characters of the movie work together on a vase. If you have ever worked with clay on a potter's wheel, you may have discovered that throwing pots is a rather interesting barometer of inner balance. The oozing clay swirling between your hands can develop into a beautifully balanced vase when events in your life seem to be going well. However, when upset or thrown off center by some situation, it becomes an impossible task to form a symmetrical object. No matter how many times you may start from scratch by throwing the clay mound back onto the wheel's center, it always seems to turn out asymmetrical and irregular in shape. This offers physical evidence of the mind-body connection between our inner balance and outer performance.

Both the movie and television industries have tried to tap the Western audience's curiosity about exploration of inner strength. One of the more successful marketing attempts placed the viewer somewhere in the dry, arid American West. The audience was immediately engulfed by a howling wind blowing dust and tumbleweeds across a vast barren desert. The camera revealed to us a lone figure emerging out of the dust. He strode across the desert floor leaving no footprints as the winds quickly erased his tracks. He walked gracefully, at an unhurried pace. He wore an old hat, and carried only a small bag, a bedroll, and worn shoes slung over his shoulders. His face, unlined and serene, revealed a man without past or future; a man living fully in the present moment. We are able to sense in him a great courage, power, and strength, that at the same time projected a quality of compassion and kindness. His name was Kwai Chang Cain. This characterization of a Shaolin priest, in the series *Kung Fu*, was Hollywood's definition of being centered. This television series, starring David Carradine, barely scratched the surface.

There are real-life examples of those who have mastered living in the present and have attained the peaceful inner strength we all search for: Mahatma Gandhi, Albert Schweitzer, the Chinese student who stood alone, directly in front of the approaching tanks during the Tiananmen Square assault, and many others who reflect the potential within each of us.

It is this inner balance and centered strength which enables the extraordinary. It is attained by inner development and acceptance of full accountability for our own actions and attitudes, as opposed to an external search and outward force or aggression. I am familiar with the techniques for attaining inner balance and centeredness, but I have not mastered the ability to remain constantly centered. However, I don't feel a need to be in control at all times.

The centered strength or inner calm occurs when we have given *equal* attention to the needs of our *three selves*, the Conscious Self, the Basic Self, and the Higher Self. The degree to which we are able to center ourselves and the amount of time we remain centered is equal to the degree of skill we have for maintaining our focus and concentration. It is unnecessary to concentrate all the time, as it is unnecessary to be centered at all times.

Objective: Moving back to inner calm and control, our point of center, after an external distraction.

Purpose: Learning how to filter external noise. (A preparatory step to learning how to filter inner noise and distractions.)

This activity was given to me when I lived in Toronto. It will be ideally suited for anyone who lives in a city where there is a subway: New York, Chicago, Toronto, London, Tokyo, or Moscow. If you live elsewhere, any noisy event will do, or put on a heavy metal CD and crank up the volume until the windows shake. It is an easy exercise to adapt to any environment. It shouldn't be difficult; all you really need is a location that produces a loud, ear-piercing noise that is difficult to contend with and makes you uncomfortable. Now how hard can that be to find in this age, hmm?

This exercise creates stress. It was not designed to be fun, but it is extremely effective in teaching and preparing us to let go of a major external distraction. It offers us a means to discover for ourselves how to regain an inner calm and center of balance, even become relaxed, while we are still standing in the middle of a hostile environment.

Exercise: Stand in an underground subway and purposely miss your next train. This will throw you off center and into a reactionary mode of behavior. Notice the surroundings and the expressions on people's faces. Feel the tension in the air. You'll likely feel the tension as soon as the train wheels begin squealing out of the station. As your train causes that horrible, ear-shattering, high-pitched sound of steel wheels screeching on steel tracks to reverberate through your body, take a deep breath. Tell yourself, "this noise cannot pull me off center." *Feel the high-pitched noise flow into your body and imagine it passing right through.* Visually imagine the painful noise as a wave or color that enters and leaves your body. As it leaves, you will be able to lower the sensation of stress. The pain of the high pitch will actually seem to drop in decibels to a level of sound that is more tolerable to your ears. Don't fight it. Don't let the sound build within you. Let it go. As the stress recedes, feel an inner calm take the place of the noise. The noise is still there, but you are concentrating on letting it pass through you and are thereby regaining your own control. See yourself responding with confidence, ease, and poise. This feeling is balance. You will notice others around you have frozen and become paralyzed by the same noise, yet you are now able to watch and view their reaction instead of being entirely focused on the noise and its impact on you. This is another element that shows you have regained your center of balance. When your attention begins to refocus on the noise keep repeating, "Let it go, just let it flow through me."

Save this experience and the sensation you felt for future re-centering after a setback or crisis. It is the exact same sensation when the floor calls you to hit your account $150,000 just before the market opens. Repeat the exercise as the next train pulls into the station. Get on the train and move on. It's behind you; just let it go if there is nothing more that can be done. Move forward.

During this exercise there is one very important element... *don't overdo it*. Don't hang around the station for the next train to try this technique a second time. Our resistance to the distraction and our ability to let it pass through us will rapidly diminish if the painful setting or situation becomes repetitive. It is similar to having a painful injection. Using this technique blocked the pain for the first few cortisone shots in my shoulder from swimming. Eventually I couldn't use the technique as I was unable to concentrate on it as the trainers pierced the same shoulder over and over again. Pain has its limits, but all stressful experiences can be tolerated for longer periods than you would normally expect to by practicing. Practice builds our stamina and tolerance to stressful experiences. As traders we need stamina to handle our trading environments.

When the disturbance is other than a physical sound, you will want to use an additional technique. This is a method I referred to on page 37, in the chapter "The Three Selves". As I walked out on the pool deck prior to an international swim meet, I defused the distractions by mentally forming a "tunnel" surrounded by a soft peripheral focus to re-center myself. I used the exact same technique when I walked past an individual in the trading room to filter him out — by forming a soft peripheral focus around me. You are remaining in control by narrowing your inner field of vision.

When you watch a sporting event, you would likely have noticed many athletes listen to tape recorders or portable CDs with headsets. By involving your other senses, in this case music, you will keep your mind and its negative chatter of thoughts to a minimum. It is a different application of the same visual tunnel technique or channel where you control your focus of awareness. Music is just another way to filter and allows an escape from a distraction or stress associated with a painful 'noise.'

The same technique can be used while trading. In some situations, to relax the tension in my neck and shoulders, or to filter out distractions which are beginning to pull me off center, I listen to a portable CD player after establishing a position. Sometimes the music you listen to can be serendipitous. One day I opened a new CD of John Williams' motion picture themes. I only scanned the contents and saw themes to Steven Spielberg's movies that I like. I didn't read the list very carefully, though. I put my headset over my ears, volume on full, kicked back in front of the computer screen, ready, music maestro, please...and the theme to the movie *Jaws* began. Ironically the locals had my position for lunch that day.

Intuition

"If I ever stopped to think about what happens after the ball hits my hands, it might screw up the whole process."
—Joe Montana, three time Super Bowl Most Valuable Player

The process described by quarterback Joe Montana most certainly applies to trading. Joe's comments show that any conscious decision-making that enters into a fast paced activity usually ends up destroying the critical timing and minimizes the result. It seems once we have learned how to do something, and the mechanics of that activity become effortless and automated, we then begin to rely on a natural sense of timing as dictated by an inner voice and metronome. This sense has been described in various ways: impulse, instinct, gut feel, insight, sixth sense, automatic response or reflex, inner wisdom. All of these words or phrases portray a direct knowing without the conscious use of reasoning. And it is this intuitive knowing that is essential to all fast paced activities that demand the cooperation of body, mind, and spirit.

You can't watch yourself fly. But you know when you're in sync with the machine, so plugged into its instruments and controls that your mind and your hand become the heart of its operating system. You can make that airplane talk, and like a good horse, the machine knows when it's in competent hands. You know what you can get away with. And you can be wrong only once.

—General Chuck Yeager,
First Man to Break Mach 1: the sound barrier.
Yeager: An Autobiography.
Reprinted by permission of Bantam Books

One explanation of intuition having greater value in fast paced and high risk environments is that our Conscious Self becomes bogged down with too much information. It is like our brains have the structure of a bureaucratic corporation. The Conscious Self is akin to the ivory tower executive staff of the corporation. Top level executives cannot be involved with all the minute details of a business; information is passed on by summary reports and executive support staff. The decision-making ability of the top executives is dictated by what filters up to them. If given incomplete, wrong, or filtered information, the executive staff will be put in a position of making decisions from erroneous facts.

In the case of our Conscious Self, we are unable to access the lower divisions and floors of our own corporate structure. Therefore, the Conscious Self is severely hampered and not fully equipped to make critical decisions because it is working with incomplete data. The Conscious Self is capable of many things, but it isn't very good at making decisions because it gets clogged up by analysis paralysis. The Conscious Self is like the trader who uses twenty different methods to determine when to buy or sell. They frequently miss trades by being over-burdened with information. They need the intuitive guidance of the Basic Self. As with most corporations, the employees, even low level employees, usually grasp the problems and are capable of figuring out what changes the corporation needs to make, long before the executive board reaches similar conclusions. We are like that corporation. Our Basic Self is our corporate grapevine, and our Conscious Self is our Executive Committee.

> Good instincts usually tell you what to do
> long before your head has figured it out.
> —*Andrew Jackson*

As the conscious mind is limited, it is the Basic Self that steps in to help us make faster, clearer, more comprehensive decisions. This occurs because our subconscious can access many more variables without boundaries of conventional measurements of time. If you have ever been involved in a car accident that you can see coming but cannot avoid, it seems to happen in slow motion. We have endless time to process all our options before the point of impact occurs with the other car. In reality, the point of impact could be fractions of a second away, yet we find the time to process the angles of impact to minimize our risk. This is our intuition at work.

It is our intuition that also provides the immediate understanding of a developing situation on our computer screens and how to react to it. That is, if we have done our homework beforehand to test for such a scenario. The Conscious Self trains and prepares us on the mechanics of trading like a flight instructor, forcing us to spend endless hours testing our indicators that become the tools of our trade. But after studying the numerous market scenarios and variable outcomes, the Conscious Self steps back and the Basic Self takes over.

Markets don't allow us the luxury of time to think. We don't have the time to give to our Conscious Self. *In such situations, analysis is paralysis.*

We all possess an intuitive instinct, yet few of us hear it or trust it to the level we should for consistent and successful results. When you intuitively feel "this isn't the best time or market level" or your instinct yells "it's wrong, get out, get out!" follow your instinct. (However, using this abusively as a crutch will be discussed at a later lime.) If the instinctive response was wrong, know it can be cultivated and developed with extensive back-testing. You may be thinking: "but isn't paper trading a better way to test the profitability potential of your skills?" NO! Paper trading has none of the risk or inner demands associated with risking real capital. Phooey to those who think they are market wizards after they show staggering profits from hypothetical paper trades. Even if you factor in excessive slippage and commission costs after the fact, *they have never been battle tested.* If you've not been tested under fire, you cannot determine or even guess how well you would do when the virtual game turns into the real battle against yourself and the markets. We lose money because of our inner vulnerabilities. Weaknesses within ourself will defeat us, not any external factor.

> It is not the same to talk of bulls
> as to be in the bullring.
>
> —*Spanish Proverb*

Evel Knievel, the oft-fractured motorcycle daredevil, was also an avid golfer. He wanted to challenge Jack Nicklaus or Arnold Palmer to a unique $500,000 skins game. The winner would gain $500,000, but the stakes would be paid out of the loser's pocket. To Knievel, the definition of pressure was not the difference between winning $250,000 of the sponsor's prize money, or only winning $100,000 by missing a six-foot putt. Pressure was the difference between winning $500,000 and having to pay $500,000 out of your own pocket. Neither golf legend accepted the challenge. Maybe that's why they are golfers, not traders.

It takes a special mindset to be a trader. Japanese candlestick analysis has integrated terms reflecting military conditions that engulfed Japan for centuries. There are "night and morning attacks," the "advancing three soldiers pattern," and "counter attack lines," to name a few.[1] Trading has long been recognized as requiring the same skills as those needed to be victorious in battle. The first futures market evolved in 17th century Japan out of the need of Samurai warlords to meet their future rice taxes. Hideyoshi Toyotomi was one of three great generals

---

[1] Steve Nison, *Japanese Candlestick Charting Techniques,* New York Institute of Finance.

attributed with bringing unification to Japan, ending "Sengoku Jidai," the 100-year period of war. Hideyoshi regarded Osaka as Japan's capital and promoted the development of commerce in that area. It has been told that warriors of Hideyoshi were positioned throughout his rice fields and on roof tops. These warriors would relay changing crop conditions from one field to the next until they reached Hideyoshi in Osaka.

It was one of Hideyoshi's war merchants that established the roots of the first centralized rice futures market. The merchant's extraordinary ability to establish the price of rice formed a centralized market on his front lawn. What was the name of this first exceptional trader? Yodoya Keian. (Hard to ignore that the name Yodoya, when spoken by a Japanese, sounds to the Western ear like "Yoda"!)

Osaka life in the 1700s was centered around making a profit; however, the class structure within this environment was strictly managed by the Japanese Samurai warlords. Yodoya, first trader extraordinaire, became too wealthy for his social rank. In 1705, his entire fortune was confiscated. His demise could have been worse. In 1642, an attempt had been made to corner the rice market, and the punishment for those involved — execution of their children, banishment of the merchants, and confiscation of all their wealth.

Despite such harsh penalties, trading grew and the Dojima Rice Exchange was formed from Yodoya's front yard in the late 1600s. Up until 1710, the Exchange dealt in actual rice, but at this time the Rice Exchange began to issue and accept rice warehouse receipts. These receipts for future delivery of rice to the warehouse were called rice coupons. By 1749, there were 30,000 bales of rice harvested throughout all of Japan, but the number of rice coupons traded would have corresponded to a total of 110,000 bales.[2] Speculative trading had to account for most of the differential.

---

[2] Hirschmeier, Johannes and Yui, Tsunehiko, *The Development of Japanese Business 1600-1973*, Cambridge, MA: Harvard University Press, 1975, p. 31.

A modern day samurai, Taisen Deshimaru Roshi, wrote *The Zen Way To The Martial Arts: A Japanese Master Reveals the Secrets of the Samurai*. The author was born in Japan of an old samurai family and taught at the Soto Zen School until his death in 1982. He himself trained under the Great Master Kodo Sawaki. In Master Deshimaru's book, on page 35, there is an exchange between a student and Master Deshimaru. This excerpt shows that the outcome for any conflict will ultimately be determined by how well we have trained our minds to be attentive.

> **Student**: Last year in Kyoto I watched a contest between two kendo masters who were about eighty years old. They stood face to face, sword in hand, sword-tip against sword-tip, without moving, absolutely without moving, for five minutes. And at the end of five minutes the referee declared the match a tie, *kiki wake*.

> **Deshimaru Roshi**: Yes. When you move, you show your weak points. Where young men would have worn themselves out in fierce thrusts and unorganized rushing about, where more mature men would have called into play all the experience of their technique, the two old masters simply fought spirit, with and through their eyes. If one of them had moved, his consciousness would have moved too and he would have shown a weakness. The first to weaken would have been utterly lost, because the other would have answered with one blow.

> It is the same in everyday life as well, you must watch the other person's eyes; when your adversary's eyes move, or are unclear, hesitate, doubt, waver, there is *suki*, opportunity, the flaw. In the critical moments of our lives we must not show our weak points; be-

cause if we do we will make mistakes, we will stumble
and fall and be defeated. This form of vigilance cannot come from constant bodily tension, for the body
would soon wear out; it must come from the attentiveness and strength of the mind.[3]

The goal is not technique, though improved technique re-
moves the distraction of doubt we have about our ability. The
aim is not physical strength, yet physical weakness hampers
our ability to focus. It's certainly not outward aggression, for
that drains our energies and leads to a loss of the control we
have over our own actions. *Everything we do to prepare to
trade contributes to increasing the attentiveness of our mind
and ultimately our ability.*

Without testing the strength and attentiveness of our own
mind in real battle in the markets, we have no foundation on
which to judge our skills. Paper traders are just fooling themselves.

So what's all this got to do with becoming a Samurai trader,
or a Top Gun pilot in the markets? All these different exercises
to develop our inner skills contribute to our trading performance.
A Top Gun pilot may fight only two or three real dog fights in
his career, but he fought thousands of battle simulations in
preparation. Joe Montana would take at least 300 snaps a week
in practice to refine his timing and technique, but his actions
during a game were instinctive. Both did their homework until
the mechanics became instinctive.

It is no different for traders. We have to do our homework as
well. Our homework involves countless hours of indicator back-
testing to build a confident reference library for our decisions.

---

[3] From *The Zen Way To The Martial Arts,* by Taisen Deshimaru, translated by Nancy Amphoux. © 1983 by Taisen Deshimaru. Used by permission of Dutton Signet, a division of Penguin Books USA Inc.

We test and retest our hypothesis and trading results until rapid-fire trading decisions became instinctive. Intuition is born from hard work. There is no way to side step this phase of development. If you are currently struggling with the technical aspects of trading, the chapters that follow will be challenging for you. However, those who know there is more to trading than technical skill, or discipline, are ready to fully benefit in the training which lies ahead.

Let's go back to the final days leading towards the Gulf War.

At this stage of my career, I was trading for a private investor who leased two condominiums that comprised the entire penthouse floor of a high-rise building near the United Nations Building in New York. Security at the building, which housed numerous foreign dignitaries, was as tight as Fort Knox. I am quite confident that the key security positions for this building were filled by Secret Service Agents. All the condos facing southeast could clearly see down to the front driveway of the U.N. Building.

Of the two penthouse condominiums, one was dedicated entirely to the trading operation. The trading room was spectacular. It was situated in what had previously been a sunken living room with hardwood floors at the corner of the building. Two entire walls were floor to ceiling glass. The trading desk was made up of two huge glass tables fitted back-to-back in the middle of the room. By day it offered a stunning view of New York; by night, it was breath taking. This room was surrounded by a sparkling curtain of city lights and shimmering building silhouettes. The immense and spectacular trading desk was not cluttered with the usual cables and paper. There were nine 35" TV screens stacked three high, covering the full width of the room. Eight screens tracked the markets, and the center screen tracked the profit/loss of all open positions on a real-time basis. (If a trader was in a losing trade, everyone on the desk could see it!) The other wall that ran the length of the room was a white board where the firm's analyst kept a running tally of support/resistance, price projections, volatility, Fibonacci levels, and custom statistics. Now you have a feel for what this trading environment was like.

Five traders were employed to trade their specialty: S&P, Bonds, Crude, Beans, and Metals. A sixth seat at the head of the table was reserved for the Principal. I traded the S&P. The energy specialist had an additional responsibility: having acquired exceptional money management skills while trading for Paul Tudor Jones, he managed the risk exposure for the firm.

Each morning when we entered the trading room, we were required to put a number from 1 to 10 on the white board beside our names. This number was an analysis of ourselves. If you felt like you were sitting on top of the world, everything was going your way, you felt healthy, strong, and had an invincible attitude ready to take on anything that might happen that day, you would give yourself a rating of 10. On the other hand, if you had been up all night with the flu, you just opened your mail and learned you have been personally selected by the IRS to experience the joy of a field audit, and you wanted to kick anything living or inert that comes in your way, you might give that day's attitude a rating of one. Most of us rated ourselves between four and eight. A 10 was rare, and when it showed up on the board, everyone took notice of it. A shuffle would occur within the firm. If the Bean trader was a 10 when I was closer to a 3, the firm's trading capital was allocated accordingly so that the Bean trader could establish positions of greater size than might normally occur. No one was motivated to falsely give themselves a 10, as a 10 also meant that you were trading a portion of the other traders' capital, and they could constantly see how your trades were doing by just looking at the middle monitor. You had to be incredibly sure of yourself to be willing to take on that extra stress. It is an interesting system that I still use today with a few minor twists. I've altered the daily rating to a scale of .1 to 1.00. The rating becomes a weighting adjustment to the probability portion of any risk management equation. It is important if you adopt such a system to rate yourself before the markets open.

This system of attitude monitoring ties directly to how tuned-in you may be to your intuition. One of the rarely declared '10' ratings that I gave myself happened to coincide with the James Baker/Tarek Aziz last ditch effort to prevent the Gulf War. You knew the outcome of the meeting would produce a ballistic market move, and the outcome would dictate the direction. Every trader in the world faced flat lines on their computer screens as we waited for them to emerge from their meeting at the Intercontinental Hotel in Geneva, Switzerland. We were all waiting for Secretary Baker's statement.

On that day, my intuition was a live electric wire. Every little thing seemed to be amplified. The first jolt after the meeting was when CNN announced that the press briefing had been rescheduled to a later time so that Secretary of State Baker could report to President Bush. That time delay alone nearly had me reaching for the phone to sell S&Ps.

You don't call the boss to tell him you succeeded, that can be relayed within a public forum. You usually only need to consult with the boss when you need to define a plan of action when you have to walk on eggshells or cover your back. While the CNN anchor babbled in Atlanta over a live picture from Geneva, you could see a reporter ask Baker a question. They did not broadcast the audio for this live picture, but sound wasn't needed. If you had an eye for detail, the answer was clear as a bell. Baker wiped his hands, left over right, right over left, and shrugged them away from his body as if he were trying to wash this whole mess off and push it away. I instantly grabbed the phone to start selling the S&P up to my full size without moving the market excessively. The other traders on the desk were still waiting to hear Baker, and they all looked in shock at me and then turned questioningly to the Principal of the firm sitting at the head of the trading table. Somewhere in my selling frenzy I yelled, "SELL! IT'S WAR!" The principal just looked at me with a questioning glance. I nodded back and kept selling. About that time, the CNN camera showed Baker walking down the hall toward the press room. To me, he had the weight of the world on his shoulders, and the Principal then picked-up on Baker's body language. The other traders still had no sense of what was coming. About the same time, the Principal looked over at the white board and saw the number 10 scratched by my name. Without any further delay, he screamed in his heavy German accent, "DO IT!" We were all fully positioned by the time Baker began his now famous, "I re...." The markets never even let him finish the word *regret* before all hell broke loose on the screens. To my great relief, we were on the right side. The desk netted a two million dollar gain within the next thirty minutes.

Many individuals who freeze at the screen, and cannot pull the trigger to execute a trade, experience analysis paralysis because they are unsure of the tools from which they base their decisions. These individuals have not put in enough time, they haven't done their homework, to build their confidence. This form of decision paralysis is simple to fix. It just takes time and hard work to answer the nagging questions. There are certainly other reasons for decision paralysis that are more difficult to address, and these will be explored in other chapters.

Intuition, I find, plays an important part when I don't understand what's happening or developing on the screen. At these times I find it is more helpful not to push for the answer. Relax, become calm, and go with the flow of your intuitive self. For years I carried around a quote from Albert Einstein. It goes something like this:

> As one grows older, one sees the impossibility of imposing one's will on the chaos with brute force. But if you are patient, there will come that moment in time, when while eating an apple, the solution will present itself politely and say, "Here I am."

When the solution does not present itself politely, the situation unfolding on the screen likely contains a wild card that I don't understand. In which case, my intuition nearly always forces me to the sidelines and out of the trade. It may mean that the exact same trade will have to be established at a slightly different level. However, when I truly have no idea about what is transpiring on the computer screen between markets, my flight-to-safety instinct is invariably the correct response.

A flight-to-safety response can be abused as an easy out to resolve an inner conflict between the Basic Self and the Conscious Self. Fortunately it is easy to identify when this tug of war happens within us. The Basic Self and the Conscious Self are usually separated by the word "But." This leads us to the next exercise.

Objective: Trading from the Left Side of Your "But."

Purpose: Learn to favor your Intuition rather than your Conscious Self.

Exercise: Simply stated, stay on the left side of your "but," and don't let what follows the "but" steer you off course. The left side of each of these phrases is your intuition. Here are a few examples:

"I could really use a break,	**BUT**	I need another winning trade to close out the month."
"I really think there is a buying opportunity right now,	**BUT**	my indicators have not given their usual confirmation pattern."
"I really want to get out of this trade I just established,	**BUT**	my broker will think I'm indecisive."

"There is a strong sell signal on the screen right now,	**BUT**	the last time I traded from that same signal I was wrong."
"Euros are in a fast market and bonds haven't moved. I should sell bonds immediately,	**BUT**	I don't know all the factors that explain why this imbalance is occurring."
"I really should go out to that party tonight,	**BUT**	I have to get up early."
"I'd really like to get into better physical condition,	**BUT**	there's no time."

You probably have the pattern firmly identified in your mind now with these examples. The challenge is to live and stay on the left side of your "but."

You can also practice your intuition by trying to predict common every day occurrences. For instance: who is calling on the phone? What does that man in the seat beside me do for a living? Will that man waiting for the train door to open walk to the left or right? It is our inner voice that can guide us through a crisis, major decision, or problem, or simply change mundane habits. Our intuition is our most reliable guide. By asking simple questions of ourselves like those just listed, as if it were a game, we learn to listen to the answer from within. It's not the answer that is important, it's learning to listen for our inner voice. *When we trade without effort, we are thinking less about our actions and listening more to our intuition.*

> How can you think and
> hit at the same time?
>
> —*Yogi Berra*

To conclude this discussion of intuition, let's return to the *Secrets of the Samurai*. This is an excerpt from a Sajshin, an intensive three-day training session.

Student: But why is spirit or mind the most important?

Taisen Deshimaru: Because in the end, it is what decides.

In the Japanese martial arts of long ago, one motion meant death, and that was the reason for the great deliberation and concentration in the movements preceding attack. One stroke and it's over: one dead man — sometimes two, if there were two strokes and both were as it should be. It all happens in a flash. And in that flash the mind decides, technique and body follow. In all modern sports there is a pause, but in the martial arts there is no pause. If you wait, ever so little, you're lost; your opponent gets the advantage. The mind must be constantly concentrated on the whole situation, ready to act or react; that's why it is most important.

Student: How does one choose the technique of attack?

Taisen Deshimaru: There is no choosing. It happens unconsciously, automatically, naturally. There can be no thought, because if there is a thought there is a time of thought and that means a flaw.

For the right movement to occur there must be permanent, totally alert awareness, of the entire situation; that awareness chooses the right stroke, technique and the body executes it, and it's all over.

Student: In kendo, for example, there is a tactic called *debana wasa*: you must attack before your opponent does, strike before he strikes. For that technique, intuition is certainly very important.

Taisen Deshimaru: It is always important, essential. If an opponent gives you a blow you were not expecting, then you have to have the intuition to parry it, that will trigger the right reaction of body and technique. But if you take time to think, "I must use this or that technique," you will be struck while you're thinking. Intuition triggers body and technique. Body and consciousness unite, you think with the whole body, your whole self is invested in the reaction.

That's why it is so difficult to make categories about the order of importance of *shin, wasa, tai* - mind, technique, body. They have to be united, not separate. It is the perfect union of the three that creates the right action; not their separation. Complete unity.

In the martial arts, kendo, the way of the sword, has always been regarded as the noblest of all because it necessitated the most complete union of all three, intuition, body, and technique.[4]

---

[4] From *The Zen Way To The Martial Arts*, by Taisen Deshimaru, translated by Nancy Amphoux. © 1983 by Taisen Deshimaru. Used by permission of Dutton Signet, a division of Penguin Books USA Inc.

Visualization

Our visions are the blueprints of our reality.

Recall a television close-up of an Olympic downhill skier standing at the top of a mountain prior to the race. Within minutes that racer will put years of training to the final test with a two minute free-fall down the icy slope of a mountain. They stand with their eyes closed near the starting line. If we watch carefully we see controlled skiing motions — weight to left, weight to right, hands driving forward — as they run "inner videos" in their mind of the course from start to finish. We know what they are doing. We can see their bodies react to the skiers' inner images. Chris Evert, Jack Nicklaus, Carl Lewis, and hundreds of elite athletes have all described their method of creating sharp, vivid images of themselves being successful *before they step out to take action*. They refuse to leave the outcome to chance; they train and rehearse mind and body synchronously. Why?

It is because what we conceive in our mind's eye is what we can accomplish. We direct and control the outcome of our own performances by first accumulating images and data that will lead to our success. Visions are our ideas in picture form. Since pictures are connected to ideas, they have energy just as ideas do. It is the energy of our mental pictures that encourages them to take form and become real actions. As a result, visions are the blueprints of our reality.

As an example, should you see yourself as a math whiz, you will likely prove this to be true the next time you are challenged by a math problem. We can also accumulate negative images. How much time do you spend visualizing past events that you want to eliminate? We tend to dwell on the issues we dislike, often visualizing and rehearsing them with great passion and intensity. If you picture yourself as unable to break out of a trading slump, you will live up to that negative image. The activity of visualizing negative outcomes is a rehearsal to fail. It also keeps the negative attitudes and energy alive that accompany these negative pictures. They hold us captive by blocking us from developing other positive images we may strive to create.

Visualization is an important technique to be used within a trading environment. It helps us prepare ourselves for numerous potential market outcomes. These inner pictures become a rehearsal for the actions we need to take in a critical situation. In the early chapters I shared with you the thought process that took place when I had a large S&P position in serious trouble during the Gulf War. I used visualization while still on the train to evaluate my options on how best to unwind a big mess. I pictured in my mind the various market scenarios that could occur once the market reopened. Then these images were used to create various plans of action for that specific market scenario. Eventually you have a plan of action for each outcome, and you have prepared yourself to the best of your ability. You may do better next time from what you learn from this situation. But that is the future, only the now counts. When prepared to your fullest potential, the anxiety is usually replaced with an inner calm. The calm is confidence.

Before I left Kodak, I had already developed a strong image of myself being successful in the financial world. That inner image was a novice's Disneyland world. However, that virtual image generated action and was soon reinforced with the installation of a real-time quote machine on my desk. This positive inner image was energized when I had my first few winning trades. The visions blurred with reality even further as I developed my command of the language associated with trading. Fact reinforced the vision and produced more actions. They began to propel one another. Soon the image and the reality merged when my Kodak peers and some Directors began to ask for my advice and forecasts. I knew absolutely nothing about the markets. In hindsight, I only acted out a stage character in full dress rehearsal. The script was written and rehearsed within my visions; my conscious self and body reenacted the rehearsal in reality. Soon I had on public record enough correct market calls that those around me perceived my knowledge as far greater than theirs. Soon all that differentiated the reality from the dream was the actual physical location and surroundings. It didn't matter that I knew squat about the markets; *I did not need additional knowledge at that time to exchange the virtual image of myself for reality.* Mentally I had already made the career change. Once I had started my new job with the junk bond firm, my Disneyland picture of what it would be like was shattered. But there again, it was shattered after the career change had already been made. I had to go forward to survive.

The reason visualization works so effectively is that you create a picture in advance of each movement or action exactly as it should be, while you are in a relaxed state of mind. The more you practice in this relaxed state of mind, the greater will be the chance that you will be able to carry out those movements during the real performance. Visualization helps to smooth out erratic performances and builds consistency because you are essentially preprogramming your actions. Constant replaying of your visions builds consistency, and that promotes performance excellence.

The Boston Celtics reached a staggering conclusion when they tried an experiment in visualization. Players were separated into two groups with the goal to improve their foul-shot percentages. One group had unlimited practice time to shoot endless foul-shots. The other group had restricted shooting time, but were taught to visualize doing the same thing. After three weeks what did the study find? Those who visualized foul-shots excelled at the free-throw line in game performance. It's time we make use of these results by taking a look at the next exercise.

Objective: Transforming Erratic Performances by Visualization.

Purpose: Consistency improves results and establishes a common foundation to return to for making enhancements.

You'll like this exercise. It will improve your golf swing, or skill in any sport you may now enjoy. To begin, you need to think of a particular aspect of your game or sport that you feel could be improved. A few examples could be your tennis backhand or serve; your golf chip shot or putting; for a dressage rider maybe the half-passe or tempi changes. Regardless of the activity you choose, you need to pick an element that will be very specific within that activity.

Exercise: Now with your mind's eye, see yourself repeatedly performing that task as you would like it to be performed. It is always helpful to watch a video of a high achiever you admire in your sport or activity. The next step is to transpose the image of yourself into this video. You see yourself in the role of the individual you admired. The hook is to then create a physical trigger or cue for yourself that acts as a reminder on command. Your eyes are closed and there is no body movement as your mind rehearses the action. (This process is entirely mental, you are not playing air tennis with an imaginary racket.) As you mentally *visualize* executing your perfect tennis backhand, create a physical reminder, such as forming a small circle with your fingers so that the index, or middle finger comes in contact with your thumb. What ever you choose, it just has to be simple. Then tell yourself, "I can repeat this form on command anytime by use of my physical reminder." By connecting the mental visualization with an actual physical action, you will be able to bring that form of perfection back into focus by simply using your reminder while waiting for the serve.

As you will discover, the outcome will produce the successful results you pictured during your visualized rehearsal. A success will itself produce another success if you use and apply yourself to the next exercise.

Objective: Visualizing Reruns of Past Successes.

Purpose: Training your mind to reproduce the environment of a success on command.

There will be trading days when everything seems to come together and go your way. You must save the feelings and actions of this day. Savor them. Practice visualizing the conviction and attitudes with which you entered your orders.

Exercise: Recall and record in your mind the confidence and ease with which you made decisions on this day. Do not forget the sensations when you are trading at this level. Rerun the experience and performance in every detail shortly after the reality has past. Create your physical reminder. It could be the one described earlier or perhaps take one of the many small desk toys we are given by vendors as a cue. Visualize this performance often to carve this day and its feelings of optimal performance into every cell of your mind. When you use your cue, it will help you to focus so you can recall this optimal performance on command. It will not repeat the performance; it will help you recapture the mindset you experienced earlier.

You have just been taught one of the subtleties of a high level performer. The skier's pre-race mental preparation should tell you a little more. Watch for his physical reminder the next time you watch an athlete rehearse for the downhill run. This visualization technique applies on the slopes, the golf course, in the corporate board room, before an interview or phone conversation. Now use it. It works on your self-esteem, your health, and yes, even in the trading room.

You should now catch on that our mindset and attitudes are what produce results, not technique. Create a clear image of what you wish to accomplish, see yourself exactly as you'd like it to be, mentally rehearse adequately, role play that rehearsal in real life, use your physical reminder, and then become that image of success for real.

Confidence

*Life is not always a matter of holding good cards,
but sometimes, of [having the confidence]
to play a poor hand well.*
—Robert Louis Stevenson

Confidence is a state of mind. It is an inner belief in our abilities and is *always* accompanied by a quiet, open and still mind. It feels like an inner calm. In fact, we can't experience a state of confidence without having the sensation of an inner calm along with it. Notice a trend developing here? We've just come across it again. We keep running into different descriptions of attitude and states of mind.

Returning to the words of Zen Master Deshimaru, *"Any conflict, whether it takes place within the body and mind or outside them, is always a battle against the self."* I don't think anyone who has ever traded the markets will disagree that trading is indeed a battle. Therefore, all battles are ultimately against ourselves; trading is an inward battle. It seems we have firmly painted ourselves into a corner that demands that we acquire a deeper understanding of ourselves and how to control and quiet the inner chatter of our minds to form an inner calm on command.

We began Part III with a script excerpt from the movie *The Empire Strikes Back*. We read where Yoda, the Jedi Master, was introduced to us in *The Star Wars Trilogy*. Yoda trains Luke Skywalker, a warrior, to use "The Force" to develop his powers of concentration, focus on the here and now, and to listen to and believe in his instincts. Now let me introduce you to the ancient Master after whom Yoda may have been modeled and a closer look at the concept of *"The Force."*

In 1728, Samurai Chozan Shissai, wrote *A Discourse on the Art of Swordsmanship* in a series of wood-cuttings.

> Life Force is the origin of life. If the Life Force detaches itself from its form, then death occurs.
>
> From mastery of action follows the harmony and balance of the Life Force; only then will the Principle of the action reveal itself of its own accord. When it is understood in one's Heart (can also be translated as 'Being') and no longer generates doubts then action and principle converge, the Life Force is concentrated, the spirit calmed, and responses follow unhampered. If the actions have not been mastered, then the Life Force will not be harmonious and balanced, the appropriate form will not ensue, and, therefore, one will not attain liberation.
>
> When there are irritations in the Heart, then the Life Force will be inhibited, and the hands and feet will not perform their function properly. When the Heart is free of irritations, then the Life Force is harmonious and peaceful. When calm and peaceful the "Life" Force is then lively and moves freely, and the Heart is without rigid form: without strength, it is naturally strong. *The Heart is thus like water and flows with the Life Force.*
>
> If the Heart (Being) is too deeply involved in technique this will interfere with the Life Force, and the Heart will not be harmonious and balanced. One might say that this is like forgetting the beginning in search for the end. Yet it is also wrong to totally discard practice and say that it is unnecessary. The function of swordsmanship lies in activity and form. If its func-

tion is discarded, what reference shall the Principle of its essence have? By practicing its function, one becomes aware of its essence, and it is in this awareness that the true liberation of the function lies. Essence and function have one origin: the Life Force. Thus, technique is practiced from the Life Force, but if technique is not mastered, the flow of the Life Force becomes rigid and the form unfree.

—Translated and reprinted in the book,
Cheng Hsin:The Principles of Effortless Power.

Yoda was not an original creation of Hollywood film makers. It took some sleuthing to dig this up and dust it off, but I think you'll agree that it was well worth the search!

Let's listen to the words of a modern-day samurai address the topic of "concentration." Could this be the origin of Yoda's renown movie line...

"NO! Try not. DO. Or do not. There is no try."

Modern Samurai, Zen Master Deshimaru writes:

I am always saying we must concentrate "here and now," create "here and now." That way we become fresh and new. You must not rest while you are training in a martial art. Doing it halfway is *no* good; *try not*, you have to *do* it all the way, give yourself wholly to it. We must not have any energy left in reserve.

Concentrating means "all out," total release of energy; and it should be the same in every act of our life.

In the present-day world what we see is the opposite; young people half living, half dead. Their sexuality is half way too, yet they think about sex at work, and the other way around as well, and so it goes with everything they do.

But if you have exhausted all your energy, you can take in fresh energy, flowing like the water in a stream.

If you try to spare your energy in a fight, you cannot win. That's one secret of the martial arts. We cannot count on *wasa*, on technique alone.

The Jedi Master, Yoda, was fashioned in the image of the elite ancient warriors, who were Samurai and Zen Masters. In one respect East and West have met in a comfort zone, through the character of George Lucas's Yoda.

In our Western culture, those of us not students of the martial arts begin to get uncomfortable and squeamish over the words Zen, meditation, or instruction on conscious methods of posture and breathing. These require a different concept of time and demand a lifetime of commitment, practice, and patience, something we Westerners have been conditioned to think of as a waste of time. That is not our fault, but it is our fault if we remain ignorant. We are conditioned from birth to pursue everything for instant accomplishment and automatic reward. Our society is geared towards fast foods, quick studies, and one-minute managerial techniques. Our impatience is a flaw, but imbedded within this flaw is our strength of spontaneity. So somehow in our preparations to do battle, or trade the markets, we need to learn how to blend our Western strengths of spontaneity with the discipline and strength of the Eastern mind. Wow, now there's a challenge, but let's think this one through just a bit further.

Our Western perspective requires instant accomplishment, but what can be more immediate and conclusive than Japanese *kenjutsu*, sword fighting? What trader alive would not wish to acquire even a fraction of the renown mental skills, or even a glimmer of understanding of the Way of a samurai warrior, or the Way of a Kendo Master? (Japanese swordsmanship) Now, "they had confidence!", we might say in the West, or a reader from an Eastern culture might exclaim; "NO! That's *shin*, spirit-mind-inspiration-wind-breath-intuition-soul-attitude... all at once."

So permit me to blend East and West further by sharing studies that have awakened me to Eastern culture and the Way of the Samurai. To those of Eastern cultural background, I mean no disrespect. I promise to be honest to the best of my ability to the teachings I have read from various *mondo*, question-answer exchanges that have been recorded between disciple and master. My intent and wish is only to drive home into the thick skulls of my fellow traders some Eastern concepts that are absolutely essential for trading and life, but are absent from our arsenal of Western beliefs and experiences. That is why Yoda became such a phenomenon within the Western culture; the character filled a void.

Yoda was teaching Luke how to quiet his restless mind to achieve inner liberation and total awareness through the practice of Zen. Zen is the practice of meditation. So the Way to quiet our restless minds is through a daily practice of meditation. Before Western readers conjure up images of smoking incense sticks and background sitar music, know that you have been tricked into doing meditation already. Sneaky of me, I know. The techniques I already described for improving focus, concentration, and practicing visualization *are techniques of meditation*. So shed the baggage that we attach to the word meditation; just let go of the anxiety resulting from our false perceptions.

It is through visualization that we reinforce attitudes such as confidence, by replaying past successes in our mind through visualization. We then learn to concentrate on the feeling of inner calm that is associated with our state of confidence. This means that this mindset is repeatable. By recreating the attitude associated with the success, we repeat the successful outcome more often.

Sometimes an individual in a position of power or strength confuses confidence with an overinflated ego. They are small-minded and weak as they are held captive by the attachments to themselves. They can be extremely vulnerable to external pressure and any ideas that challenge their inner perception of security and status. Their projected self-confidence is about as firmly rooted as a house built upon quicksand. In a corporate environment these individuals are frequently the back-stabbers, the ones who quickly step in and take credit for someone else's work, or play a vicious game of boardroom politics. They are best left to step into a hangman's noose of their own making. Eleven years at Kodak was long enough for me to see a few fast trackers eventually hang themselves. No one set them up; neither did anyone offer a back door exit for them. They finally painted themselves into a lethal corner.

Confidence does not in any way border upon an attitude of arrogance. When you meet individuals with a strong need to brag about their accomplishments to build themselves up, or to diminish others, beware. When they implode, they typically try to take others down with them. Give these individuals some distance so you don't get sucked in by their own implosion in the trading room.

So it seems clear what confidence is not, but what is the best way to illustrate what it is? Development of a confident attitude is exceptionally well-defined in the movie *Cool Runnings*, the story of the Jamaican Bobsled Team at the Calgary Olympics. The film shows how everyone, including the Jamaicans, believed their attempt to enter the Bobsled event was laughable. The odds were against them; they had never set foot on ice. Then the Olympic committee lowered the qualifying time in the preliminary round in an attempt to block this team from entering the Games. Instead of giving in, the Jamaicans tapped their confidence, knowing they had foot speed that the other teams did not have. Their running start helped to place them in the top qualifying group. This movie is their story of how their pride and confidence grows. It is not tied to winning a thing. They never had a chance of winning. The film shares with us how each individual finds his own center of balance and confidence, which in turn nurtures the team's pride in themselves and their country.

When you find the joy and fun of testing yourself to perform to your fullest ability, without measuring yourself against someone else, you will be able to relax; in essence you become liberated from the need to conquer.

The visualization technique can be used to build our state of confidence. We have learned that we will perform as we see ourselves in our mind's eye. There are a few traps to watch for, such as forming false expectations. Another trap is forgetting the successes and focusing too much on the setbacks.

While we can build our confidence by visualizing our successes in minute detail, it is equally important to build upon our ability to form an inner calm. That inner calm has to become a retreat that we can enter whenever we are in need. Trading certainly creates a turbulent storm within ourselves.

One exercise that was offered earlier allows us to reduce the painful noise associated with the screeching wheels of a train in the subway. You learned how to allow this noise to flow through your body, rather than hold onto the discomfort and let the noise build up within you. If you have practiced this exercise, you have learned how to let go of the noise and the discomfort. (These exercises all help to build upon one another... if you skipped that exercise you need to go back... you aren't ready for the one coming up. If you can't let external noise flow through you, you won't be able to let go of noise within your mind. That is where we are heading next.)

As you stood on the station platform letting the noise of the screeching train flow through your body, the sensation you felt was similar to lowering the decibels of that sound and most likely the pain associated with the sound. This exercise prepared you to deal with physical noise, an external source of turmoil. Now we need to address the inner noise of our thoughts. As with external noise, the body does not have to hold onto inner turbulence. In fact, we must let go of it, if we are to win the battle against ourselves when we trade. As a result we must learn how to return our minds to a state of calm and relaxation, regardless of the source of the noise, discomfort, or distraction.

The method used to free ourselves of mind noise is another meditation technique. It is quite easy. When we sit comfortably, quietly, preferably with eyes closed, our mind begins to listen to the various thoughts attached to the emotions in our mind. We think of thoughts that frustrate, anger or trouble us; we will also have happy and serene thoughts. Simply take a quiet moment, let these thoughts come forward, and listen to them. Don't judge them. Don't dwell or become attached to any particular thought. Avoid becoming tense. Don't resist or react in any way. Let the thoughts flow into your conscious awareness like a movie unfolding before you. *Your job is to be aware of them, not judge them.*

These thoughts flowing under our conscious mind all have the power of subliminal persuasion. Like the subliminal messages of an advertisement, we are manipulated and subtly influenced and motivated without conscious awareness. As confidence is a state of mind, reducing or releasing subliminal factors allows our confidence to exist without contradiction or challenge. We will be able to improve our focus and *do*, rather than try. Subliminal sabotage distracts from our ability to commit fully to our trading activities. Confidence is always accompanied with a sensation or feeling of inner calm.

If you are a child of the seventies, you may have experienced the ritual of being given a mantra for Transcendental Meditation. It's just a hook, a gimmick, a tool to aid our concentration and prevent our attention from wandering by using a repetitive sound or word. Some cultures and techniques focus on a pin-point image such as a candle flame. We have the exact same sense of tranquillity and inner calm when we stare into a camp-fire; or a roaring fire on a cold winter night. (I don't think the glass of wine hurts this setting either.) By focusing on the fire we allow our thoughts to flow freely through us without attach-ment. As a result we feel an inner calm as our bodies relax.

Everyone has the ability to just sit for a few minutes with their eyes closed. The objective of meditation is learning to focus and give full attention to the current moment. This is not the time to take a vertical nap. We need to give our full con-scious attention to watching these inner images. When we be-come distracted by allowing our attention to drift off with a random thought, we need to refocus. We need to allow our-selves to return to our inner observation post to view our thoughts. The more we practice, the easier it is to return to our inner sanctuary where we allow our minds and bodies to expe-rience calm. It requires tremendous commitment to stay de-tached, but the objective is not to be confused with trying to stop our thoughts. *Thoughts come and go and that is exactly what should happen.* Effort is not expended to stop these inner thoughts from flowing to our conscious awareness. Maybe only 10 minutes every day is needed, but it requires some practice daily.

If you still need to ask, "So why bother doing this? What's in it for me?", recognize that at the very minimum, this technique is a stress release. Anything a trader can do to lower his stress level a notch is worth doing.

With regular practice, meditation offers us several important skills we need in a fast-paced environment. Practice allows us to become less distracted by random thoughts and improve our ability to focus on the present moment with inner strength, centeredness, and balance. We also waste less energy and have greater focus for the task at hand. We are more aware of what is happening, similar to increasing the depth of field with a camera. As an added benefit, when we meditate we connect with our Basic Self and strengthen the communication link we have with our intuition. As a result meditation expands the use of our senses. Meditation is the practice of pure awareness and allows us to experience a state of mind that can effortlessly absorb huge volumes of information. And for those of you who asked, "What's in it for me?", a greater ability to absorb huge volumes of information is not a frivolous skill to develop as a trader. Right?

So the next exercise is specifically designed to make it easy. You won't even have to leave the trading room.

Objective: Achieving Inner Calm through Meditation.

Purpose: To increase our awareness and to assimilate greater quantities of information.

One way to allow yourself this break and not even leave the trading room is to make a tape cassette recording for yourself. Put the headphones on. Turn the cassette player on. Tune out the trading room. The recording can be of your own voice reading the instructions that follow below, or one of the many environmental recordings such as waves rolling up onto a beach, or any peaceful sound track of your choosing. People are funny when you have a headset on. They know you can't hear them, so they don't disturb you. If you close your eyes for a few minutes, they think you are just listening to music. Anyway, it takes away some of the restrictions we feel that make us uncomfortable in a Western culture.

Exercise: Set aside as little as 10 minutes.

1. Sit with your eyes open or closed. Adjust your posture so that you are comfortable. Perhaps put your hands at your sides. Begin by taking a few very deep breaths, allowing yourself to exhale fully to push out tension.

2. Imagine your body relaxing, starting with your toes. Bring a feeling of relaxation into your feet, calves, and thighs, then up into your abdomen and lower back, chest, upper back, and shoulders. Always start from the toes and relax upwards to your shoulders. Now relax your hands, arms, neck, head, face. Let the muscles around jaws and eyes relax. Let gravity make each part sink and become heavy. Do this until you feel physically comfortable and your emotions begin to calm and quiet.

3. Adjust your posture so that your energy can flow more easily up and down your spine. Inhale a full deep breath into your lower chest, moving your shoulders as little as possible. Breathe into your lower chest several times; notice how you feel. You will likely have a sensation that the pain and tension in your neck and shoulders is diminishing with each exhale.

4. Straighten and lift your upper chest with a deep breath, so your spine is more upright. Notice as you do this you may also want to adjust the back of your head to the most comfortable upright posture.

5. Watch as thoughts and images flow into your consciousness. If you wander with a single thought, let go of it. Be aware of your thoughts, but don't judge them or become attached.

6. Take several breaths to focus on your relaxed state. Realize by relaxing and attaining an inner calm, you have lowered your pulse from Mach 5 to Mach 1.

7. Now, open your eyes and refocus again on your surroundings. Take off the headphones.

You will find that you are able to both focus and concentrate more effectively than before your relaxation session. From earlier discussions you already know the value of these benefits.

Conscious Breathing

"Don't forget to breathe!"

I was startled when a judge yelled, "Don't forget to breathe!" as my horse and I moved past the judge's stand prior to riding a Dressage test. The truth is I need a recording of that judge to replay whenever market volatility increases.

I forget to breathe when I trade, as well. Only after a period of time do I become consciously aware that I am holding my breath. Guess what holding your breath does for your stamina and ability to focus and concentrate? You guessed it. It has a detrimental effect. It is not an uncommon problem. Many of us hold our breath unknowingly, and most of us are extremely inefficient about how we breathe.

Singers and athletes are given lengthy instruction on how to breathe efficiently. Few traders have benefited from that instruction, unless they have also studied the martial arts. Students of the martial arts require the highest level of instruction. They have good reason; their very lives depend on their ability to breathe correctly. A strike that falls on someone while they are exhaling is benign, yet the same blow delivered when they are inhaling can kill.

With limited observation skills we can see that our breath and our emotional state of mind are mirror images of one another. When we watch someone breathe, we can sense that person's emotional state of mind fairly easily. When we feel calm and relaxed, we breathe evenly, slowly, and with ease. When we're upset, our breathing patterns will be out of rhythm and balance. If we are sad, we will inhale forcibly (an unconscious attempt to replenish depleted energy levels). Frustrated and angry, we will exhale more forcibly (an unconscious release of excess energy). During a trade, if we become fearful or exceptionally tense, we can stop breathing altogether.

Breathing imbalances have a wide array of negative influences on us. They can aggravate any medical conditions we may have, hamper our efforts to receive and process information, limit our ability to concentrate, and contribute to stress. Due to the pressure associated with trading, and just day-to-day life, most of us naturally tend toward constricted, shallow breathing. Compound that inefficiency with a trade that is going against us, and suddenly our cardiovascular system is no longer capable of contending with the oxygen needs that our brain requires to handle the emergency. We may react too slowly to effectively minimize the capital damage. Worse, we might freeze and watch a bad trade turn catastrophic. And we all know that it takes many, many trades to recoup from one very serious blow to our account.

Ordinarily, we breathe fifteen to twenty times a minute, but we breathe superficially, using only one-sixth the capacity of our lungs. Full breathing takes place at the level deeper than the thorax or even the diaphragm. One can learn to breathe more slowly, five or six deep, calm breaths a minute.

> **Objective:** A Conscious Evaluation of your Breathing Right Now.

> **Purpose:** Establishing a baseline from which to compare at a later time.

> **Exercise:**

> 1. Put one hand just below your neck. Place your other hand on your diaphragm. (Above your belly-

button and just below the "V" of your rib-cage.) Notice your breathing right now. Are you slouched over? Do you normally breathe through your nose or mouth?

2. Take three conscious deep breaths. Inhale through your nose, exhale through your mouth. Which hand moved? If only your top hand moved you are a typical shallow breather, using only a portion of your lung capacity. Now inhale and try to push your lower hand out rather than moving your shoulders up.

3. Exhale fully. Feel your shoulders, chest, belly and entire body relax and let go of tension. Exhaling fully will create a pressure within your abdominal muscles.

4. Make the breaths very slow and deep, but not to the point of strain.

Let me guess, you had trouble with the exhale, and you first squirmed to adjust your posture. You may also have discovered that you are an inefficient breather. That's your starting point. Now we need to address increasing lung capacity to increase efficiency. An exceptional exercise to help explain this technique is one every competitive swimmer in the world will know. Swimmers spend their entire training lives learning how to breathe. When I teach people to swim, breathing is the hardest thing for most to learn. It is because we do not know how to breathe on land. So you put someone in water, and it becomes a major obstacle. Every swimming coach in the world emphasizes breathing out for a longer and longer duration. Swimming power comes from exhaling, not inhaling. We can adapt this training to an exercise on land.

Objective: Increasing Lung Capacity

Purpose: Greater Efficiency of our Cardiovascular System. (So we can concentrate far more effectively!)

Exercise:

1. Go out for a walk. Count each step you take. Left, right, left. That would be a count of three. Inhale on a count of one, then exhale throughout the next two strides. Repeat.

2. Once you get the idea of breathing in rhythm to your steps, begin your interval training. Repeat as you walk a full block. Inhale on the count of one, exhale throughout strides two and three.

4. Then extend to a five count. Inhale on the count of one, exhale throughout strides two, three, four, and five. Repeat this count of inhaling on a single stride and exhaling throughout the remaining four for at least another block. It takes time for the body to relax and catch on.

5. Continue increasing the number of steps until you reach your comfort limit, maybe to a count of seven or nine. At your limit you are pushing yourself to exhale throughout the duration of the remaining strides before you can inhale again on the count of one. Stay within comfortable boundaries. The objective is to work up to a count of 15.

6. Now do it backwards. If you worked up to seven, drop it to five. Take a breath on the count of one, then exhale throughout the next four strides. From five, drop it to three where you started. It is always important to work back down to your starting point.

Let me tell you up front what you are going to experience. At first the exhale will feel very forced. Either too slow or too fast, certainly not in sync with the count of 'one' when you feel like gasping for a breath. Breathing imbalances accompany irregular breathing patterns. So it is understandable that any rhythm you try to force upon yourself will feel out of sync. This feeling does pass fairly quickly. For this reason it is extremely important to give yourself enough time at one specific count to allow your body to comfortably fall into sync with that particular rhythm. It just has to be a distance far enough to allow yourself time to feel at ease before the count changes. If you never feel comfortable... don't change! You will also find that it is the exhale that allows a sensation of calm to flow through your body.

Let's conclude this discussion with the teachings of Master Deshimaru. This excerpt shows that breathing techniques, an integral part of the martial arts, can help us in our battle with the markets.

> It is important to concentrate on breathing out, on spreading and distributing, because breathing in, stocking up energy, happens unconsciously and automatically.
>
> The Japanese martial arts use this way of breathing out (yang), if possible while the adversary is breathing in (yin), because he is then at his most vulnerable. Through intuition, and that's the most important point, one must take advantage of the instant when the opponent, *breathing in*, shows his weak point.
>
> You yourself must breathe out when you attack. In karate a blow received while breathing in can be dangerous. So you must seize the opportunity while the adversary is breathing in, because then he reveals his weak point, his empty space. The opportunity always comes while the other person is breathing in because the body becomes lighter then, less concentrated. The in-breath of the other person offers an opportunity which your mind-body must know how to grasp. To attack while the adversary is catching his breath, show-

ing his weak point, the flaw in his defense, *his attitude*, that is the key.

Breathing in is one great *suki* or opportunity, and too much tension, or too little, is another; in a tournament, it is impossible to maintain the same intensity of concentration indefinitely. At some point the attention wavers, and we show a fault, a *suki,* an opportunity, which the opponent must be able to seize.

This question of opportunity arises in every contest, however, not just in the martial arts - in argument, business. You must not show your weak points, either in martial arts or in everyday life. Life is a fight! When opportunity presents itself, you must leap upon it without thought.[1]

---

[1] From *The Zen Way To The Martial Arts*, by Taisen Deshimaru, translated by Nancy Amphoux. © 1983 by Taisen Deshimaru. Used by permission of Dutton Signet, a division of Penguin Books USA Inc.

Assertiveness vs. Aggression

"The real pros, those who are winners,
do what's required to score,
then immediately hand the ball to the referee."
—Mike Ditka, Former Coach of the Chicago Bears

Ironically, one of pro football's most aggressive players and coaches is the person who most eloquently defined the difference between assertive and aggressive action. These comments were expressed by NBC analyst Mike Ditka concerning players who were showing off after a touchdown. His observation is exceptionally pertinent for a comparison of assertive and aggressive attitudes given the inherent aggressive nature of football.

The spread between an assertive attitude and an aggressive attitude is a polar extreme. Assertion is positive, aggression is negative. Negative attitudes drain and deplete our energy reserves. They are also significantly harder to sustain.

John Skiian was a special man. He was my most influential teacher, coach, and a surrogate parent. He's no longer with us. Together we resolved the toughest obstacle I had to face as a swimmer. Later, without his knowledge or help, I had to tackle the same problem when I first started to trade. It was the same obstacle, and the same solution. You see, I excelled at the 150 meter Backstroke. (If you swim, you'll see the problem immediately.) There were only two Olympic backstroke events close to that distance: the 100 and 200 meters. I wasn't fast enough to sprint 100 meters and lacked the stamina for the 200 meters.

It was the era of the East German machines. You had to sustain the effort, as you do with the markets. There was never any hope of dominating the event early and then holding off a late surge from behind. The late surge began when the starter's electronic beep began the race. The pace would build from there.

It was John Skiian who uncovered that I was trying to annihilate everyone else in the pool. The defeat was a result of attitude, not technique. The aggressive attitude to win through domination left me exhausted by the 3/4 mark of the race. Physically there was nothing left. His change in focus made a tremendous difference when all else had failed.

In Webster's dictionary, *assertion* is defined as "a behavior that emphasizes self-confidence and persistent determination to express oneself in a positive way." The assertive attitude originates from an inner strength. It is thereby sustainable for considerably longer periods of time and will have a positive impact on our staying ability and stamina. The assertive player is in sync with the conflict around him and enjoys a sense of joining and fusing with the environment through self-control.

Being in sync and harmony with a market is one of the most important aspects for successful trading. There is an inner rhythm in your gut that tells you when you are in sync. Your intuition shouts "pivot point!" with limited technical input. You scale in and out of your positions with fluid actions. It becomes a dance with the market as you shift from long to short. It may even be similar to attaining the status of Top Gun pilot, exceptional skill accompanied with inner calm, self-control and unshakable strength.

Before your balance sheet can tell you, your gut tells you: you lost it. "It" being that elusive harmony with the market. If we need to aggressively dominate the market, we cannot dance in sync with it. Being in sync requires a sense of inner calm and self-control. We have all heard buzz phrases like, "the market is always right;" "don't fight the markets;" and "play by the market's rules to win." We've all heard these phrases, but why do we disregard them?

The problems lie with motivation, tactics, and attitude. An aggressive behavior includes a sense of ruthlessness and domination and is frequently accompanied with a driving need to annihilate an opponent. It is not enough to excel and then just walk away, or as Mike Ditka said, just pass the football back to the referee. Aggression requires an outward focus and an opponent or counterforce to be aggressive toward. The trap of adopting this mindset is that outward aggression depletes our energies. It generates tension, stress, and fatigue and usually ends up backfiring on us. In sport, the opponent nearly always replies to aggression with an aggressive counter attack. The counter attack always seems to come just when we have depleted our energies and made ourselves vulnerable. The markets are also very capable of swinging a counter punch just when our energy reserves are fully depleted.

When those energy reserves are depleted, we are most vulnerable to making mistakes. For example, do you have nine small winners and then proceed to give the profits all back to the market on the tenth trade? It is important to understand that aggressive trading cannot be sustained. It leaves us extremely vulnerable to counter market moves that we cannot react to when our defenses are down. That's why a team's aggressive attitude may win one of the quarters within a football game, but may not lead to victory. Trading is even harder. There is no two minute warning. We need tremendous stamina to sustain each day's competition into infinity.

A different and more successful attitude is knowing that we can win, *but we do not have to dominate*. How? By changing our focus from outward to inward and concentrating on asserting our trading skills, strengths, and abilities. Asserting ability will take less energy and produce less tension and strain. What is more important is that assertion is always a more relaxed mindset than attempting a victory through aggression. Therefore assertion is more closely aligned to the mindset we adopt when we are in sync with the market.

An attitude that focuses from inner strength also indicates that we are in control and take responsibility for our own actions. By having a focus that is directed inward to achieve, we establish a firm platform from which to learn, improve, and grow. This only occurs when we are in control and accountable to ourselves.

Trading is a war, but the markets have all the ammunition relative to our limited reserves. We have to rely on our inner smarts to win a few battles, and then recognize when to step aside when the odds are against us, not waste energy attempting to win the war. If you really think about it, the final outcome of this war has already been decided. Markets 1, Traders 0.

Aggression, with its outward focus, becomes entirely dependent upon the actions of a counterforce or opponent. Failure is directed towards the opponent with better skills, greater speed, strength, whatever. The opponent was the cause of our failure. When we are aggressive towards a trade, we provide ourselves with the same scapegoat of excuses. "No one could have predicted that action from the Fed;" "no one is winning in this market;" "the pit locals have control." They, they, *they* all over again.

The excuses are directed toward outward events. We write them off as out of our control, so we end up losing the opportunity to learn from them. As a result, we do not learn because we are not accountable. The aggressive attitude is a stagnant growth curve. If you lost, what do you do next time? Try to be more aggressive, of course. The resulting energy drain and tensions increase. It is a no-win foundation for achieving success. On the other hand, winning through an inner focus of asserting our own abilities provides the foundation to improve.

We are accountable only to ourselves on how we use our abilities and accept our skill level as always growing. If the market takes an unpredictable zig when we zag, it is not a failure. It is an opportunity to increase and add to our knowledge and skill. As a result we learn, we change, we grow, and we move forward. The aggressive trader can only try to learn how to become more aggressive.

This is the exercise my coach John Skiian gave me, that got me onto the winner's stand. It was given to him by a Japanese coach. It works.

> **Objective:** Conscious Awareness of Focus; Inwards vs. Outwards

> **Purpose:** Changing attitudes from domination over an opponent to winning by exceptional execution of your own skills.

> When we admire certain traits in others, we frequently have similar traits. In ourselves, these traits may be dormant. The first step is to visualize these traits in others so that we can later find them within ourselves.

> **Exercise 1:** Identifying with an assertive individual or animal.
> You will need a small piece of paper and pen by your side.
> Relax, close your eyes. Visualize a person or animal that exemplifies assertiveness to you. It could be a cheetah, jaguar, dolphin, some other animal. It could be a person, a famous person, leader, or friend. You want to see qualities of power, confidence, and strength.

Imagine all the qualities of your selected animal or person that make them powerful, both physically and mentally. Picture this person or animal at their best. Visualize their actions in minute detail. Now define the characteristic traits they demonstrate as they assert their abilities. Most will find traits such as courage, focused attention, and self-confidence. Feel the attitude they display and the mindset they seem to adopt.

Now that you have seen these qualities in your mind's eye, you need to write down these traits on paper immediately. Not only must you see them in your mind, you must put them into a tangible list that you can see and touch.

Make a list now. (We'll use your list for the next part of the exercise.)

Exercise 2: Role playing to help you adopt the assertive traits of the character you have chosen.

After visualizing the assertive animal or person of your choosing, you wrote down the traits that you admired.

Now picture yourself being that person or animal. Visualize the actions and feel the strengths and mindset required to role play that individual in your mind.

Role play and literally act out the mindset you felt to assert confidence, power, and unwavering focus. By consciously adopting that mindset, and then following through by *role playing your visualization*, you can teach yourself to focus and utilize that attitude when needed. There will soon come a time when you will no longer be role playing that part in a real life play; you will become that person or portray the attitude and strengths of the animal you first selected.

The next step, when you face an opponent, is to draw upon this inward rehearsal. This progression of visualizing what you want, breaking down the traits, defining the components, and then role playing the part, is precisely how to become what you want. Once you've felt it, you can become it.

It's attitude that makes a winner and a champion. An inner focus means you are in control of your own actions. When your focus is directed outwards, you relinquish control, and you will always blame your shortcomings on external factors or your opponent. By denying accountability for the outcome, you *can't improve*. Now become accountable for your actions. No excuses remain. It's up to you.

Courage

"One small step for (a) man, one giant leap for Mankind."
—Captain Neil Armstrong, Apollo XI

You can achieve most goals by taking small continuous steps towards that goal. However, we eventually come across a missing bridge in our life's path that requires one giant leap, or we fail to move forward.

The decision I faced to leave the Kodak "mothership" was one of the chasms I encountered. At that time, I was struck by the number of people who said, "I wish I had the courage to do what you are doing." I did not understand at that time what they really meant.

I do now. Many of those individuals are essentially doing the same jobs today as when I left Kodak. They are trapped and have abandoned their own dreams and aspirations. Some have become bitter; others just became prematurely old and resigned from life itself. *Calculated risk-taking is living.* Life without risk is merely existing. Living life to the fullest means pushing our abilities, emotions, and potential right to the very edge. Chuck Yeager coined the phrase that said it best, "pushing life to the outer edge of the envelope."

There's no comparison between what's lost by not trying
and what's lost by not succeeding.
—Francis Bacon

In Jean-Paul Sartre's play *No Exit*, three people are trapped in one room without windows. After considerable time in this confinement, a door opens to freedom. But they end up staying in the confined windowless room because the unknown has become too great a risk to face. This does happen. Many of us choose a known suffering over the possibility of an unknown freedom.

So if living is calculated risk-taking, to increase our odds for a positive outcome, how do we control the anxiety and fear that accompanies risk-taking? The answer is courage. Courage is not the absence of fear in the face of risk, courage is the ability to control the fear that accompanies risk. So the key is learning how to manage anxiety by fully analyzing, then understanding, and then fully accepting the implications of an associated risk. When a big risk contains hidden opportunities, or we deduce that the worst probable outcome isn't a fatal setback, we suddenly find the courage to take on that calculated risk. It is this progression of thoughts that builds our confidence, diminishes our anxieties, and then allows us to take a great leap of faith.

> ...risks are the spice of life...You accept risk as part of every new challenge; it comes with the territory. So you learn all you can about the ship and its systems, practice flying it on ground runs and glide flights, plan for any possible contingency, until the odds against you seem more friendly. You know you can be hammered by something unexpected, but you count on your experience, concentration, and instincts to pull you through.
>
> —General Chuck Yeager,
> First Man to Break Mach 1: the sound barrier
> *Yeager: An Autobiography.*
> Reprinted by permission of Bantam Books

Sometimes we can diversify the risks by choosing to make shorter-term goals that mitigate the worst case scenario should we fail. For example, you could establish a smaller position on a risky trade. This is one approach, but I'd rather continue addressing the more difficult situation when we face an impasse getting to our next milestone.

Objective: Learning from Past Adversity

Purpose: Assessing risk for the future.

In the television show *Northern Exposure*, there was a brief segment where the following story was told by the Inuit woman. It went like this.

> An old warrior spoke of the time his son's only horse ran away.
> The neighbors all said it was bad luck.
> But the next day the horse returned and brought five horses with him.
> The neighbors all said it was good luck.
> As the son was trying to ride one of the wild horses he fell off and broke his leg.
> The neighbors all said it was bad luck.
> As it turned out, soon after the accident, military troops swept through their village and took all the able-bodied warriors with them to war. The son was spared.
> The neighbors all said ...

The moral of this story is that things aren't necessarily what they seem.

Exercise:

1.   Write down a painful risk you took in life, or business, that later became a blessing or worked out on your behalf.

What felt most difficult about it originally?

2.   Write down your initial fear(s) prior to taking the risk.

3.   Did the fear materialize? Was it justified?

4.   How did you feel after taking the risk?

5.   What do you see as the primary benefit of an otherwise painful situation?

6.   Write down what good or positive lesson it offered.

7.   How did this action affect your life then? Now? How will it (or did it) impact you in 5 years?

These steps teach us how to reevaluate past risks we faced, and then to apply the same progression towards analyzing a current risk. Anxiety diminishes with thorough preparation. In fact you may find the anxiety shifts from the risk of taking action to the risk of stagnation through inaction. When we know that we can live with our decision and can accept the consequences of the worst case scenario, the inner calm returns and courage moves in to push us forward.

Aspects of a Successful, Professional Trader: A Self-Test

Throughout this book we have been working together to understand the importance of attitude and concentration. We have traveled a great distance together. We have learned through the words of ancient and modern samurai that all battles ultimately are against ourselves. It is only fitting that you now face a midterm test. It is not a test to mark the conclusion of our training session, but a means to establish a measurement and foundation to help define the next action plan for improvement. Areas where you score poorly must be changed. *Your very survival as a trader will depend on it.*

The following list was given to me by Joe DiNapoli in a private trading seminar offered by Coast Investment Software, Inc., 6907 Midnight Pass, Siesta Key, Sarasota, Florida, 34242. This list was given with the following instructions:

> Rate yourself on each of the following items between one to ten. Ten is outstanding or exceptionally strong, five being average, one being exceptionally weak or absent from your characteristic traits all together. When you rate yourself with a five or less, that aspect, if left unattended, will become your undoing as a trader.

I played Joe's game. I rated myself on each item in the list. When it came to "an ability to release tension," I gave myself a 2 and a pat on the back for being honest. I chuckled, and then proceeded to do nothing about it.

About a year later I was extremely sick, an emotional basket case, and in need of hospitalization. I hit bottom, total burnout. At the time of that seminar, Joe warned me that this would happen. He knew it would happen, he said, because we were so similar and he had taken the same path of self-destruction. I didn't heed his warning for a second. I've got staying power, confidence, inner focus, nope, won't happen to me. (Ego speaking.) Unfortunately, it is not enough to know intellectually what we have discussed so far, you have to live it.

When the implosion came, I was told by two doctors to get out of my trading job or the job would do it for me. My employer didn't need any medical reasons, I was tail-spinning into the deepest financial hole I had ever experienced. I ended that year down 22% in my futures account. That was the year everything in my life went astray. As Joe said to me, "You're finished, you're done. That's the easy part. That's already been decided. Now you have to get out for at least six months and think things through. Go do something else. Go live on unemployment. Go write a book or something. Every trader who amounts to anything goes through this phase. No one escapes. When it happens, you step away thinking you'll never trade again, but you'll be back. And when you do, you'll come back a true professional and make tremendous profits."

He was right. I was an addict, uncomfortable when I didn't have a position on, and therefore out of control. I had to learn how to break the control the markets had over me. Been there. Done that. Moved on. The progression that was required to learn that lesson was extremely painful, led to tremendous hardships along the way, and quite literally could have ended my life.

Rest assured it will happen to you, if it has not already. Now rate yourself on each item defined on Joe's list. Then create an action plan to address the weaknesses you uncovered. We have covered the techniques you need to work on any weaknesses that you uncover. And heed my warning, you will eventually

Aspects of a Successful, Professional Trader: A Self-Test

	Low				Avg.				High

Independence: 1   2   3   4   5   6   7   8   9   10

(Do you need to call and ask others what they think about the market, or do you make a decision in total isolation from everyone else?)

Stick-to-it-ive-ness: 1   2   3   4   5   6   7   8   9   10

(Be careful not to confuse this with compulsion and addiction.)

Discipline without anguish:

1   2   3   4   5   6   7   8   9   10

(Trading the wrong time frame can contribute to a lower score here.)

An ability to take the Responsibility for Your Own Actions:

1   2   3   4   5   6   7   8   9   10

An ability to learn from your Mistakes:

1   2   3   4   5   6   7   8   9   10

Your ability to Release Tension:

1   2   3   4   5   6   7   8   9   10

A Sense of Humility:

1   2   3   4   5   6   7   8   9   10

(Excessive egos must be down graded here.)

Knowledge of the Market:

1   2   3   4   5   6   7   8   9   10

Experience in the Market:

1   2   3   4   5   6   7   8   9   10

Knowledge of Money and Self-Management:

1   2   3   4   5   6   7   8   9   10

Realistic Expectations:

1   2   3   4   5   6   7   8   9   10

Your ability to act on what You See:

1   2   3   4   5   6   7   8   9   10

address these weaknesses. If not now, you will certainly develop the need later when that weakness becomes your self-destruct button.

This section began with a excerpt from *The Empire Strikes Back*, and it is time to return back to Yoda, Jedi Master. If not before, you should now grasp the full depth of the meaning of Yoda's words. You are becoming a Jedi Trader, as you learn to liberate your mind from distractions and become aware of all around you. You are in essence becoming a Zen Trader. You have learned that with inner control and focus, you can build and nurture your skills and abilities. You have become accountable for your actions. You have learned much... *but your training is not complete... we have yet to discuss the dark side of "The Force."*

THE EMPIRE STRIKES BACK

EXTERIOR: DAGOBAH - DAY

With Yoda strapped to his back, Luke climbs up one of the many thick vines that grow in the swamp. Panting heavily, he continues his course - climbing, flipping through the air, jumping over roots, and racing in and out of the heavy ground fog.

YODA: Run! Yes. A Jedi's strength flows from the Force. But beware of the dark side. Anger...fear...aggression. The dark side of the Force are they. Easily they flow, quick to join you in a fight. If once you start down the dark path, forever will it dominate your destiny, consume you it will, as it did Obi-Wan's apprentice.

LUKE: Vader. Is the dark side stronger?

YODA: No... no... no. Quicker, easier, more seductive.

LUKE: But how am I to know the good side from the bad?

YODA: You will know. When you are calm, at peace. Passive. A Jedi uses the Force for knowledge and defense, never for attack.

LUKE: But tell me why I can't...

YODA: (*interrupting*) No, no, there is no why. Nothing more will I teach you today. Clear your mind of questions. Mmm. Mmmmmmmm.

Artoo beeps in the distance as Luke lets Yoda down to the ground. Breathing heavily, he takes his shirt from a nearby tree branch and puts it on.

He turns to see a huge, dead, black tree, its base surrounded by a few feet of water. Giant, twisted roots form a dark and sinister cave on one side. Luke stares at the tree, trembling.

LUKE: There's something not right here.

Yoda sits on a large root, poking his Gimer Stick into the dirt.

LUKE: I feel cold, death.

YODA: That place .... is strong with the dark side of the Force. A domain of evil it is. In you must go.

LUKE: What's in there?

YODA: Only what you take with you.

Luke looks warily between the tree and Yoda. He starts to strap on his weapon belt.

YODA: Your weapons ... you will not need them.

PART IV

The Dark Side of Trading: The Obstacles, Addictions, and Inner Anxieties

We have seen the enemy
and they is us.

—Pogo

The time has come to face the Market Wizard hiding behind the curtain of Oz. The control panel that ultimately dictates all our trading wins and losses is located right between our ears. Our trading performance depends on how well we have learned to tame our own inner demons. Our P/L will never be determined by our ability to forecast the markets. Some analysts call market moves exceptionally well, *but that doesn't mean they can trade that move.* Why? Because trading does not depend on our indicators, methodology, or even our level of experience. Even with solid money management technique and analytic skills, there can be no success, because technique alone will be insufficient. It comes down to how well we understand ourselves under intense fire, and how well we've learned to calm our darker side when the stakes become exceptionally high. You have read the words of ancient samurai warriors to modern day champions and know it all boils down to the same single question, "Are you sufficiently liberated from your inner anxieties, addictions, fears, and deepest emotions?" We have indeed come face-to-face with the enemy, and it is within us.

A word of caution to those who have just jumped directly to this section without having read the prior chapters. You may be eager to read the concepts that follow because the chapter headings read like the most direct way to the bottom line, *but you are not equipped to make the needed changes in yourself.* The prior sections have prepared the reader through a time-tested progression of developing mental skills and attitudes to be open to the discussions that follow. There has also been a subliminal bridge constructed to help you straddle the boundary of Eastern and Western cultures so that we may now address a fairly difficult concept for those of us living in the West. In essence you are limiting your awareness and are trading with only half a deck.

If you lack the patience, or drive for the preliminary work, or are still always focused on the future and never the present, that's OK, too. Accept you are still focused on the technical mechanics of trading. There is nothing wrong with this. The Chinese say, "a journey of a thousand miles begins with a single step." You are chipping away the tip of an iceberg whose real mass lies below the surface of the obvious. You have a thousand miles to go, one step at a time. These aerodynamic trading techniques will let you fly a part of that journey.

It is only *when*, and not *if*, you experience a major trading slump, or reach total burnout, that you will become convinced that there is much more to trading. Eventually we must let go of our beliefs that trading success depends entirely on money management and the mysteries locked within the charts. Hopefully this rude awakening occurs before experiencing burnout. However, if you are as stubborn as I was and have to hit bottom, know that on the other side of extreme pain is inner freedom.

Emotions

*We tend to think of the rational mind
as a higher order, but it is the emotional that marks our lives.
One often learns more from ten days of agony than from
ten years of contentment...*

Some Men are more Perfect than Others —Merle Shain

Can following strict money management guidelines for stop placement also control our emotions? Many traders believe so, but can it? I recall one trade, out of thousands in that terrible -22% year, that forced me to reevaluate the relationship between money management and emotions.

When the S&P market opened on October 5, 1992, I was already 20% short. Additional selling near the open increased the existing position to 55% short. Suddenly, without warning or news, the S&P market began plummeting in full points towards the first limit down at -12.00. This was not a market to chase and instincts warned me not to add to my existing position. I elected to sit back and monitor the fall, having caught the start of the move.

Somewhere near -9.00 S&P points it became very apparent that sitting on the sidelines 55% short was not sitting well with my employer. Soon I went against my instincts and began to sell into the shallow retracements to extend my exposure to 73% short of what I'd normally trade.

Why only 73% short and not up to 100%? A sanity check prevented me from establishing a normal position at that time. Keep in mind that there isn't a single market scenario that will ever justify exceeding your sanity check boundary. There are always two independent calculations for risk assessment: one is for stop placement, and the other is an attempt to calculate an absolute worst case scenario should everything, and I mean *everything,* go wrong. If you could not get out of the market for some unforeseen reason, where might the dust finally settle so that you could halt the financial damage? In my worst case scenario, I try to ensure a catastrophic loss will not exceed 10% of my total capital available for trading. That way you can still trade another day should everything blow up in your face. You pray that you never experience your worst case scenario. A 1% or 2% capital exposure is still high for any single position. However, every professional trader eventually will experience Armageddon.

So on this October day, I only established a 73% short position as the worst case projected a 10% capital loss if the market closed just above the previous day's close. With the market currently in a free fall, it had to be a low probability. Anyway, I would hardly sit back and do nothing as the market rallied 12 or more points against me. I would say the odds for this worst case scenario developing on this day were slim to none.

The S&P market was soon locked limit down at -12.00 points. Trading would then be halted for thirty minutes and the session would reopen with even wider limits at -20.00 points.

The trading halt is supposedly designed to let traders contemplate the errors of their ways and cease such foolish capitulation. In reality, when the market is truly in a serious decline, it will only serve to make things worse. The trading curbs in the DJIA will force mutual funds to short the S&P to hedge the losses developing in stocks. There will be a day when the S&P market will lock at the first limit down, and then immediately fall to lock limit down at the newly expanded limit. We will experience several days like this sometime in the future, but October 5, 1992, was not the start of this anticipated large scale collapse.

My eyes were glued to both the Reuters and Telerate screens. The two independent quote services had been installed to ensure backup service should one system fail or go down. We even had battery power backup to minimize that potential problem. I traded from a private office that was very isolated and distant from the main trading room shared by several traders. There was never any reason to communicate between these different trading areas within the same firm, so it would not have been known by anyone that the information displayed by Reuters and Telerate in my office was very different from that being transmitted by CQG throughout the main trading room.

On that sunny day of October 5, 1992, both Reuters and Telerate in Boston displayed that the S&P market was locked limit down. *In reality, the pit in Chicago was developing a ballistic S&P short squeeze rally!*

The first alarm occurred when the Telerate screen gapped up recording a trade +4.25 points off the low. My first reaction was that this was just a bad tick. Looking over to the Reuters system, they still showed the market was locked limit down. Relief overcame me as my suspicions were confirmed about the erroneous market quote. However, in the fraction of time that it takes to glance over to the Reuters system and back to the Telerate system, the Telerate chart had expanded the first bad tick into a rising fast market. I had three different phone lines that could be used to access the floor. I grabbed the private dedicated line that was a direct link. The phone automatically dials the number. I waited for the connection to be completed. Instead I heard:

"We're sorry. Your call cannot be connected as dialed. Please try again."

"SAY WHAT? IT CAN'T BE!"

While the phone fails to connect to the S&P floor, the Reuters system began to mirror image the Telerate system showing a ballistic rally unfolding with the market now up +5.40 points

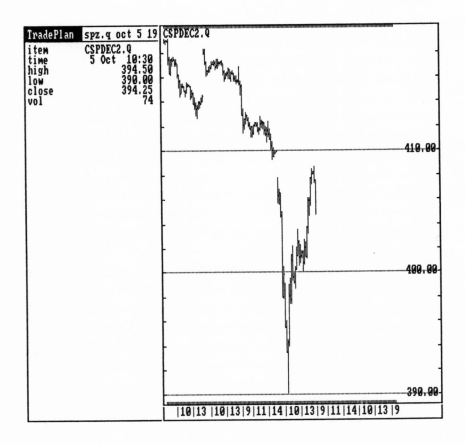

TradePlan	spz.q oct 5 19
item	CSPDEC2.Q
time	5 Oct 10:30
high	394.50
low	390.00
close	394.25
vol	74

15 minute bar chart of the S&P, October 5, 1992
(Chart courtesy of Telerate)

off the lows of the day...and still climbing. "GET ME OUT OF HERE!"

I grabbed the second phone that was a conventional public line. Again I used the speed dial setup to attempt to reach the floor. There was the familiar sound of the automatic dial, a connection, but then... "We're sorry. We are experiencing diff...." SLAM.

Now bordering on panic, I grabbed the third phone line on an independent circuit to contact the floor. There was the familiar sound of the automatic dial, a connection, but then... "We're sorry ...." SLAM.

OK, keep yourself together... the market is now +7.00 points off the low *and still climbing.* However, the market is a full 5 points away from the catastrophic worst case scenario that was calculated. SO THINK! What's the common element between these three independent phone lines?

YES! They are all MCI lines and pass through the newly installed main switchboard. There must be a problem with the switchboard that went on-line only last week. The traders had all been given instructions how to use a predial code to bypass the cost saver network that utilized the main switchboard, so the instructions were extracted from the top drawer of the desk and immediately executed. A pause, the connection, and then, "We're sorry..." SLAM.

OK, maybe it's MCI itself or the building. I can use the dedicated phone jack for the modem that is still serviced by AT&T. BUT HOW?! The other phones on my desk were all hard-wired directly into the wall and could not be disconnected. Just then I recalled having seen a standard phone in the corner of the office. I dove for the modem line, but restrained from ripping it out of the wall and possibly destroying my last link to the outside world. SNAP. The plug fit. (Many offices use two different phone jack standards as ours did. This could have been fatal! You can also see why it is important to have cellular phones for your backup.)

Another problem... I didn't know the number! With the speed dial feature on the other three phones there was no need to memorize the phone number to the floor. Fortunately I had once anticipated this problem and had *etched* the number to the S&P pit on one of the computer frames. (Paper can drop off, pencil can be rubbed out, pen smeared; etch it!) I dialed the number and finally made a connection to the floor.

All the while the market had continued its rocket ascent. A short horizon Elliott Wave pattern showed that the market had just ended a small fourth wave down within a vicious third wave extension. This was the best place to cover the entire position, but the market would not have been able to absorb the entire size of this order graciously. I entered an order to unwind half of the position "at-the-market," something you just don't do unless you are throwing in the towel to save your hide at any cost. By this time, it was my hide that was in jeopardy—and it was going to cost! I had never entered such an order and the floor knew it. "Repeat that order." "You heard it... *'at-the-market'*." The market runs against me another 1.25 points, then the rest of the position was unwound at any gracious retracement that could be found. In hindsight, the whole position should have been thrown into the pit at the same time. Bad situations just get worse. The trading session eventually closed that horrendous day just slightly off for the day. Incredible.

Total damage: -8.7% of my total capital in only four hours of trading. Poof. Everything that could go wrong, did. It was the first time I had ever experienced the Armageddon scenario. The only saving grace was that the risk management calculations had actually worked. The risk management criteria had also served to keep my emotions in check so that I could think through the crisis without uncontrolled panic. *I did not believe it could ever happen to me.*

The phone company later determined that the phone service between Boston and Chicago had been seriously affected by a fire at a major switching station. The MCI representative tried to dissipate my anger: "But madam, the disruption in service was only for a limited period of time — less than an hour!"

This "brief" service disruption explained the quote differences between vendors. Reuters and Telerate were adversely affected by the same major fire. CQG was not affected, as its data feed used a different technology. (Yes, I now install different data feed technologies for backup as well.) The worst had happened and I had lived. There would be another day. I had substantial capital remaining to dig out of this major loss. I knew I could come back. Things were going to be OK. *Or so I thought then.*

It took little time to discover that while I had the positive attitude to dig out of this hole, and retained confidence in my technical indicators and trading ability, there was still something very wrong that I did not understand at the time. Attitude and technique were suddenly not enough. What was missing was the stamina and energy to continue doing battle with the markets. Soon, suppressed emotions began appearing in the form of physical illness. The comfort zone with trading hundred lots soon dropped to 50 maximum, then 10, finally just 5 cars would lead to the same mad dash down the hall to the washroom. I was sick. Without knowing it at the time, I had come face-to-face with physical exhaustion and emotional burnout. I had depleted all of my reserve energy. The fight and energy were gone, and I didn't know how to go about healing myself. What I didn't understand was that in a competitive environment there are three facets, not just the two of technique and intuition. I did not have need of the third aspect as my former competitive experiences had always involved the support of team members, a coach, a corporate mentor, or peers for moral support. No one was there this time. *Why did I physically fall apart? Why did I lack the energy to bounce back? Why couldn't I find the energy to fight back? Why was this time so different?*

All my "whys" were answered through further study of the martial arts. In the martial arts, there are three essential training aspects: *wasa*, technique; *ki*, energy; and *shin,* mind/spirit/ intuition. We have already explored the training similarities and benefits for traders with the technique and intuition aspects of the martial arts. We learned that ultimately it is our state of mind and intuition that takes precedence over technique.

It is *Ki*, energy, the second aspect of martial arts training that ultimately dictates the strength and power of our state of mind and intuition. *Ki* is the power of our inner energy flow. *Ki* can also be abused and damaged. The trade I just described was not catastrophic to my trading capital, but was total annihilation of my *Ki*, my inner strength and energy.

When we think of someone who is weak, we might picture someone who speaks very softly, their body language shows introverted qualities such as slouching over, and they have trouble looking others directly in the eyes. They may appear physically frail as well and have what I term as 'a dead fish' handshake. Such individuals have a weak *ki*. Their inner energy flow is very weak. We do not come into this world with a weak *ki*, so what causes the change?

Emotions are a pure energy moving through us without obstruction. This is not the energy that allows us to lift weights, work hard, or swim long distances. It is a "feeling" energy that moves us to pursue these activities. As infants, we didn't know what anything was, but everything sure looked interesting. With unobstructed emotional energies we felt naturally motivated to explore, touch, taste, move, learn, act, and discover. Unobstructed emotions don't imply we always felt happy, but when we felt sad or afraid we let the feeling flow, and then let go of it. We could quickly return to our natural state of free flowing openness and joy.

So what happened to us? Now we are ashamed to show anger, embarrassed to show sorrow, reticent to express joy, and some of us are so out of touch with our emotions we no longer know what we feel. We become so used to living life in shades of gray that we forget what life felt like in vivid color. We are taught to suppress our emotions since our childhood, but in order to reexperience the aliveness, the excitement, and the incredible motivation we felt as infants, we need to clear the obstructions that block the free flow of feeling energy.

The physical law of *conservation of energy* states, energy can neither be created nor destroyed. Energy can only change from one form to another. Light can change to heat; heat can turn into mechanical work; a latent idea can manifest itself into an action. In fact our ideas, thoughts, feelings and emotions are themselves energy. We can't even wiggle our toes without having first thought of the action. The energy of our thoughts makes all action possible, and every cell of our body is constantly eavesdropping on our thoughts. That's why positive and negative attitudes can have such an impact on our health and our abilities. Generally we are unaware and take little notice of how we go about sabotaging our goals and abilities by misusing our own energy. *All the energy in the universe already exists and it cannot be increased.* So when anyone speaks of increasing their energy, they are really trying to learn how to make *their existing energy more accessible.*

So our job is getting the rocks and obstructions out of our energy hose so that the "water," our natural energy, can flow without obstruction. When we flow more freely with our natural energy, things seem to go our way and become easy for us to do. We feel strong and sure of ourselves. The way you feel when you are having a 'ten' day is ultimately what we would all like to experience more often. Suppressing emotions won't produce more days at a 'ten' energy level, because this only shifts the inner obstruction to a new location. What we really want to do is clear the obstruction so that we have more energy accessible to us. Navigating through the dark side of trading is really a journey of self-discovery, to remove our inner obstructions so that we become stronger.

To most of us, the word *emotion* refers to feelings or sentiments: positive ones like happiness, joy, and excitement, or negative ones like anger, sorrow, envy, depression, and so forth. As emotions are an energy, we can feel and sense these feelings from other people. Our energy fields are not isolated islands; they interact with those around us. Energy is dynamic. That is it doesn't stay put. All you have to do is study electrical energy to see how energy fields move around. They attract, repel, move, and interact, just as our own energy does. A room full of people creates an energy field that can be positive or negative, depending on everyone's intent. We've all had the experience with our families or other groups of entering a room and immediately sensing an energy field. Have you ever heard the expression, "cutting the tension with a knife?"

According to the laws of electricity, electrical energy flows from a positive to a negative. Our brain energy is a measurable electrical energy that abides by the same laws. Our energy flows from a positive state to a negative one, and not vice versa. This means when you have a positive energy and come in contact with a negative energy, like lots of negative angry people, one of two things will happen. One is that the negative energy will drain you of your positive energy. You will feel tired and may become negative as well, or your high positive energy will cancel out the negative. When I experienced the loss on October 5, those around me, of the firm, became extremely antagonistic and negative. The principal himself proclaimed I would never recover from such a loss. Instead of support, there was only an intense energy drain, and soon I was so physically ill that there was no way of healing within this environment.

That negative environment would literally suck the life out of your positive energy state. It will be extremely important to remember this when we discuss other aspects of the dark side of trading. What we are striving for is to nurture our positive energy and make it more accessible to us. This is how we develop a strong *ki*.

Master Yuno of Japan, who excelled to the 8th dan in *kendo* (swordsmanship) taught that preparation for any battle requires that you let go of your own inhibitions and fears. He teaches that this is the only way to bring about inner strength and enormous energy, *ki*. This is illustrated in a Zen parable told by Master Yuno.

> Chi Hsing-tzu was raising a fighting cock for his lord. After ten days, the lord asked, "Is he ready?" Chi answered, "No, sir, he is still vain and flushed with rage." Ten days passed, and the prince asked about the cock. Chi said, "Not yet, sir. He is on the alert whenever he hears another cock crowing." When the prince's inquiry came again, Chi replied, "Not quite yet, sir. His sense of fighting is still smoldering within in him." When another ten days elapsed, Chi said to the lord: "He is almost ready. Even when he hears another crowing, he shows no excitement. He now resembles one made of wood. His qualities are integrated. No cocks are his match — they will at once run from him."

Stress, Compulsions and Addiction

Nothing so needs reforming
as other people's habits.
—*Mark Twain*

The inner discomfort, turbulence, and pain we feel from pent-up and obstructed energy is what we call stress. We are forced to find ways to reduce the stress to provide an escape from the discomfort, but relief is only temporary. The escape behavior is an energy pressure valve and when the pressure builds back up, along with the discomfort, our need to find relief returns. The compulsive habit can easily become a cyclical extreme that develops into an addictive behavior. Some energy release valves can develop into physical substance abuses while others can be psychological dependencies that are just as addictive.

Psychological dependencies can occur when we systematically overstimulate our natural adrenal system. It is the sharp adrenaline rush followed by the sensation of relief or relaxation that becomes addictive. Thrill seeking is frequently a common ground for adrenaline junkies. The fears associated with high-risk behaviors such as skydiving, bungee jumping, driving fast, jumping horses, and even amusement park rides, all fit the pattern of an adrenaline rush originating from fear, followed by a release of tension.

Horror films also have similar elements as high-risk behaviors. These films contain fearful images that hold us captive to the screen; relief comes when the film ends or the director gives us a brief reprieve. Surprisingly, comedies that bring tears to our eyes and cause side-splitting pain are similar to horror, in that laughter provides the mechanism for release of tension. These can all be important and useful stress releases.

Other outlets for stress reduction are overeating, sex, over-exertion, and stress related illnesses and injuries. These behaviors all follow the cyclical progression of adrenaline rush followed by relief or relaxation. Overeating is probably the most common outlet for lowering the body's energy level. We crave to eat sweets or pastries, cause a steep rise of blood sugar, then experience a corresponding drop. That doesn't imply that just because we have an urge to binge on junk food, enjoy a good wine, or occasionally get sick, that we have a compulsive or addictive behavior. It simply means that these activities provide us with a means to reduce our pent-up energy.

When the need to attain temporary stress relief becomes a compulsive extreme, it can develop into an addiction. A bungee jump, a horror movie, a downhill mountain bike race can be an excellent release. Trouble is just around the corner, however, when we "live" for the release itself. All truly addictive behaviors, whether physical or psychological or both, serve to release blocked energy from the body. As long as the inner obstructions remain, the pent-up energy will return, and along with it the renewed discomfort and pain that necessitates our need to find some way to release it.

We cannot see our energy, *ki*, but we certainly do feel it. Our perception of feeling high or low energy does not reflect our abundance or lack of energy surrounding us, but rather points to our own ability to access it, to feel "The Force", as Yoda would say. A good analogy is that we are always surrounded by air, but we still have to access it by breathing. While that access can be obstructed when we have a cold or hay fever, we can be invigorated when we are in good health and breathe in the fresh, crisp, fall morning air of a pine forest. When we feel most energetic, we feel alive. When our *Ki*, our energy is blocked, we drag, have difficulty thinking, lack motivation, and feel "dead."

You will recall that high energy fields flow to lower ones, or positive energy flows down to negative ones. When you are constantly surrounded by a negative energy field, such as angry or hostile associates, you are in serious trouble. You will find ways to release the stress, but will also deplete your *Ki* in the process. This leads to an energy crash and is fatal in any competitive environment.

Typically we minimize our discomforts by finding some kind of outlet for relief, but soon our inner obstructions once again lead to stressful pains and inner turbulence that drives us again to find an outlet for relief. The habit becomes a repetitive cycle. To break the cycle, we need to break down the obstructions.

Our inner obstructions come in three primary forms: mental, emotional, and physical. Mental obstructions include worries, concerns, regrets, resistance, judgments, and past associations. (HOG!) These thought forms all impose a tension on the body that blocks the free flow of energy. Like the analogy of water flowing through a hose, obstructions take away strength from the final output of the hose, thereby weakening our *Ki* and ability.

Emotional obstructions center around forms of sorrow, fear, anger, envy, jealousy, depression, irritation, frustration, and rage. Though these feelings are generated by the mind, we feel these emotional obstructions specifically within our body. They lead to physiological changes, such as breathing restrictions and imbalances, that also block the flow of energy. If you take a moment to think about these emotional obstructions, there is an element of time associated with them. Fear is always of a future event and about the possibility of being hurt. Anger on the other hand, arises in relationship to a past event, such as having been hurt. The exercises in the second portion of this book become extremely important for developing our skills to focus on the present moment, for they help to minimize these emotional obstructions. The individual techniques or exercises also provide us with the means to let our unconscious let go of suppressed and deeply held inner obstructions so that we can at least become aware of them. Then, when they step forward into our conscious awareness, we can do something about the obstacle.

Physical obstructions stem from injuries, poor posture, and restrictive movements that are likely by-products of the mental and emotional obstacles we carry. Stress-produced illnesses and injuries are not themselves a physical obstacle, but a symptom. Those of us who unconsciously use illness or injury as a stress release outlet do it by default. We become ill because we avoid or neglect other stress release outlets that are beneficial, such as exercising. Not every illness or accident is a subconscious decision to release stress, but when we develop patterns of illness or injury, then we need to work on achieving new levels of well-being. That may require a lifestyle change.

My one-way train commute to Wall Street from Connecticut consumed 90 minutes to two hours for one direction. Eventually that takes a physical toll on your body. I was constantly fighting off colds, flu, and respiratory problems one after the other. As soon as the commute was removed from my schedule, so were the string of illnesses.

In our day to day lives we experience both acute and chronic obstructions. Acute obstructions are induced from temporary issues or difficulties. Our chronic obstructions tend to lie far deeper. They are hidden, repressed, and have likely been with us since our childhood.

Though acute obstructions are painful and sometimes swift and dramatic, they generally have a very obvious source: "What do you mean the Fed just raised the discount rate again!" "I just broke my toe." "Ahhh, that was *my* parking spot!" And my most frequent one at the end of the month..."My American

Express bill is for how much?!" Our acute obstructions are somewhat fluid as they rise and fall throughout the circumstances of our daily lives. We can elect to routinely overuse one of our stress reduction outlets to find temporary relief from our pent-up and obstructed energy, or we can clear the obstruction. For acute obstructions, time will heal the broken toe, we will find ways to resolve our financial pressures, or we will find another parking spot. (Unless you live in Boston!) Some of us will resort to chocolate, as I do, when I need a release from the drudgery of analyzing government bond spreads. But what about chronic obstructions?

Chronic obstructions in the body, mind, or emotions reflect deep tensions, pains, and unresolved issues. These obstructions fester within us as physical memories and deep turbulences. They remain with us no matter how good our current circumstance may be. It can be a beautiful day, things could be going our way, yet we will always see the "ugly" side of everything as we view the world through distorted glasses. Deeper fears and chronic obstructions need help from a twelve-step program: Gamblers Anonymous, Narcotics Anonymous, Alcoholics Anonymous. There is need for a Traders Anonymous group. Anyone who has been forced to take a cold, hard look and actually focus in the mirror and see themselves in pain and trapped within the dark side of life, tends to develop an aura of authenticity about themselves that I admire. They no longer play "let's pretend." I'm not a twelve-stepper, but I do know the first step is recognition of the courage it takes to acknowledge our more addictive patterns. Addictions are a symptom and the more abusive and chronic addictions require help from trained specialists. The bad news is: trading can be an addiction. The good news is: unlike alcohol and drugs, the cure does not have to mean giving up trading permanently.

The exercises we practiced earlier offer us the means to identify and clear out many of the obstacles from within our own energy flow. The greatest difficulty is always identifying our obstructions so that we can then do something about them. Striving for a kind of emotional simplicity then is a valuable element in the creation of our goals. If you are unaware of your emotional patterns, look at the pictures of your life. What do the pictures of your environment look like? Do you see lack of space, confinement, discord, disagreement, lack of unity, failure, or repeating patterns of conflict in your life? Be willing to acknowledge that our inner obstructions will have a connection between our fears and the pictures we see of our environment. As an example, the fear of success will go on creating the similar pictures of failure, one after another, until it is corrected. The fear of success is the obstacle that develops stress, which in turn leads to compulsive behaviors that we need to escape the pain.

It is hard for us to strip down, simplify, and focus our thoughts over a period of time in order to quiet the inner jumble of blaring radio stations within our minds. Concentration requires quietude, perseverance, and self-control. Concentration is a discipline. The reward for having the discipline to practice the numerous techniques described earlier is that our minds learn to focus on only what we desire to create. We do not have to be trapped within a bubbling stew of unwanted and self-destructive thoughts.

The techniques and methods offered to you for visualization have another value. Visualization captures the energy of ideas. When there is only a vague notion of an idea that is hard to bring into the forefront of our thoughts, remember that everything we see existed first as an idea that we entertained. Visualization brings us into focus with the fuzziest and deepest notion of an idea, as it links us with our Basic Self, similar to the process our dreams create when the Basic Self is given freedom from the controls of our Conscious Self. However, only visualization lets us remember all the details that surface.

Dreams are less useful and quickly recede out of our conscious awareness.

Likewise, when you want to move your focus away from an inner obstruction that you have now identified as an obstacle, you need to work on changing the ideas as well as the self-image in your mind. It is very much like looking at a 35mm slide projected on a screen. What you see on the screen comes from a slide within the projector. Any markings you make on the screen will not alter the original slide in the projector. It's like trying to cure an illness by retouching the X-rays, as comedian Jack Benny, the legendary tightwad, once suggested as a way to save on the doctor bill.

Since visualized pictures are direct connections to the energy fields of our ideas, visualization also offers us the means to reprogram and neutralize the undesirable energies. For example, how much time do you spend visualizing past events that you want to eliminate? We all have a tendency to dwell on the issues we dislike, often visualizing and re-living them with great passion and intensity. This only helps to keep the undesired energy 'alive,' and works against the energy of any other positive images we may strive to create. Our undesired energies fuel our compulsions which in turn trap us within our addictions. The escape is not found by looking outwards. The escape from the pain of our stress and addictions can only be found within ourselves.

Ego and Self-Judgments

The true value of a human being
can be found in the degree to
which he has attained liberation from the self.
—*Albert Einstein*

Ego is the only rational explanation for one particularly expensive lunch on Wall Street. In fact, this astonishing lunch was not for a crowd of people, not even for an extravagant couple; just for an individual trader. A trader who entered a single bond order, established NO STOPS, then left the building for lunch. *That lunch ended up costing $27 million..... without the tip!*

This memorable lunch occurred in the Summer of 1991. You have already met the diner in an earlier chapter. He leased the double penthouse suite with the awesome glass trading room overlooking the Manhattan skyline and the United Nations building. That day the Principal of the firm entered a private order unbeknownst to the main trading desk. This was common. However, this time he entered an order *to double his original bond position every two ticks that the market moved against him.* Then established no stops... and walked out of the building for lunch!

Sure enough, the Federal Reserve elected to use this very day and lunch hour to intervene within the markets. A fast market was soon underway against him... and the brokers that had been given this order executed his instructions to the letter!

<POOF> He was blown out of the markets in his private account. As a result, it started a chain reaction as the desk was notified that the private account now had insufficient funds to cover his trade. All positions for the trading firm had to be closed immediately. The business accounts were frozen by the time the Principal returned from lunch... 90 minutes and $27 million later.

The next day, the situation was even more shocking than the events that forced the business to shut down. A mad scramble of vendors and creditors were busily stripping the offices. They were ripping out the computer screens, walking away with the furniture, literally stripping the entire penthouse floor. There was a panic unfolding as creditors worked to get back any asset they could lay their hands on. They were like vultures stripping a carcass. Somewhere in the scramble, the grand glass trading desk had been cracked, and scars marked the walls where the large computer screens had been rushed out of the room. A lone secretary was left standing on guard, trying to fight off the onslaught of vultures from raiding the files and business records. She lost. The grand hardwood floors of the sunken trading room were covered with dead wires and cables from the once highly productive nerve center of a high powered finance center. <POOF> Riches to rags.

I recall shaking and showing signs of shock... not because I had lost my job, which was bad enough, but because I had witnessed the destructive power of the markets first hand. My shock was the sudden realization and acceptance that *this could happen to anyone when their ego was in complete domination and control.*

The firm's principal was aggressive, dominating, and had an ego so large and explosive that the broker who took the fatal order would not have dared to ignore his instructions. He was verbally, mentally, and sometimes even physically, abusive. His every trade would translate into a personal victory or great defeat and was a reflection of his own self-worth and self-esteem. When our ego is in control, we all attach our very soul to a win or loss. Losses become devastating, crushing blows. He had to conquer all who ventured into his personal battlefield — the market, or die in the attempt. In the end he opted for the latter, and his business vanished along with all those it supported.

Much energy is wasted when ego motivates an individual to constantly defend his greatness. Ego forces you to compare your skills to others around you. There is a constant need to live up to self-centered illusions that create unnecessary and inhibiting anxiety and tension. The trader or athlete who needs to boast and impress others is usually doing so out of feelings of deep insecurity and uncertainty, wasting a lot of energy in the process.

Enormous power can be reserved by limiting the desire for possessions, praise, and other external attachments. Such desires and attachments to medals and trophies, money, sponsorships, and accolades are a great disadvantage because such desires create tremendous inner tension and pressure. *Ego* literally translates into *the limited self,* the *small self* in several Asian languages. It also implies we need to learn how to surrender and abandon our desires to obtain credit or acknowledgment, to win others' respect, love, and approval. *The key is detachment.* The more you detach yourself from yourself, the more effective you become. That's hard to do, but it is true.

The less we focus on having to prove ourselves, and the more we assert our skills with confidence, the better we perform. Talented free-agent rookies, struggling to make a pro team, often doom their chances with mistakes born of trying too hard to prove themselves. One such free-agent walked into a New York Jets training camp several years ago, vying to replace a retiring all-pro linebacker. He stood on the sidelines for several plays. As he waited, a highly acclaimed draft-choice, competing for the same job, confidently focused on executing the specific drills as they were defined. When the free-agent's chance finally came, he was ready to explode — the other guy wasn't even trying! On the first play from scrimmage, he blew over the tight end; crashed into the backfield, and nailed the totally unsuspecting quarterback. The quarterback was Joe Namath. This true story about trying too hard was that free-agent's first and last play as a New York Jet. He shouldn't have sacked that quarterback; he was cut on the spot.

Ego is significantly worse than an obstacle that hinders or blocks our energy. Ego becomes a fuse leading to our own self-destruction. The $27 million 'lunch' is an example of how our egos can misguide us into believing we can do no wrong. We get sloppy and lose our fear. Which is worse: no fear or excessive fear? I can't answer that. One makes us too sure of ourselves, and the other paralyzes us. Both are undesirable qualities as both limit our abilities. However ego is likely more damaging because when we focus on ourselves, we also isolate ourselves from the positive influences of others around us. We tend to have trouble letting others help us which only adds to our isolation. Not only do we waste our energy, we restrict and undermine our efforts to replenish our energy when we become run down.

To a large extent, we make or break ourselves. Our ego demands that we judge ourselves based on how well we impress others and perform up to our own delusions and expectations, a sure formula for self-destruction when the markets are involved. All that we have discussed about tendencies of aggression and having to victor over something or someone to feel better ourselves, can be attributed to an overly possessive ego. The need to win becomes our measure of self-worth, a burden too great for anyone's shoulders to carry. We may choke at a critical moment, we may miss a signal on the screen, or block out the inner voice of our intuition when it tries to yell, "Get out of the market... NOW!" Our own self-criticism turns our thought patterns from "I will win" to "I must not lose," a sure game plan for heavy financial losses. We cannot profit in the markets by being defensive and fearful of losing. Of course we are going to lose sometimes! How else do we learn?

Ego promotes harsh self-criticism which is just a setup for failure and misery. The mind begins to constantly find ways to confirm negative self-talk and sabotage our chances. Those who have images of success or those who visualize failure will both be right. We live up to the image we have of ourselves and go no higher. A win that exceeds what we believe we deserve within our Basic Self will soon lead to a loss in order to reestablish our inner balance and self-image. We will actually sabotage ourselves to find our inner balance. A friend of mine who once modeled in her teens is constantly struggling with her self-image and perceptions about her weight. As a teen-aged model she was a skinny rail, but as a very strong and muscular athlete training for the Olympics, she struggles with feelings of being overweight. Despite body fat measurements that scientifically prove otherwise, she is on a never-ending diet that undermines her athletic abilities.

Another example of unconscious self-sabotage is frequently demonstrated with lottery winners. The experience of winning large sums of money develops considerable stress when the new millionaire's self-worth is unable to accept this new image. Some winners lose it all in a very short time. When you have gains in your trading account beyond a certain amount, does it "burn a hole in your pocket"? Do you actually feel more stress as the profits in your account grow, less stress when an error in judgment wipes out some of those gains? I used to roll gains over into my Sterling or Yen account so that my domestic account was always digging out of a marginal hole. The change in emphasis from adding to prior winners, to digging in to come from behind, makes all the difference I need to avoid unconscious sabotage. When the foreign accounts were ahead I'd split those profits into new accounts as well (always hedging the risk exposure to foreign exchange fluctuations).

Traders can have a problem similar to lottery winners. As an exercise, rate yourself on a scale of one to one hundred to qualify how deserving you feel you are of all the best that life has to offer. When we are very honest with ourselves and tune into our deepest feelings, we will give ourselves less than one hundred. It shows we have to work on our sense of self-worth when we feel uncomfortable with the highest rating.

The cartoon character Pogo summed it up perfectly: "We have met the enemy, and they is us." Through lack of acceptance and disapproval of self, we become our own judge, jury, and executioner. We feel an obligation to punish ourselves for being 'bad' or undeserving. Our unrelenting self-criticism then inhibits our courage, confidence, concentration, hope, motivation, and excitement. We eventually distrust ourselves and abandon our developing skills. We are forced to give up when our ego is dissatisfied and unfulfilled. We move on to the next project in an effort to alleviate the inner turmoil and meet the needs of our ego.

It is helpful to evaluate your own behavioral patterns as pictures again. The many choices we make to bring our environment into balance with our self-image creates a window into our unconscious. Can you picture yourself blaming a poor performance on your indicators, your money management system, your job, your neighbor's dog that kept you awake all night, maybe a slow computer? In those pictures, the blame will always be directed to an external factor. Recognize these patterns for what they are — ego oriented. Next time you have a loss, change "It was because of my computer" to "That trade hurt like crazy, but I learned I now need to develop..." The shift in focus will mean you can actually do something about it rather than just find fault or blame.

One of the things we are most attached to is our point of view. This baggage becomes rooted within our egos. I know when a friend of mine stops looking at the market and makes statements like, "I don't care what the indicators say.. it's going down," that market is likely destined to rally. I am guilty of the same thing. As soon as I start to skip over numerous models because there is no doubt in my mind what is going to happen, the market runs me over. Overconfidence and ego seem to go hand-in-hand. An open mind, a calm mind is willing to consider other points of view before drawing any iron-clad conclusions.

Finally, once a decision is made, should a trading loss occur, it is not constructive — indeed it is highly destructive — to denigrate yourself with epithets such as "I'm such an idiot," "I'm so stupid," and so on. Besides a poor inner image, our inner, or outer speech can also cut us down. We need to listen to what we are saying to ourselves. If we are always finding fault and reason for failure, we are giving ourselves negative reinforcement. To neutralize negative impressions rephrase the negative. An example would be "I can't because I don't have the money." A more positive approach is "I'm short of cash right now but am doing ___ to change it." With the beginner's mind, it is important to accept that we are all students and some days our best will not be good enough on a particular day. Without the baggage of ego we will learn, we will grow, and we will improve without self-limiting boundaries.

Fear of Failure

"Young man, we have not failed 5000 times,
we have successfully determined
5000 ways the light bulb will not work."
—*Thomas Edison*

In our Western culture, it is said that "winning isn't every-thing, it's the only thing." As professional traders, we know there will be periods when we will develop a string of errors, but tolerance of trading setbacks and losses will vary widely among employers and clients. Some employers do not mea-sure a trader's performance as it relates to the action within the markets. That means if you just trade one futures market and that market spends the year in a narrow trading range, you would likely only have a few opportunities to produce high return trades.

Unrealistic expectations may lead to pressures that require higher capital risk exposure. This is a tough way to stay on an institutional desk for a long period of time if erratic risk man-agement creeps into your trading approach. Wild capital swings are as lethal as adhering to strict money management practices that produces a flat-line on your equity curve. If not fired, there are lesser "punishments" such as drastic capital reduction to limit your account size, or removal from a high profile desk, or office, to one with limited action and commissions. For some traders, their fear of these "punishments" causes such tremen-dous stress and tension that the anxiety itself actually helps to produce unwanted results. Losing is viewed as so devastating that it causes them to discontinue their efforts or quit the industry all together.

This mentality is responsible for much of the fear of failure both traders and athletes experience. Failure cannot be avoided, and it certainly is not shameful. The greatest traders in the business have all failed at one time or another, and so will we. The difference is how you handle it. There is a Buddhist saying, "The arrow that hits the bull's-eye is the result of a hundred misses." With every miss we gain new knowledge. I don't believe I'd have the sixth sense and intuition that I do have today had it not been for lots of errors in my chosen trading area — the very short time horizon in the S&P market.

Fear from past errors adds an element of caution. When circumstances begin to feel familiar and you hear yourself saying, "I've seen this before, this move is taking too long to start unfolding, GET OUT!" Don't waste any further time to debate the alternatives. Do it. Then back-test your indicators or decision criteria to build your confidence that you indeed made the best decision. Trading instincts can only develop through experience under fire. Competent money management skills are necessary to survive the early years and to offset the lack of experience and knowledge while first learning to trade. It is only through our failures and mistakes that we are given the opportunity for improvement. It is the most effective method for most of us to go beyond our present level of performance.

Perceptions about a trading performance will vary greatly. We cannot control other people's yardsticks for evaluation. I was still reeling from my worst year, when a principal in a major Chicago firm asked, "You only ended the year down how much? That's nothing for this year!" That individual then offered me a base salary of $100,000 and 30% commission paid quarterly on a $5 million discretionary account.

I turned it down. I needed time away from the markets to regroup. However, I'll admit that particular phone call and job offer did a great deal to speed along the recovery process and reinforced a truism: nothing is ever as bad as it seems or as good as it seems. We cannot control other people's perceptions and judgment extremes, so focus only on what we can control — each individual trade.

When you experience a large gain, do you find yourself playing the game, "Now-if-I-extrapolate-that-gain-forward-in-time-by-multiplying-it-by-the-number-of-weeks-remaining-in-the-year." Do you realize how you just set yourself up to fail? If you find yourself doing this, you just lost your focus for the present and have created a distraction. Just concentrate on what you can control: when to enter the next trade, or when to exit the present one. Accept that we will miss several big market moves along the way and are destined to miss numerous bull's-eyes.

Two currency desks of a major bank in New York were located in separate areas. One desk always outperformed the other by a large margin. It was later determined that the primary difference between these two desks was the approach taken by the head traders. The head trader of the higher performing desk did not focus on or become obsessed with negative outcomes; he simply rewarded his desk for finding the solutions to dig out of inevitable setbacks, failures, and complex market scenarios. Freed from the pressure of always having to be right, traders on the more successful desk were more relaxed and less fearful of failure. As a result, they outperformed the other desk that was always obsessed with preventing negative outcomes. Environment within a trading firm is everything. You can't do your job if you are afraid a bad quarter will cost you your job.

Excessive fears of failure can be paralyzing. It might be caused by the trading environment or insufficient confidence in your trading methodology. Fear of failure can also be ego associated. Only you can work through ego problems; you're not going to listen to anyone else anyway. If the problem is insufficient back-testing because you don't know how to back-test market signals, learn. This is a learned skill. There is no excuse for not doing it. Change the negative speech within you from "I don't know how," to one that is more affirmative, such as "I don't have much experience with back-testing my indicators, and I'm doing____to do something about it." This shift in focus from the negative to moving a step forward to learn makes a world of difference. Then when we have a trading loss and learn from the experience, we gain the knowledge of when and where we need to be more alert.

Fear is a natural emotion, a survival instinct that is extremely useful for a trader. Some fear acquired from past errors is necessary to be able to trade well. If you try to fight or force your fear away, it just creates a counterforce that makes you more tense and anxious. A little fear can be a good thing. The element of fear that accompanies an activity can contribute to an adrenaline rush as we discussed earlier. It needs to be controlled. We often feel fear when an enormous task has to be undertaken. Rather than looking ahead, try dividing it up into much smaller and more manageable segments. Exercise, preparation, doing everything you can to unveil the unknown, and defining the worst case scenario are all methods that work towards eliminating or reducing our fears. Don't forget the exercise of visualizing past successes. This is a particularly effective method for dealing with fear.

A friend of mine is learning to sky dive, but her free-falls are made with an instructor, and she doesn't jump alone. Otherwise it would be too dangerous. The sky diving school in Florida has the following slogan on the side of their plane: "You go up, you come down, no problem." But if you find yourself sitting on the edge of the plane preparing to jump, and then freeze, that's a big problem.

When you ask yourself: "What's wrong with me?" "Why am I so scared?" "Other traders can handle this market, so why can't I?" Listen to this fear. This is our Basic Self telling us, "Don't continue." If you are feeling much more anxiety than just caution, and instead feel endangered, ask yourself why you're feeling that way. Have you prepared yourself sufficiently for the trade you are about to make? Do you have all the information you need? Are you out of your comfort zone? Let yourself be afraid and recognize when fear offers a sanity check of advice.

Fear as a sense of caution and alertness is beneficial, and *the only thing we have to fear, is not fear itself, but having no fear.* Some fear is essential, or we too may place a take-out order for a $27 million lunch!

Fear of Success

You must do the very thing you fear most.
—Eleanor Roosevelt

Success-phobia is rampant in trading. If there is a perceived imbalance between what we believe we deserve and what we have achieved, then we may follow a substantial gain with a devastating loss by unconsciously sabotaging our trading style. Sabotage for other people may take the form of illness or injury just as they approach the brink of making a major breakthrough.

One does not have to have an imbalance between self-worth and good fortune to experience unconscious sabotage. The enormous stress associated with success itself may contribute to a later performance decline because we become erratic and inconsistent. Success brings with it numerous negative factors. Friends may step back unable to deal with their own feelings of envy. Other traders or business associates may become hostile towards you as they begin to view you as a threat to their jobs or as an authority figure. As you excel further, there are additional performance pressures and expectations to exceed or repeat the prior success. No wonder people fear success; it can actually bring about hardship. When John McEnroe defeated Bjorn Borg at Wimbledon, he seemed to find the victory more of a burden than an accomplishment. In his own words, "I couldn't handle it well, and I don't know why." His game deteriorated for some time after that victory until he learned how to handle winning.

When we are successful and have the illusion that we have "arrived," the initial rush of happiness usually fades. This initial rush from success is soon replaced by discomforts and anxieties that threaten other aspects of life that are important to our inner balance; family, friends, job associates. After all, if we are really good at something, we all tend to devote more time to that aspect of our life to become even better. This can only mean other aspects will suffer.

The business world is filled with situations that create, cultivate, and teach us fear of success. With each new position comes the added responsibilities, the extra hours on the job, new tensions, anxieties, and stress. One individual at Kodak was promoted to the position of vice president at the age of thirty-five. The new position radically changed his life, not only at work but at home as well. Peers at work became back stabbing enemies. Everything became more complex as he grew more accountable to a greater number of people. For his first five months he ran the halls constantly fighting low grade illnesses. His performance suffered and took a nose-dive as he became increasingly unhappy. His family life was nonexistent, and his children began to treat him more as a stranger than father. All the commotion around the new job had taken a great toll. He eventually resigned from his position and the company. He currently has a much lower paying job as a traveling sales representative. He is aware that he is terrified at the possibility of ever being a success again. As soon as he excels he begins to miss deadlines and finds the sales within his territory begin to slip. These symptoms all point towards a fear of success, and he will likely sabotage any effort to succeed in the future.

Learning to win is as important as learning to lose. Maybe it is even harder to learn to succeed because we certainly don't consciously sabotage our own abilities. Fear of success is one of the most difficult weaknesses to recognize. Probably most of us have resisted success at one time or another. Becoming totally committed to excellence often means taking time away from something else that may put us in a position of painful repercussions. Family, friends, other obstacles get in the way, and we may get bogged down and fail to develop other skills we may have. If you turn your back on your talent, you create another pain that you have to contend with: growing older and constantly wondering what might have been. Regrets from not having pursued and developed a skill can actually become an even greater burden than the difficulties that come along with success. The choice is ours to make. If you have the slightest inkling or notion today that you may have regrets later, "go for it," while you are still capable.

It may surprise you that fear associated with success is very common. One of my coaches gave a small quiz that involves a list of questions. Should you answer 'yes' to any of the questions, then it indicates a possible fear of success. Consider each of the following:

1. If you succeed, do you think you will experience pressure from someone to perform even better in the future?

2. If you succeed, do you think your life will become more complicated in any unpleasant way?

3. If you succeed, do you feel anxious about the inevitable decline that may follow?

4. Do you fear the enormous amount of work that stands before you and the commitment you will have to make to yourself to be successful?

5. Would you feel anxious or frightened if your success meant that you would have to be accountable to a greater number of people?

Answering "yes" to any of these questions may help you uncover feelings of stress and anxiety associated with success. Consciously or unconsciously you may decide to simply stay put and not pursue these skills leading to a discomfort. Simply because you have an ability is hardly a sufficient reason to go for it. We all have to decide what level of success makes us fulfilled. The decision has to be a conscious one.

Integrity

*Integrity supersedes all else because
it puts the circumstance of the trade,
the event, or an opponent into a position of irrelevance.
You place yourself above the circumstances
of a given situation, and this self-power
is what leads to extraordinary performance.*

The darkest side of Wall Street is without question the "dart of the deal." It's not the "art of the deal," but the poison dart of which you must beware. They are everywhere and transcend all levels, from simple back-stabbing to extremely intricate schemes involving huge sums of money. The Wall Street environment will expose you to a host of temptations and challenges to your integrity. Any time you combine runaway egos, greed, and enormous capital, you're swimming with sharks in mine infested waters. That's a given.

Money comes and goes. We succeed and we fall short, but what does not have a cyclical nature is our integrity. Once it has been lost, it can never be regained. Sure huge sums are made through artful dodging and short horizon intellectual brilliance, but those individuals eventually implode as a result of their own schemes or by an anonymous tip to a regulatory agency from one of the many enemies they have cultivated along the way. What goes around, comes around...without fail.

An event I witnessed raised many questions about the meaning of integrity for me. Some believe this event was ground zero when the detonator was armed for the S&L implosion that shook the financial bedrock of the United States. The events led me away from trading fundamentals and stories, to technical analysis, where I could escape the endless "stories." This particular story weaves an intricate web and still leaves many — perhaps most — questions unanswered. The key players have all faded into the background behind new events and new headlines. So just take this as a tale told through the eyes of a novice; fate just happened to put me in the right place at the right time.

The events of the day began when the senior partner from our firm and I stepped out of our hotel into the searing heat of a humid summer afternoon in Dallas, Texas. Our meeting was scheduled to begin at 2:15 PM and we decided to walk, but by the time we had walked to the curb we could feel our suits already clinging uncomfortably to our bodies and perspiration dripping down our backs. Today would become a memorable day, but not because of the record breaking temperatures for August 15, 1988.

David and I decided to save our suits and hailed a cab for the three blocks to our first scheduled creditors' meeting at the former head office of the First RepublicBank Corporation (FRB). FRB had filed a petition for relief under Chapter 11 of the Bankruptcy Code on July 30, and the court had already assigned its offices to the newly appointed U.S. Trustee. The bank had reported on July 19 a $758 million second-quarter loss. Following a $1.5 billion deficit in the first quarter, Texas's largest bank had a stunning $2.26 billion loss for the first half of 1988. The previous year, Manufacturers Hanover had posted a $1.14 billion deficit. The Manny Hanny federal bailout had put tremendous financial strain on the Federal Deposit Insurance Corporation in Washington. The FDIC itself was beginning to struggle. David and I had been sent to Dallas to represent our firm's substantial interest in this failing bank. The timing of our firm's purchase of FRB bonds would later prove to be an important factor.

We crawled out of our cab and walked toward the shimmering, glass-walled building that reflected the high-tech, Dallas skyline. The interior of the building retained the image of the once prosperous bank. The marble floors were still highly polished, and the plants were well-cared-for throughout the lobby. Maintenance was still performed as if business continued as usual. Only the people were missing. With the exception of the creditors filing into the building for the day's meeting, there were no longer signs of the enormous activity that once hummed through this financial center. The employees had all vanished, innocent victims of circumstances beyond their control and understanding.

The cramped elevator only added to my feelings of anxious anticipation suppressed with nervousness. A robust man in his early fifties held a cigar in the corner of the confined space. The smoke filled the car and made the trip to the ninth floor an eternity. As the elevator doors opened, we were met by security officers who carefully verified our identity and then directed us toward Room 9E-21. It was once the executive dining room and struck me as rather Spartan for the clientele it had once hosted. The room was fairly large and, though we were very early, it was already filled with people. I didn't know who any of these individuals were, so David pointed out a few. The room was filled with portfolio managers of well-known insurance and mutual funds throughout the United States. Numerous others representing all segments of the U.S. financial community had traveled to Dallas to represent their individual interests in the bonds which were now in default.

Our firm was one of the largest bondholders, but in creditor hierarchy, my colleague and I were viewed no higher than vultures — scavengers of the bond community. Once people discovered who we were they would gradually fade away from our table to sit with old acquaintances, meet with a colleague, find a new acquaintance, or just grab a coffee, never to return. This was a far cry from the warm reception I was used to when I worked for Kodak. When we said we represented a junk bond firm based in Greenwich, Connecticut, I detected noticeable panic in the eyes of our fellow bondholders as though our image could somehow be transmitted like the black plague. You see, a great many individuals and firms still carried the FRB bonds at par ($1.00, sold in lots of thousands) or better on their books.

They were not required to mark-to-market the price of the bonds on their books each day, or even quarterly. Bondholders didn't have to report the current market price of any issue on their books until the bonds were sold. That meant investment funds reported to their clients the purchase price (closer to one dollar,) rather than the then-current price of 23 cents on the dollar for Senior debt. Subordinate bond prices were much lower than that. So many in the room would elect to carry these bonds to their grave or leave the problem on someone else's shoulders by moving to a different job. Our firm's efforts to purchase more of these distressed bonds had put additional pressure on the other creditors. So no one would want to be caught sitting at our table. It would raise questions among the other creditors if our tablemates had cashed out their bonds to us at these distressed prices. As a result, we were left with our own private table, though the room was extremely crowded as the meeting got underway.

Two days preceding FRB's filing for bankruptcy, a *Wall Street Journal* headline read on July 28, 1988, *"First RepublicBank Bailout — Plan Choice May Be Near: Wells Fargo Bid Reported."* Correspondent Richard B. Schmitt reported that Federal officials were very close to choosing a bailout plan for the insolvent First RepublicBank Corporation. The prize was certainly not the defaulted real estate loans, but the credit card income flowing through the bank's holding company. That was the real cash cow for the bank; for that matter, most any bank. It was the holding company that housed the goose that laid that golden credit card revenue stream. Everyone was trying to structure a bailout plan so that they would end up in control of the golden goose. The remaining divisions and subsidiaries would be spun off in numerous directions as they were non-performing assets. The prize was the goose. This was no small goose. FRB was the state's largest bank, with total assets reportedly of $26.8 billion.

Citicorp of New York and Wells Fargo had submitted bids for the holding company to the FDIC. NCNB (now NationsBank), had already established that they were keenly interested as well. The battle for the bank was heating up, and the final outcome was dependent on the calculations and decisions made by the FDIC. The ultimate cost of this bailout for the FDIC was expected to rival or exceed the record 1984 rescue of Continental Illinois Corporation, of Chicago. The current estimates were now pointing to about $1.7 billion.

The bidding war was high stakes roulette for the FDIC. Their reserves were low from several preceding bank bailouts. Creditors believed the best bid was Wells Fargo's, but it might have been the most costly for the FDIC. Wells Fargo was well known for making acquisitions that were turned over for a quick profit. A quick turnover would mean higher costs to the FDIC as the non-performing assets would be spun off to a separate bank, likely requiring immediate write-downs and a rapid hit to the FDIC's cash flow. That was something the FDIC had to avoid.

For a while, it even looked as if FRB was aggressively still trying to restructure itself. Federal regulators had received a new recapitalization proposal in which FRB eliminated its plans to spin-off the bulk of its non-performing assets. In so doing, it was trying to show it was willing to reduce FDIC's exposure to the immediate write-downs. It would then attempt to raise one billion dollars in new stock to recapitalize the bank holding company, feathering the nest of the golden goose.

This figure of one billion dollars soon weaves an interesting thread through this story, the point being that FRB was desperately in need of *exactly* one billion dollars.

The recent FRB default allowed all debtholders to demand immediate payment of principal and interest. Full payment was neither possible, nor expected. However, what we the debtholders were prepared to settle for, and what the stockholders thought they were likely to get, were two polar extremes.

It had been only six weeks earlier that we had attended the last stockholders' meeting. Their naiveté was saddening. They failed to understand that the stockholders had no real power. We were holders of substantial Senior notes and floating rate paper. Our firm, along with all other debtholders, fully intended to *cram-down* on the stockholders. The '80s were full of well publicized corporate takeovers. The banks that fell victim were not as widely known, but the practice of cramming-down on bank stockholders was no different from the way it was in a hostile corporate takeover. Both the Preferred and Common stockholders would be given token new shares — suitable for framing, but little else — in exchange for their present nearly worthless shares. On the other hand, the bondholders expected to fare quite well and repeat the favorable settlements that had occurred with Continental Illinois Corporation and First City Bank in Houston. No asset would exist once the creditors that gathered for this meeting had divided the remains.

The stockholders' meeting six weeks ago had put faces on the victims that later haunted me. One elderly man stepped forward to the mike in the main aisle of the auditorium and described how three generations of his family had always believed in and supported Texas business. *All their funds and investments had been deposited or invested in the largest bank of Texas* — the First RepublicBank. Surely this bad spell would pass if only the stockholders could come together with a plan. Waves and waves of stockholders expressed their hope and their grief at the plight of their bank. Texas pride had taken a serious blow. Only a year ago the bank's shares had been trading above $26 a share after a merger of the First RepublicBank (FRB) and InterFirst Corporation (IFRB). This day their shares traded at $1.25 on the New York Stock Exchange. Many of those folks, from oil tycoons to hourly wage earners, suffered a serious financial blow as their stocks plummeted, but they seemed more upset that this once great Texas financial institution would soon be acquired by non-Texans. This seemed to cause even greater anguish than the fact that their failing bank was sinking fast and dragging them down with it.

The bravado and naiveté of the stockholders could be summarized by the rallying speech of a young business woman. She was highly polished in her Armani suit, Mikimoto pearls, and Bally shoes. She stood before the mike and displayed confidence as she prepared to speak.

"On market open I intend to purchase 150,000 shares."

People began to move to the edge of their seats and squirm.

"If we all step into the market on Monday and add to our existing shares, we will be able to muscle the price of our shares back up by showing the market that we, the stockholders, still believe in and stand behind our Texas bank!"

The squirming stockholders erupted into applause and cheers. The principal of our junk bond firm just shook his head and grinned. Images of Oliver Stone's movie, *Wall Street,* came to my mind. Michael Douglas won an Academy Award as Best Actor for his role as Gordon Gekko. His speech at the stockholders' meeting was the highlight of his Academy performance. It captured the essence of the '80s' takeover frenzy. I'm sure you remember the one...

I am not a destroyer of corporations...
I am a liberator of them!
The point is, ladies and gentlemen,
that greed, for lack of a better word, is good.
Greed is right. Greed works.
Greed clarifies, cuts through, and captures
the essence of the evolutionary spirit.
Greed in all of its forms... greed for life, for money,
for love, knowledge, has marked the upward surge of
mankind, and greed... you mark my words...will not
only save Teldar Paper, but that other malfunctioning
corporation called the U.S.A. Thank you very much.

Well, no thank you. This meeting was when I first realized I
wanted nothing to do with the junk bond industry. (Ironically,
one of my farewell presents from my Kodak colleagues was the
poster from the movie *Wall Street*.)

Sadly, as in Oliver Stone's movie, these stockholders were
completely unaware that they didn't have a chance. Their
scheme would only cause a momentary blip on the screens of
equity traders around the world. Like water, markets seek their
own level, and the stock would surely sink back to $1.25 in no
time. Most were unaware that the stockholders' meeting was
simply an outlet for them to vent their frustrations and anger.
Their fate had already been written, and they could not change
the course of events that were about to unfold.

It was believed that the FDIC had been tipped off that the
bankruptcy was about to be filed prior to the actual court filing,
because it moved with astounding speed in one of the most
complex seizures on record, involving the First RepublicBank's
40 banks with 130 banking sites across the Lone Star State.
The speed with which it seized assets was deemed incredible
for any corporation, let alone the government. The previous
year, Congress authorized the FDIC to seize the assets of insolvent banks and manage them for up to two years while a buyer

was found. Regulators certainly wasted no time exercising their new-found power in this situation. *The New York Times* (July 27, 1988) reported, "Such action, in effect, eliminated the voting power of the stockholders and bondholders, giving the regulators virtual control in finding the buyers."

The August 2, 1988 issue of *American Banker* documented the events surrounding the seizure. Immediately after the bankruptcy was filed, regulators quickly seized the assets, then *transferred them to a federally chartered bridge bank*. One week after this transfer, a new entity was named by the FDIC — NCNB Texas National Bank. The FDIC had nationalized the Dallas-based First RepublicBank Corporation which, quoting *American Banker*, "Mark[ed] a regulatory evolution that promises trouble for investors.....and a spate of controversy for regulators." The controversy erupted in full with the press release announcing the FDIC would give NCNB an *initial $4 billion federal assistance*. In addition, *American Banker* quoted then-FDIC Chairman William Seidman as saying "the holding companies are no longer going to be protected." (That meant the golden goose was no longer the property of the creditors.) Seidman was further reported as saying that the regulators were able to create a warehouse for First Republic member banks and devise a management and purchase contract that contained "performance incentives for NCNB."

Interesting, but what were these incentives? Why wasn't this incentive offered to any of the other bidders? It turned out that NCNB would be dropped down to a 34% tax rate, which created a shelter of almost $1.5 billion in taxable earnings as calculated by Morgan Stanley in *American Banker*. Apparently none of the other bidders submitted a tax plan, and this element significantly eased the FDIC's cash flow burden compared to alternate plans. In addition to this "performance incentive," who got to keep the credit card holding company? You guessed it, the FDIC.

Significant Time-Line of Events:
First RepublicBank Corporation

Jan. 19, 1988   FRB reports $656.8 million loss for 1987.

Mar. 17, 1988   FDIC announced $1 billion six-month loan to FRB sub-
                  sidiary banks guaranteed by FRB, IFRB and collateral-
                  ized by pledge of stock of FRB subsidiary banks. The
                  FDIC assures depositors and creditors they are protected.

Mar. 18, 1988   FDIC Note Agreement executed.
                  $1 billion dollars wired to FRB.

Mar. 24, 1988   Mr. Pastor, Vice Chairman of FRB, resigns.

Apr. 12, 1988   FRB announces estimated $1.5 billion loss for 1st Quar-
                  ter of 1988; The Chairman resigns as CEO of FRB and
                  is replaced.

Apr. 29 to
May 31, 1988   29 banks merge... a cash shuffle.

May 13, 1988   FRB defaults. FRB announces suspension of interest
                  payments on FRB and IFRB long term debt.

June 28, 1988   FRB Annual Stockholders Meeting.

July 19, 1988   FRB announces $758 million 2nd Quarter loss.

July 29, 1988   40 FRB banks declared insolvent and placed in receiver-
                  ship; NCNB Corp. agrees to buy 20% stake in a 'new'
                  Texas bank that will take over FRB's assets with $4 bil-
                  lion in FDIC assistance.

July 30, 1988   FRB and IFRB file petitions for Chapter 11.

Aug. 3, 1988   FDIC seizes IFRB credit card bank.

Aug. 15, 1988   Bankruptcy Court hearing in Dallas with creditors.

NCNB got a tax incentive and a low interest $4 billion loan to take over First RepublicBank's non-performing assets that the FDIC didn't want to get stuck with and, in the deal, NCNB upgraded from a regional bank to a national power. In so doing, it immediately became one of the largest banks in the United States with an expanded market in states where it had been previously restricted from entering. The FDIC gets the goose that lays the golden eggs. Everyone's a winner. Or are they?

The August 15 meeting began with the usual introductions and then copies of the bankruptcy petition listing the top 20 creditors were distributed throughout the room. We had acquired a copy prior to the meeting. It showed a very serious discrepancy. Our firm was nowhere to be found on the list. We had been omitted, but should have been listed as the second largest Senior FRB creditor. That raised a very interesting question. Was the due diligence for this bankruptcy filing actually prepared earlier, prior to our purchasing activity? That six weeks would have placed the due diligence for bankruptcy filing near the time of the final stockholders meeting. Had the meeting been a carefully rehearsed stage show by the newly appointed executive officers with the inconspicuous FDIC directing? Right away, this whole mess suggested that a much larger plan was at work.

Of course, no one else knew the creditor listing had a massive omission, and even we didn't suspect what would transpire next.

The meeting grew quieter, as the attorneys began to draw the schematic of First RepublicBank and InterFirst Republic Bank (IFRB) subsidiaries. The intricate flow-chart on the white board showed the cash flow between the FDIC and the two banks. On March 18, 1988, one billion dollars was distributed to FRB in two tranches; $800 million went from the FDIC to the Dallas Bank, and $200 million was wired to the Houston Bank. The loan was promised for six months. As the circuitous charts were drawn, the room fell silent.

Well before the six month term concluded, the $200 million from Houston was transferred to the Dallas Bank. Inexplicably to all observers (outside the FDIC, the Fed, and the bank's newly appointed CEO, at least), the Dallas Bank then wired its $800 million and Houston's $200 million to... the Federal Reserve! Then, shortly after FRB wired the billion dollars to the Fed, the FDIC called their loan against the bank. The bank had already repaid the government — the Federal Reserve had it. But the result was technically a default.

After the FDIC took over the bank, the Fed wired back the one billion dollars into the IFRB credit card holding company, thereby keeping the Golden Goose on life-support...so eventually that money 'fluffed' the troubled nest of the FDIC when it retained ownership of the holding company. The Fed could not wire funds directly to the FDIC to bail them out, but this had the same net effect — a Fed bail out of a cash strapped FDIC by injecting $1 billion into the FDIC's newly seized credit card company.

With this revelation, the meeting broke into total disarray. The largest known players took their shot at the attorneys, raising a slew of issues and questions. In time, the room quieted down. It was only then I realized we still had not clarified who were the top 20 bondholders. Since we had been omitted, there might be others. So taking a deep breath, I raised my hand. When acknowledged, I explained to the entire room that our firm had been omitted from the creditors' list, and we would have been the second largest FRB creditor of the Senior 11¼% Notes of 1989. I suggested we go through the room and establish a more accurate accounting of who owns what. The suggestion was met with nods of approval from around the room. An elaborate inventory roll call began. It appeared our firm was the only one that had been entirely omitted.

Then from the far back corner of the room, a slender man, not more than 5' 3", stood up. He spoke with the utmost cour-

Flow of Funds From the FDIC's
$1 Billion Subordinated Loan to FRB

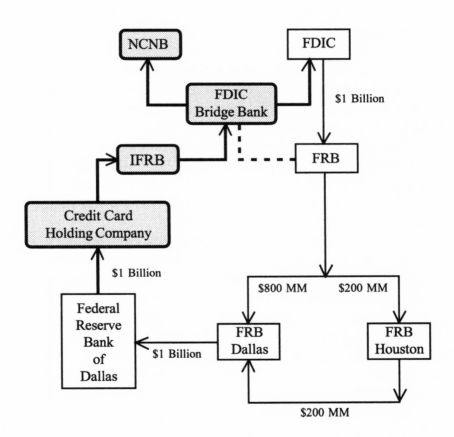

tesy and with the soft cadence of a Japanese accent. He gave his name and asked if he might be permitted to ask a question? In his soft, slow, heavily accented voice the man asked, "Am I correct in understanding that one billion dollars was wired by the FDIC to the bank, then wired on to the Federal Reserve in Dallas? As a result, when the FDIC's one billion dollar 'loan' was called against the bank, they defaulted?"

Not a sound could be heard as all eyes had turned back to the podium.

"At this time, these appear to be the facts. Yes."

The man in the back corner began to speak once again.

"I was sent to this meeting on behalf of several interested parties in Japan. Collectively we hold ### bonds. I will return to Japan and report today's findings."

The Japanese holdings were so staggering that the room went into shock. While I had not understood the wider ramifications, I clearly understood that Japan was the number one creditor by a country mile. This federally-chartered, federally-insured Texas bank was effectively owned by Japan. (Japan was also the prime lender to many S&L companies across the U.S.)

Turning to David, I asked him, "What does this mean?"

It means, he said, that the Bank of Tokyo and a host of other Japanese banks have just been stung by the Fed and FDIC. Japan will start pulling their money out of solvent American S&Ls as soon as possible.

If the FRB default scared the Japanese into withdrawing their support of the S&Ls, the industry would be threatened. What was believed to have been a domestic bank default had suddenly expanded into an international crisis.

David's next words were chilling,

> ...the fuse has been lit for an S&L implosion. Within three months this country will be in the midst of an S&L collapse. The crisis we have seen so far is only the tip of the iceberg in comparison to what's ahead.

It made no difference that later due diligence uncovered additional cash flows that would have helped the bank along with other less damaging facts. The fuse was lit and could not be smothered out. David's time estimate wasn't quite right. It was less than a month later that *The Wall Street Journal* reported the S&L crisis had expanded to epidemic proportions.

Integrity is our inner core. It is a source of power that leads to extraordinary performance. Each of us has a different definition of integrity as defined by our Basic Self and Higher Self. When you wake up one morning and are uncomfortable about what that person in the mirror is about to do on any given day, it is time to move on. The story I have just related raised questions for me about what value the entire junk bond industry had to offer. I had spent my entire working career with Kodak building other people's businesses so as to grow ours. It was a healthy win/win relationship. I valued what we did and what we were about so my goals and milestones were a joy to reach for and attain.

The industry I was first exposed to when I entered Wall Street revolved around a world of winning at the expense of others. This caused my motivation to fade and the inner spark and drive to be a part of the Wall Street environment to die. I had little interest for digging in to uncover the fatal clause, or covenant, within a corporation's bond indenture that would become their undoing or demise. The whole element of cramming-down on others for a financial win created an inner conflict I could not resolve. The underlying factors contributing to each new pending bankruptcy had to be told and retold throughout the day in order to make a junk bond trade. My inner selves could not deal with these endless negative stories in order to find the next vulture that wanted a piece of the kill. It was distasteful. In fact, everything about that industry was a source of inner conflict and contributed to a loss of my inner balance. No one can be successful if his efforts are not fully compatible with his sense of integrity. When I began to trade futures based on technical analysis, I discovered that I began to direct my focus again to asserting my skills. As a result, I began to learn, improve, and apply my growing skills with confidence.

The markets are so large, I've since discovered that you can tell the world what trades you are making and if you win, so do the traders shadowing you. I finally achieved a balance that has re-established the healthy win/win relationship I had once known at Kodak. Each trader needs to find his own market niche that nurtures his own inner balance. Those that fail to do so may make big names for themselves for a while, but a fast unscrupulous rise can just as easily be followed by an equally volatile free-fall. I think most of us would prefer to play the trading game forever, and longevity requires inner balance to survive.

Slumps

There are two kinds of swimmers;
those who have already experienced a slump,
and those who will.
The only difference is time.
—Coach John Skiian

Like people, slumps come in all shapes and sizes; short ones, long ones, little ones, famous record breaking ones, and ones that come and go, never having been noticed. The only sure bet is that at some point in time we are all going to experience a period when all the skills we have worked so hard to develop and fine tune just seem to abandon us. The world recently witnessed one of the most heartbreaking slumps in Olympic history finally end. Together we sighed in relief as Dan Jansen won his Olympic Gold Medal in speed skating in 1994. Although he held every World Record and had dominated the sport for years, it was not until the last race of his career that he won the medal that had eluded him in three Olympic Games.

During a slump, we try to force our skills back and create added pressure, tension, and anxiety. Our very efforts to attempt to dig out of our slump can actually make the slump worse and last longer. Therefore, the key to breaking a slump is not to become rigid and fight the down cycle, but relax, just go with it.

I have a trading rule, passed on to me by several traders, that helps to break the chain reaction associated with a slump before it has time to set in and establish a major downtrend. After three intraday trading losses, I'm out of the market for the rest of the day. When I have three day trades wrong in a row, I'm out for a minimum of three days. The reason this rule is so valuable is that it takes three days to change any attitude or state of mind. Assertion may gradually melt into an attitude of aggression that makes us become rigid and fixated on our own point of view about the market. Take three days off. Don't even look at the screen or read a newspaper. Then come back and take a fresh look when you have refound your center of balance and reestablished an inner calm that allows you to once again flow with the markets.

Short horizon traders frequently refer to the three period rule: if after you have established a position, it must start to go in your favor by the end of the third period, or you close the position. In other words, if your primary time horizon to trade is hourly, then you have three hours to be proven right or the time rule will force you out. This rule has saved me on several occasions. However, if you trade from 2-minute charts, you'll need to adjust this rule to a period that makes more sense.

Slumps require a period of healing, a period of time to distance ourselves from the setbacks and to allow the frustration to fade. Then through visualization, we can call upon the skills we practiced to regain our center of balance. Some people visualize their mistakes and then go about setting small rituals to let go of them. Some see the slump as a physical object. Picture that object on the face of a tennis ball and go smash tennis balls for a few hours. You'll be too tired to be frustrated. The next step is to reinforce your confidence and take a period of time to go back and test your indicators to provide reassurance that the methodology was correct, but the odds simply swung over to the house's favor for a while. It can be extremely helpful to discuss trading anxieties with a trading mentor. Mentors are invaluable, especially a friend who has similar methodologies. The next step is to visualize in very explicit detail the sensations and events that occurred when your trading was flowing easily with the markets. That is why we practiced visualizing these periods when we were successful, for now we need to reprogram ourselves by role playing our way out of the slump.

Not only is it essential to reprogram ourselves through visualization, but we also need to closely monitor our patterns of speech as well. Are you telling yourself how stupid you were, adding insults to injury? If so, stop. Get out a piece of paper and write a new phrase that is less damaging. Remember the discussions about how to reprogram ourselves? Now is the time. (Remember Edison did not fail, he succeeded in finding 5,000 ways not to make a light bulb.) Rewriting a negative statement into a positive one is a method known as developing affirmations. Here are a few examples that may be used for breaking a slump.

> "Less effort is more assertive."
> "I did not fail; I just learned how to..."
> "When I give up defending my market view, I will then be able to yield and blend with the rhythms of the market."
> "I feel relaxed, loose, and flowing with all elements in my life."

Some slump periods will be caused when our Basic Self has been ignored, and it has a temper-tantrum to get our attention. Our efforts are sabotaged, and we have no chance of winning without our Basic Self agreeing to the game plan. So think for a moment. When did you last take some time off to just go and have fun?

When utilizing the Elliott Wave Principle, my first warning usually occurs when the market internals begin to slide, shift, and step slightly off track in very short intraday price patterns. The next stage is frequently accompanied by muscle tension and pain in my neck. When I am unable to see a new pattern emerging within the price data, I try to shoehorn mistracking short horizon patterns into the larger Elliott Wave pattern in a longer time frame. Eventually if the early warning signs are not heeded, the market simply runs me over. The time I need to study a price pattern is inversely proportional to my confidence in the direction of the market. This period of inner uncertainty and confusion is usually controlled by intuition. When the market just doesn't feel right... that's a time to step to the side. For short horizon traders, just go for a brief walk. Take a few deep breaths and concentrate more on relieving the muscle tightness in your neck and chest, rather than contemplating new ways to assert your opinion upon the markets. If you want to be aggressive towards the markets, beware, you already know who will win that battle.

Deeper, more lengthy slumps require additional time to explore the root cause. The very first step in breaking the pattern is to STOP TRADING! You need to take time off. That means get away from the markets. Don't try to track any market's progress through print, electronic media, or office contacts. Just go away for a while so you can change your current daily patterns.

Take time for yourself to heal and relax. Then before re-entry, consider rereading and practicing the exercises in this book. The method you need to identify why you are off center in your trading is contained within these pages, but it will require adopting the beginner's mindset once again. Return back to being the student and not the expert. There is a reason that coaches use these exercises in the order you encountered them in this book. They work.

Look over the self-evaluation scores that you gave yourself in "Aspects of a Successful, Professional Trader: A Self-Test." The items that you recognized as being below a grade of 5 are likely a source of the current slump you are experiencing. Do something now about changing your lifestyle to beef up the weaknesses revealed in that self-test, before you reach the next step and chapter, "Fatigue, Denial, and Injury or Illness." Failure to accept change at the "slump" stage leads to a quick slide downhill towards burnout.

Fatigue, Denial, Injury/Illness, and Burnout

Pain is the most heeded of doctors:
to goodness and wisdom we only make promises:
we obey pain.
—*Marcel Proust*

Denial occurs when our Conscious Self tunes out the needs and desires of our Basic Self. This results in various feelings of discomfort. Though we believe we've "gotten past that," whatever "that" might have been, we still may not be able to freely express our emotions or acknowledge our feelings about "that." Denial encompasses both suppression and repression. Anything less than full recognition and expression of emotions is denial. However, once we find a way to break through a denial barrier, our Basic Self rewards us with a tremendous release of energy that accompanies a release of tension, anxiety, and even physical pain.

Our skill for denial has been finely tuned since childhood when we learned to avoid blame or punishment by saying, "I didn't do it." Blame, along with the responsibility, was deflected towards a sibling or neighbor. As we grew older we learned to avoid blame by finding other reasons and causes to deflect responsibility away from ourselves. By deflecting the responsibility, we found ways to "get past that," but we suppress our feelings and eventually lose touch with them, which in turn further contributes to our stubborn beliefs that we are now "past that."

In cases of deeper denial, we choose to selectively forget incidents and feelings. We suppress these memories in an attempt to protect ourselves from painful setbacks or experiences. Sweeping these under the carpet only serves to build more densely packed inner obstructions and offers no permanent solution. Remember: our Conscious Self thinks, while our Basic Self feels. As prior pages discussed in much detail, we cannot trade on technique alone; intuition supersedes technique. By suppressing our feelings, we actually disconnect ourselves from our Basic Self and thereby lose the support and commitment from our Basic Self. This contributes to increased anxieties, and in extreme situations, decision paralysis. We may freeze before our computer screens as we become captive in our declining self-confidence and weakening *Ki*. We become disconnected from our guiding inner voice, our intuition, and create inner turmoil by losing our inner balance.

The way out of such anxiety is to find a way to reconnect our Conscious Self with our Basic Self. One way is to ask a question that helps to peel away some of the outer barriers. Try to fill in the blank. "If I knew what I was feeling now, I'd say I felt _____." Knowing that our negative emotions fall primarily within one of three categories, we can also use this knowledge to help us as well. "Is the feeling I am experiencing closer to fear, anger, or sorrow?" Follow any new awareness with compassion and forgiveness. Recognize that we do the best we can with what we have to work with on any given day. Then, as we clear our obstructions and balance our body, mind, and emotions, our "best" gets better all the time.

Another problem with denial is that we relinquish accountability for our own actions if we always deflect cause or blame for our trading mistakes outwards. We no longer have the Beginner's Mindset and fail to learn and grow from setbacks. The shift to an outward focus transforms assertion into aggression. We in essence set ourselves up for defeat.

Fatigue is a serious factor for traders. For example, you've been trying to catch the start of a major decline for a week, only to find the market chops you up within a triangle pattern. The battle to find the high resumes, and when the market finally breaks, it only leads to another choppy decline, and you're left scrambling to trade anything the market will hand you within a complex consolidation. The cycle repeats itself for several weeks, and soon weeks stretch into months. No real trend, no clearly defined impulsive price structures reveal themselves. Just sideways chop. Eventually when the market finally breaks down with conviction you are exhausted from the long battle to establish gains within a difficult and lengthy consolidation. Battle weary, fatigue begins to slow your reaction time and leads to calculation errors that lead to opportunity costs from having missed portions of the market's move. Frustration compounds the fatigue factor. I'm sure this all sounds familiar to anyone who traded the S&P in 1992 where triangles and choppy price action lasted the entire year. Such conditions take their toll on our mental and physical well-being.

Fatigue will always be a factor in trading. It is important to disconnect from fatigue; in other words, give this demon a face or name. As a swimmer I was taught to make the exhaustion some kind of entity so you can let go of it. Early in the book I demonstrated displacing discomfort when I broke my finger in a swim meet. The same technique applies to trading fatigue. "Fatigue—it's you again. Maybe you want to hang around, but I have a job to do here. You'll have to wait until I finish." Laugh about a funny moment, find a way to relax and divert your attention, and avoid developing concern over your fatigue. You may be tired, but you can finish the trading session strong. Whatever method you use, know that to push through fatigue you must not resist but yield by deflecting the discomfort. The moment you become rigid with the markets through fatigue will be the time you are positioned to take a serious hit. The market will prevail. The reason is that your anxiety and tension will greatly increase when you try to resist your fatigue, causing even greater fatigue.

Fatigue is a warning that we are not paying enough attention to the needs of our Basic Self. It is a warning we need different food and more rest. Clearly while trading we cannot take more time to rest, but fighting or becoming angry and frustrated will only distract us, or make us lose our confidence, enthusiasm, and courage. Since we know our bodies respond physiologically to the images in our minds, we can help to dissipate the anxiety and tension brought on through fatigue by visualizing ourselves being relaxed, fluid, calm, and flowing with the markets. The visualization exercises are by far the most effective technique for dealing with acute fatigue, but they are only a temporary bandage to hold you together until you can do something about the earlier warnings. These warnings must be heeded and changes made, if not now, soon, before descending further towards burnout.

When ignored, fatigue contributes to illness and injuries. That is the next progression for our Basic Self to cry out, "Attention, something is not right here!" Fatigue makes us careless and makes us prone to make a mistake. I love tennis but have broken the same ankle five times playing the game. I always used the sport of tennis as my stress release; however, I did nothing to relieve fatigue. Each incident where injury occurred was the direct result of being overtired, yet still believing that all I had to do was push through the weakness. Instead of strengthening over time, my body broke down.

After several fractures, you learn a lot about the different phases for healing. Injured athletes and traders go through the same five stages of healing. The first stage is denial. We tell ourselves, "No, not me, there's no problem. It's not that serious." Then when reality hits, we are unable to perform optimally, or not at all. The next stage is anger. "Why me, why now?!" This seems to be accompanied by panic, which only serves to intensify the pain of the injury or discomfort of an illness. As the pain deepens, we enter a phase of bargaining. We make outlandish promises that "if the pain subsides and I recover, I'll never do_____ again, ever." I frequently promised to take more time off, but never did and therefore experienced this progression numerous times. Eventually the promises and begging prove futile, depression sets in, and we begin to feel sorry for ourselves. Having passed through the first four stages of healing, we finally arrive at acceptance. "I'm injured or ill, but I could use the rest before I get on with my life." Only when we reach acceptance can we truly begin to heal. However, the more stubborn our character, the more likely it will be that we have to oscillate back and forth for a while within the first four stages before we break free into acceptance.

When we are ill or injured it is extremely important to seek the advice of a professional we trust and respect. Even if it is only reassurance a doctor gives us, this helps to reduce the stress associated with the questions we face during the panic stage of our healing. We fill ourselves with stress by asking, "How will I get by until I'm healed? How long will it take? What if this is more serious?" We can help our recovery by gathering as much information about our situation as possible.

The techniques of visualization and meditation have medically been proven to speed up the recovery process. Now is a very important time to practice these techniques described earlier. Times of injury and illness are perfect times to evaluate your situation. Try to understand what your pain is trying to tell you.

Should the warnings of repetitive illness or injuries, fatigue, and stress be denied and unheeded, the next phase is skid row — burnout.

It is a rude awakening to lie in a hospital bed extremely ill, or work through the shattering fragments of bankruptcy, or mentally heal from an emotional trauma or loss. It is a struggle to find a new foundation on which to rebuild. Burnout requires time to heal. A personal evaluation and acceptance that changes must be made are finally accepted. When you experience hitting bottom, the denial and false self-delusions fade. We become aware of our weaknesses followed by a phase of self-pity and depression. This is not the time to beat ourselves up. We need compassion and understanding, but most important of all, distance through time. The exercises offered earlier in this book will help you to uncover what needs to be changed, show you how to go about making these changes, and then provide you the means to find your way back to center balance.

While the experience is painful, it will lead to a higher awareness, and the superficial will no longer be able to pull you from your center of balance. You will soon discover the richness of living in the present by letting go of the past. You will no longer miss out on what today offers for worrying about what could have been or what might be in the future.

> We crucify ourselves between two thieves:
> regret for yesterday and fear of tomorrow.
> —*Fulton Oursler*

Painful as it is, burnout can be a doorway to freedom. It's the same door I had to pass through, and I can only offer compassion, encouragement, and through this book, the means to reach the other side. The exercises work. Do them.

PART V

The Olympian's Mindset
Applied to Trading:
A Real-Time Demonstration

A rich man, fond of felines, asked a famous Zen
ink painter to draw him a cat. The master agreed and
asked the man to come back in three months. When
the man returned, he was put off, again and again,
until a year had passed. Finally, at the man's request,
the master drew out a brush, and, with grace and ease,
in a single fluid motion, drew a picture of a cat
— the most marvelous image the man had ever seen.
He was astonished; then he grew angry.
"That drawing took you only thirty seconds!
Why did you make me wait a year?" he demanded.
Without a word, the master opened up a cabinet, and
out fell thousands of drawings — of cats.
—A ZEN Story

Swimmers will stroke through thousands of miles of water
to perfect their stroke to break 30 seconds for a 50 meter sprint.
Top Gun pilots will spend countless "flight" hours confined in
computerized simulators to prepare for those few real missions
they may experience in their entire lives. Anyone, regardless of
how often he is called upon to excel within a high risk environment, will have been conditioned and fine-tuned with countless hours to achieve his desired level of excellence.

Spectators misinterpret proficiency as a skill that comes easily for the achiever. This illusion results from endless hours of
practice that streamlined and polished away the rough edges of
inefficient technique. It is the work, the practice, the ups and
downs that lead to the same apex, our goal — the complete
balance between our technique, intuition, and energy so that

we can extend and push ourselves into a new level of achievement. Complete and total balance is rare, but with practice, we can experience this extraordinary inner harmony more often. In trading we strive to achieve a oneness with the markets so our gut feel and the market's moves are in unison.

What follows is a sample of what can be achieved when we are in sync with the market. We have discussed the skills and mindset required to excel in a high stakes environment, now is the time to stop the talk and start to *do*. The time has come to apply the skills offered throughout this book to our trading.

Regardless of the time horizon or market you prefer to trade or invest, weekly, daily, hourly, or even shorter, the principles are the same. The only difference is that the shorter your trading horizon, the faster will be your decision criteria and the greater will be the demand on your intuitive timing. The shortest, and perhaps the most demanding time frame to trade is from one and two minute charts.

The following S&P charts are one and two minute bar charts. These charts have not incorporated "hindsight analysis." The charts and accompanying trade decisions are as they occurred April 20, 1995. The time stamps record when these signals were transmitted to hundreds of institutional traders around the globe simultaneously by Bloomberg, Knight-Ridder, Reuters, Dow Jones/Telerate, and other independent quote vendor services. No changes have been made to the original buy/sell signals that follow. In addition, the trades were real.

Both very short and longer horizon traders are striving to achieve the same goal — more frequent profitable trading sessions. To achieve this goal we have to progress towards our daily milestones with continued work, patience with our own development, and a whole lot of persistence. However, once you've experienced your first trading session, in your market and time horizon like the one that follows, you'll need no further convincing that the principles offered throughout this book work and are well worth continued effort to master them.

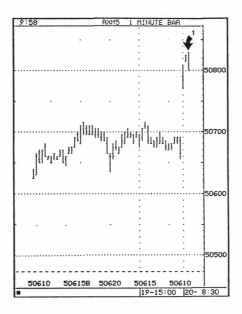

[1][S&P] Thurs. 9:32am DJIA last: 4214 June S&P last: 508.20 (SHORT) Selling 100% at current levels with a 508.90 stop. A five wave pattern up from 503.10 is now complete.

Observations: Chart [1] shows a strong market with an opening gap that led to an early fast market condition. Selling in front of a fast market rally might seem reckless or require tremendous courage. In actual fact, this market opening applies to the discussion offered in the chapter entitled "Courage." This is an example of calculated risk-taking. The fear and anxiety that accompanied the risk was neutralized when preliminary analysis identified the precise location of a formidable resistance zone just above the market. The market rallies right to the underside of this invisible barrier, offering a selling opportunity. If the market were to continue to rally through the resistance area, I will know immediately that the short position is wrong. As a result, the capital risk is viewed acceptable.

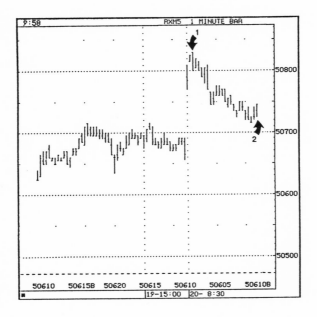

[2][S&P] Thurs. 9:54am DJIA last: 4219 June S&P last: 507.25
(FLAT) Paying current levels for 100%. A seven wave decline to the .618
retracement of the advance from the 506.55 low... expect further gains.

Observations: In chart [2], the market declines but fails to
fill the opening gap, which may indicate that the decline is complete. In addition, the retracement was a 61.8% retracement of
the previous rally, which past experience has proven is a very
high probable pivot area for the market to turn sharply. A defensive strategy is to unwind the short position to realize an
immediate profit. Executing this order applies the exercise
"Trading from the Left Side of Your 'But'" on page 158 in the
chapter "Intuition." Stay on the left side of this "but" statement:

The market is stalling at the .618 retracement jeopardizing my current gains, *but* if I hold on to the position, the market might break down and increase my
profits.

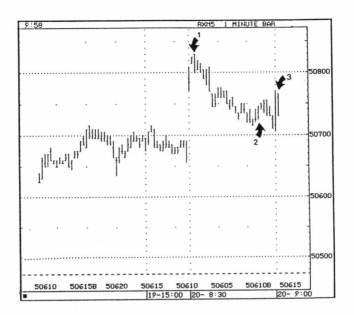

[3][S&P] Thurs. 10:01am DJIA last: 4218 June S&P last: 507.60 (SHORT) Repositioning again... selling 100% with a 508.60 stop. Reviewing cash S&P and the DJIA, the decline is not over as a larger five wave advance has just ended in the DJIA.

Observations: The price data that followed after the 9:54am update was identified as a specific Elliott Wave pattern that warned the rally is only a small correction or bounce up from the .618 support level. (The pattern is called an Expanded Flat.) This pattern leads to a resumption of the prior trend. The market is immediately sold. This trade is simply applying technique with confidence based on prior successes.

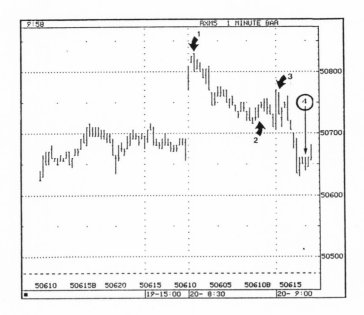

[4][S&P] Thurs. 10:10am DJIA last: 4213 June S&P last: 506.50
(SHORT) Minimum target for a zigzag decline is 505.85.

Observations: The number four in this chart is circled because no trade is initiated, only a comment is transmitted to traders around the world. All time bars with black arrows show where and when a market order is entered. In the 10:10am update above, supporting technical indicators did not warn of a bottom, so further losses are probable. This is no time to doubt your indicators. Confidence comes from having back-tested similar indicator positions to increase the odds for success. If there is a pause to question the indicator's accuracy, then more homework is indicated to remove the obstacle — *fear of failure*.

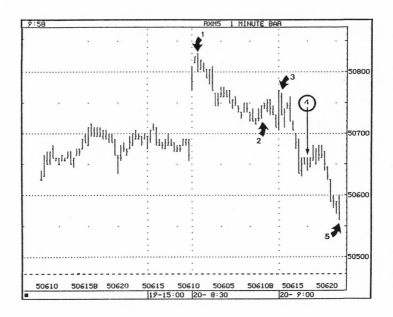

[5][S&P] Thurs. 10:20am DJIA last: 4210 June S&P last: 505.80 (FLAT) Paying current levels for 100%. The DJIA has five waves down the decline isn't over... but a bounce should develop from this target level.

Observations: Other stock market indices such as the OEX and DJIA have already declined to their price targets and formed bottoms. The high correlation between these indices warns that the S&P futures market is lagging. A rally will soon develop. While the position is unwound to protect the profit, the position is not reversed at these levels as the S&P price data warns that the current lows will be tested again. A range is defined.

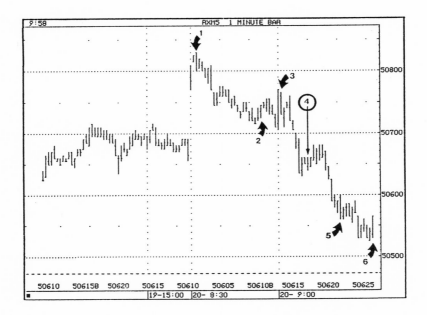

[6][S&P] Thurs. 10:32am DJIA last: 4205 June S&P last: 505.45 (LONG) Paying current levels for 50% with a 505.10 stop. Retracement levels...(505.75-.90), (506.25), 506.45, 506.80, (507.05-.15).

Observations: A new market low does develop and a short position is established. When the market traces out a move you had visualized, the follow-through to establish a position becomes easy. However, I am not confident that a major bottom is in place so a smaller position is established that exposes less capital.

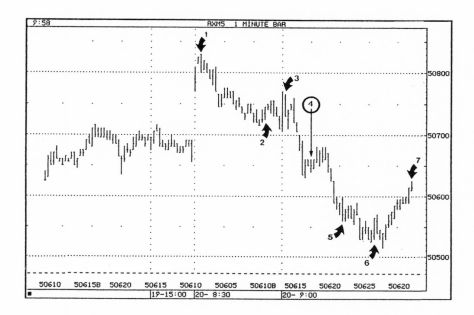

[7][S&P] Thurs. 10:45am DJIA last: 4206 June S&P last: 506.20
(REVERSE/SHORT) Selling 150% at current levels to get out of the current long — reposition short. A 506.80 stop. The very small decline from 505.70 to the last low at 505.15 is a wave b decline within a flat pattern. The advance is therefore wave c up...

Observations: As the rally unfolds, the small decline that follows price bar [6] to a new low is suddenly given a new interpretation. The new interpretation has to be quickly substantiated and requires immediate action. Then the 50% long position is unwound and an additional 100% is sold to reverse. The market has advanced to the 506.25 resistance level identified in update [6]. The 506.80 stop is incorrectly placed. The resistance levels over the 506.25 area are 506.45 and 506.80, as defined in [6]. The stop is placed over the next resistance level, but entered directly at the 506.80 zone. It should have been corrected if the error had been detected. Fortunately, this small slip did not become a factor.

To have the mental freedom to completely reverse your position and opinion requires a centered balance without bias. The chapter "Centering" described how being centered contributes to inner control and how new events or information cannot pull you off-center to cause a distraction. In addition, if we become too attached to our viewpoint about the market's direction, the small piece of new information might easily have been missed. It shows how *Ego* can limit our ability to process information.

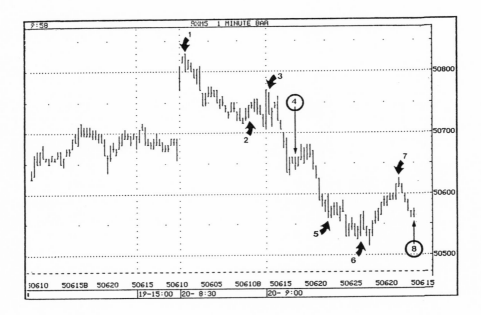

[8][S&P] Thurs. 10:50am DJIA last: 4209 June S&P last: 505.70 (SHORT) Potential targets for further weakness... 505.10, 504.50, 503.45... Cancel the 506.80 stop and replace at breakeven... 506.15.

Observations: The stop is lowered and new objectives are calculated. Caution is needed that a break in concentration does not occur when the market starts to move in your favor. The favorable move does offer a chance to take three deep breaths as described in "Conscious Breathing."

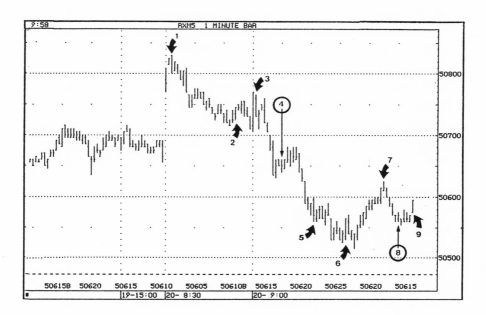

[9][S&P] Thurs. 10:55am DJIA last: 4207 June S&P last: 505.90
(REVERSE/LONG) Paying current levels for 200%...reversing.... Cancel
the stop, a new 505.30 stop. Hourly technical indicators are EXTREMELY
oversold...and this pullback from the 506.25 high is stalling at the .618
retracement of the advance from the low.
(10:56 addition) New targets for a rally are...506.25, 506.65, 507.35.

Observations: The brief pause in the market allows an opportunity to check the longer time horizon charts and hourly
indicators to maintain perspective. If focus and concentration
had been eased in [8], this new information would not have
been attained.

This is actually a vulnerable point for a trader. The market
has proven prior assumptions and trades to be correct. The risk
is a break in concentration at this moment or relaxing with a
sense of false security that contributes to an error. Ego begins
to step forward and overconfidence could become detrimental.

Another risk is slipping away from the present moment to start thinking about the odds of being right again. As soon as we question ourselves if we can continue the string of successes, we break the trend. The question and distraction can be filtered by using the technique described on page 111 in "Distortions of Reality and Ability."

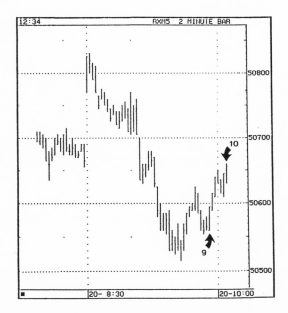

[10][S&P] Thurs. 11:05am DJIA last: 4209 June S&P last: 506.45 (FLAT) Potential zigzag up to the 506.50 high... selling 100% at current levels. Cancel the stop.

Observations: While the position is covered with a profit at these price levels, it should have been reversed. Stamina is beginning to become an issue. The exercise described on page 136 is useful in increasing our concentration. When the first small error is made it is acknowledged. When it happens again I know that's the time to take a short break. Now where did that paper airplane go?

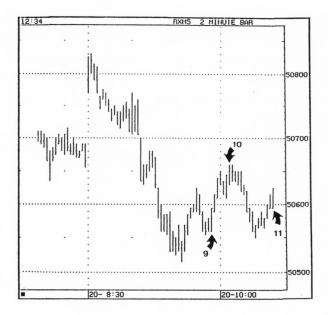

[11][S&P] Thurs. 11:35am DJIA last: 4215 June S&P last: 506.00
(LONG) Paying current levels for 100% with a 505.55 stop. The target is
507.35.

Observations: A new position is established fourteen minutes later. Note that the entry is a little late. The rhythm is still
there but actions derived from intuition are beginning to slow
down. Fatigue has become a factor.

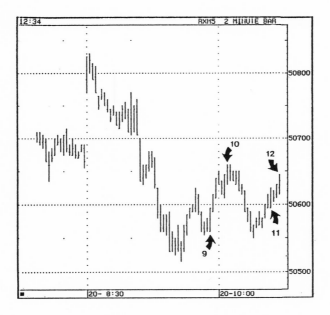

[12][S&P] Thurs. 11:40am DJIA last: 4216 June S&P last 506.20
(FLAT) The target is wrong... a bearish triangle is developing and the advance from 505.50 is wave c up. Selling 100%.

Observations: Finally, self-doubt from fatigue causes a judgment error. The Basic Self might well have been contributing to this decision to step out of the market by going flat. Triangles allow a break in the very short horizon so the trickster mind is likely wishing for a triangle. Technically the internal structure from point 10 to the next low is a five wave pattern. This means that a triangle pattern will never develop. The assumption is wrong.

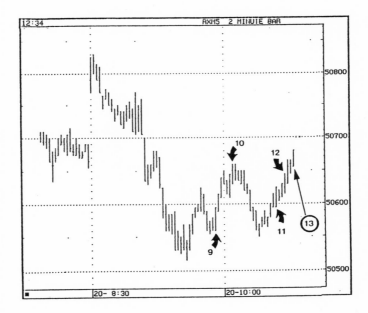

[13][S&P] Thurs. 11:46am DJIA last: 4218 June S&P last: 506.70 (FLAT) OK..not a triangle... also means the 507.35 target is likely correct.

Observations: As the market breaks above the high established in point [10], the triangle pattern is negated and the error is realized. Staying centered is essential. Missing one point in the tennis match is not a source of concern. I am still ahead. Don't let the error become a distraction.

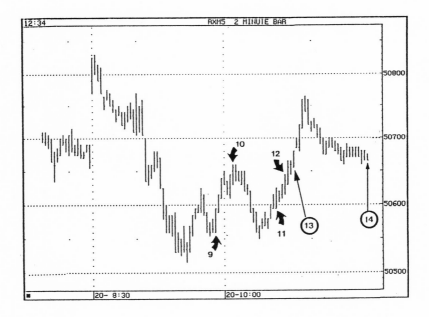

[14][S&P] Thurs. 12:37pm DJIA last: 4216 June S&P last: 506.80
(FLAT) The current pullback is viewed as another fourth wave down, im-
plying another advance in the S&P to 507.50 should then lead to a deeper
correction.

Observations: Chart [14] simply shows a re-evaluation is
occurring. It is a chance to regroup and refocus for the next
round. This is a similar situation to when the blackjack dealer
has to shuffle the deck to create a new shoe.

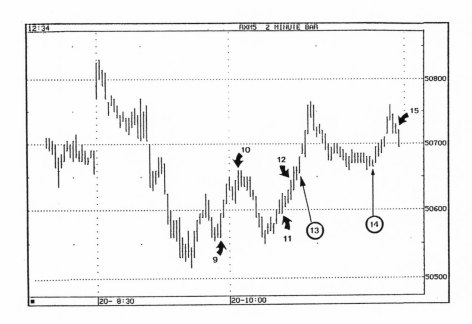

[15][S&P] Thurs. 12:58pm DJIA last: 4223 June S&P last: 507.10 (SHORT) Selling 100% at current levels with a 508.70 stop. Extremely close...just one small fifth needed in the DJIA to end the advance from 4157.... S&P could be done.

Observations: A new short position is established with the market's next pivot. The commentary shows attention to detail has returned. The brief break helps to alleviate the fatigue factor by relaxing and staying out of the market since update [12].

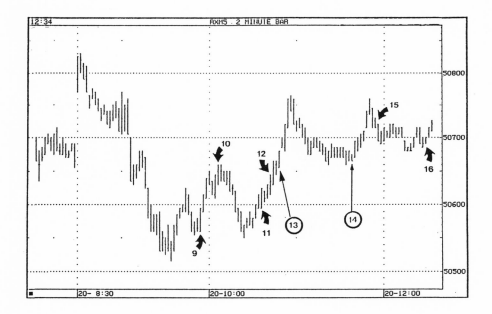

[16][S&P] Thurs. 1:28pm DJIA last: 4222 June S&P last: 507.00
(SHORT) Paying current levels for 50%...staying 50% short...and leaving
the 508.70 stop for 100%. DJIA and SPM both suggest fourth wave triangles from the 4227 and the 507.65 high. The triangle only projects a
fifth wave to 508.00.

Observations: The battle has been renewed with a second
wind of energy.

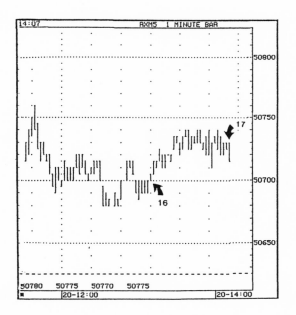

[17][S&P] Thurs. 1:55pm DJIA last: 4227 June S&P last: 507.30 (SHORT) That's the thrust up in the DJIA and cash S&P...futures are very slow to move...selling 50% at current levels. (It could be that futures are still within the triangle pattern)... The stop remains at 508.70 for 100%.

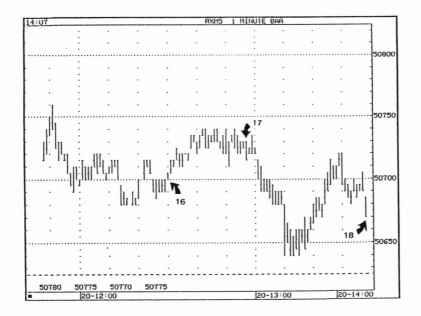

[18][S&P] Thurs. 2:38pm DJIA last: 4227 June S&P last: 506.80 (REVERSE/LONG) Paying current levels for 200% with a 506.25 stop...cancel the 508.70 stop. Wave e down developing now...more to follow in the next update...

Observations: While only the price charts are reproduced in this chapter, the methods supporting Elliott Wave analysis are RSI, custom momentum indicators, and Gann analysis. The method or technique in use is not the issue, but that the tools offer an instinctive message for the trader.

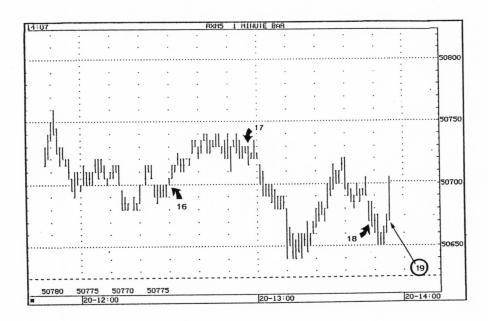

[19][S&P] Thurs. 2:45pm DJIA last: 4226 June S&P last: 506.70
(LONG) A contracting triangle pattern from the 508.30 high...wave e down
developing...largest open interest on record going into expiration...excess
puts. Favors a +2.30 S&P pop on open tomorrow...hence reversed.

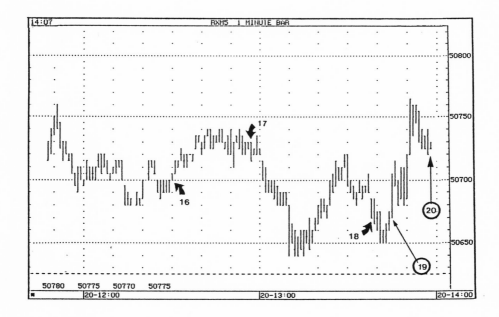

[20][S&P] Thurs. 2:58pm DJIA last: 4231 June S&P last: 507.25
(LONG) Targets...508.05, most likely 509.00...then expecting a move back
to 505.15.

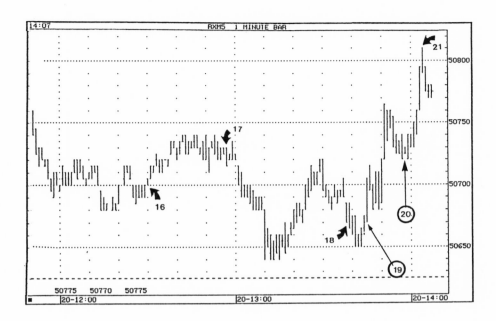

[21][S&P] Thurs. 3:05pm DJIA last: 4233 S&P last: 508.00
(FLAT) That's the first target... I don't want to be long until 509...selling
100%...cancel stops.

Observations: The trading session continues but the position is entirely unwound when scaling back would have been
more appropriate. This is fatigue showing itself as a factor
again. However, by going flat there is a better chance of selling
into the market's high preceding a much larger decline to 505.15
as referenced in chart [20].

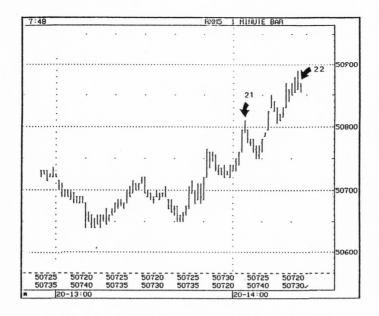

[22][S&P] Thurs. 3:24pm DJIA last: 4242 June S&P last: 508.70
(SHORT) Selling 50% at current levels with a 509.80 stop. Expiration
activity could top this market...my daily indicators are kicking up to the
underside of extremely bearish patterns.

Observations: The market just narrowly misses the 509 objective. An error is made as 100% is not sold into this target
area.

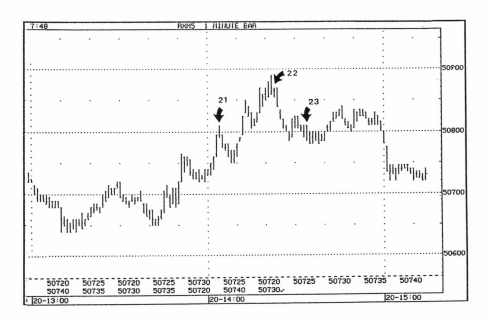

[23][S&P] Thurs. 3:30pm DJIA last: 4240 June S&P last: 508.20
(SHORT) The decline does not look corrective...selling another 50%...same
stop...at 509.80.

Observations: The additional 50% is sold. The timing for
establishing this leg is incorrect. I find impatience usually accompanies fatigue. Had the market not been near its close,
additional judgment errors would have once again developed
as the cycle repeats itself.

This trading session netted a realized gain of +5.75 S&P
points, with an unrealized gain on the open position of +1.15.

PART VI

Conclusion:
Why Struggle for the Top if it Can Only be Temporary?

As we have seen, our greatest market challenge is not out there in the external world, but within us. These inner hurdles generate most of the obstacles and difficulties we encounter. Be patient with who you are right now, but promise yourself to work tirelessly to illuminate those saboteurs working against you. They are sneaky, beware. They hide and disguise themselves as "lack of initiative" or "low motivation." Our trickster minds and Conscious Self will demand a logical reason for stepping out into the unknown. Perhaps I should say stepping inward to the unknown?

When I failed to make the Olympic team, the most common question I was asked then and still today is, "Was it all worth it?" It took time and maturity, but in the end, the answer is a resounding "YES!" True, I did not reach my intended goal, my original destination. However, the journey through many winding trails and dark open pits uncovered a strength of character and abilities that might otherwise have gone unknown. Without these challenges we would not become any stronger or wiser. Looking back, it was these small steps into the unknown that became the most clearly defined and detailed memories. It is certainly worth it, if only to stand fleetingly on a top pedestal and then move on ahead to a new challenge as someone else moves into the spotlight. At the end of the day, it is the journey you must relish and not the destination.

The following inscription, given to me by a former coach and tucked safely away in a fine old bent wood box, puts it all into perspective. This is the definitive answer to the question, "Is it worth it?"

You cannot stay on the summit forever;
you have to come down again.
So why bother in the first place?
Because what is below
does not know what is above,
but what is above
knows what is below.
One climbs, one sees.
One descends, one sees no longer,
but one has seen.
There is an art of conducting oneself
in the lower regions
by memory of what one saw higher up.
When one can no longer see,
one can at least know.

—Source Unknown

INDEX

Symbols

10K and 10Q reports 54

A

absence of fear 196
absolute balance 17
account inactivity 69
accountability 141, 190-191, 193, 202, 268
action plan 199-200
acute obstructions 224-225
addiction 63, 201, 205, 207, 221-222, 225, 227
addictive behavior 221-222
adrenal system 221
adrenaline 63, 101, 221-222, 240
aggression 141, 153, 187-191, 203, 230, 232, 264, 266, 268
Alcoholics Anonymous 225
Alpha waves 99
American Banker 255
analysis paralysis 148, 157
anger 13, 89, 176, 203, 215-216, 218, 223, 254, 268, 270
anxiety 8, 31, 37, 49, 81, 100, 115, 118, 164, 173, 196, 198, 231, 237, 241, 246, 263, 267-268, 270, 277
Armageddon 210, 214
Armstrong, Neil 201
arrogance 174
assertion 187-190, 264, 268
assertive traits 192
assessing risk 197
AT&T 213
at-the-market 214
Atlanta, GA 59, 156
Atlantic City, NJ 97
attitude monitoring 156
Auerbach, Red 61, 64
Aziz, Tarek 156

B

Bacon, Francis 201
Baghdad, Iraq 33
Baker, James 156, 157
balance 15, 17-19, 30, 32, 46, 52, 67, 80, 91, 101, 116, 124, 139-143, 170, 175, 177, 182, 184, 188, 233-234, 244, 261, 262, 264, 268, 272, 275, 276
Bank of Tokyo 260
Bannister, Roger 17, 27
Basic Self 30-32, 34-36, 45, 46, 48, 63, 99, 101-104, 106, 108, 110, 113, 124, 136, 141, 148, 149, 158, 178, 226, 233, 241, 261, 265, 267, 268, 270

battery power backup 211
Beginner's Mindset 5, 9, 24, 70, 72, 235, 266, 268
Benny, Jack 227
Berra, Yogi 159
Beta waves 99
bidding a market up 79
bidding war 251
Blackjack 94-98, 125
blood sugar 136, 222
Bloomberg 276
boardroom politics 174
body language 157, 216
Borg, Bjorn 243
Boston, MA 61, 77, 98, 165, 211, 214, 225
Boston Celtics 61, 165
Braun, Julian 95
breathing 172, 181-186, 204, 222, 223, 284
breathing imbalances 182, 184
breathing restrictions 223
breathing technique 185
bridge bank 255, 259
Buddhism 28
Buddhist 238
burnout 32, 45, 200, 208, 215, 266, 267, 270, 271, 272
Bush, George 156
buyside 53, 68

C

Cain, Kwai Chang 141
calculated risk-taking 196, 201, 277
calm 13, 19, 20, 31, 32, 37, 49, 139, 141-143, 157, 164, 169, 170, 173, 175-179, 181, 182, 185, 188, 198, 203, 207, 235, 264, 270
capitulation 210
card counting 96, 97, 125
cardiovascular system 182, 183
Cardwell, Andrew 62
Carlson, Bryce 95
Carradine, David 141
center of balance 80, 175, 264, 272, 284
centering 19, 37, 77, 80, 113, 122, 139-145, 175, 177, 223
centralized market 151
cerebral drag 4, 18
change 102-104, 107, 108, 117, 118, 121, 124, 137, 139, 148, 159, 165, 166, 185, 188, 191, 199, 207, 216, 217, 223, 224, 233-235, 240, 244, 254, 264, 266, 270, 272, 276
changing attitudes 191
Chi Hsing-tzu 219
Chicago, IL 54, 55, 71, 142, 211, 214, 238, 251
Chicago Bears 187

Other Titles from New Classics Library
(a division of Elliott Wave International, Inc.)

Elliott Wave Principle — Key to Market Behavior — by Robert R. Prechter, Jr. and A.J. Frost. This best-selling book, now in its seventh edition, has been completely revised and updated, although it still contains every word of its original 1978 forecast, which called for a great bull market in the 1980s. One sitting with this classic text and you'll understand why it has been translated into six languages, and sells thousands of copies each year.

At the Crest of the Tidal Wave — A Forecast for the Great Bear Market — by Robert R. Prechter, Jr. In his first new book in 17 years, *At the Crest of the Tidal Wave* presents the sequel to Mr. Prechter's extraordinary 1978 forecast. You will never read a more in-depth look at what a mass psychological turn of this size will mean to investment markets. You'll also learn how to prepare for the difficult financial times ahead.

R.N. Elliott's Masterworks — The Definitive Collection — by Robert R. Prechter, Jr., editor. Gives you the three ground-breaking works, long out of print, in which R.N. Elliott first described his discoveries to the world. You'll also read a detailed biography of Elliott not previously available anywhere, including rare photographs and excerpts from his letters and early writings.

R.N. Elliott's Market Letters (1938-1946) — by Robert R. Prechter, Jr., editor. Presents Elliott's real-time analyses and forecasts of market action, along with numerous essays on the application of the Wave Principle. Extensively footnoted and cross-referenced by Bob Prechter.

The Complete Elliott Wave Writings of A. Hamilton Bolton — Foreword by Robert R. Prechter, Jr., editor. Includes Bolton's book *Elliott Wave Principle — A Critical Appraisal*, all of his annual Elliott Wave articles for *The Bank Credit Analyst*, personal letters, articles and rare photos, plus a memoir of Bolton written by A.J. Frost.

The Spiral Calendar and Its Effect on Financial Markets and Human Events — by Christopher L. Carolan. *The Spiral Calendar*™ is Christopher Carolan's discovery that major turning points in the markets are often related by exact time relationships. This book demonstrates the connection between the lunar cycle and the emotional behavior of investors.

Fibonacci Numbers — by N. Vorobev. A thorough analysis of the mathematical properties of the Fibonacci sequence. Moves from "beginner" level to advanced equations. For serious students of Fibonacci relationships.

**For more information on upcoming titles or to order,
Call 800-336-1618 (U.S.) or 770-536-0309**

DAILY AND INTRADAY MARKET ANALYSIS
available on The Bloomberg, Knight-Ridder,
Reuters, Telerate and UniLink

S&P specialist Connie Brown writes the daily and intraday analysis for *The World Stock Market Outlook*, and the S&P section of *The North American Financial Outlook*. She is part of a team that covers every major world financial market.

You can receive our comprehensive market analysis on-line. Each *Outlook* described below gives our short term market analysis using the Elliott Wave Principle and other supporting methods. You will receive detailed commentary, support and resistance levels, wave analysis and more. These tools will give you valuable assistance in implementing your strategies.

We will transmit our *Outlooks* to you Monday through Friday, and supplement them with intraday updates as needed, 24 hours a day.

THE WORLD STOCK MARKETS OUTLOOK
Commentary on all major stock markets around the globe.

THE NORTH AMERICAN FINANCIAL OUTLOOK
Offers commentary on the major financial instruments in the U.S., including capital, currency and metals markets.

THE GLOBAL INTEREST RATE OUTLOOK
Detailed commentary on interest rate markets around the world.

THE INTERNATIONAL CURRENCY OUTLOOK
Analysis of major spot currency and cross rate relationships.

THE GLOBAL ENERGY OUTLOOK
Analysis of major New York, London and Singapore energy markets.

THE INTERNATIONAL METALS OUTLOOK
Analysis of precious and industrial metals on all major world exchanges.

THE WORLD COMMODITIES OUTLOOK
Follows agricultural, softs and meat futures contracts traded in the Far East, Europe and North America.

For further information or to receive free trial
subscriptions to these services:

CALL 800-472-9283 (U.S.) or 770-534-6680 or FAX 770-531-6681

ELLIOTT WAVE INTERNATIONAL
200 Main Street, Hunt Tower, Gainesville, Georgia 30501, U.S.A.
